T0205998

Lecture Notes in Computer Science 11709

More information about this series at http://www.springer.com/series/7409

Andrea Kő · Enrico Francesconi ·
Gabriele Anderst-Kotsis ·
A Min Tjoa · Ismail Khalil (Eds.)

Electronic Government and the Information Systems Perspective

8th International Conference, EGOVIS 2019
Linz, Austria, August 26–29, 2019
Proceedings

 Springer

Editors
Andrea Kő
Corvinus University of Budapest
Budapest, Hungary

Enrico Francesconi
National Research Council
Rome, Italy

Gabriele Anderst-Kotsis
Johannes Kepler University of Linz
Linz, Austria

A Min Tjoa (iD)
Software Competence Center Hagenberg
Hagenberg im Mühlkreis, Austria

Ismail Khalil
Johannes Kepler University of Linz
Linz, Austria

ISSN 0302-9743   ISSN 1611-3349   (electronic)
Lecture Notes in Computer Science
ISBN 978-3-030-27522-8   ISBN 978-3-030-27523-5   (eBook)
https://doi.org/10.1007/978-3-030-27523-5

LNCS Sublibrary: SL3 – Information Systems and Applications, incl. Internet/Web, and HCI

This Springer imprint is published by the registered company Springer Nature Switzerland AG
The registered company address is: Gewerbestrasse 11, 6330 Cham, Switzerland

Preface

The 8th International Conference on Electronic Government and the Information Systems Perspective, EGOVIS 2019, took place in Linz, Austria, during August 26–29, 2019. The conference belongs to the 30th DEXA Conference Series.

The international conference cycle EGOVIS focuses on information systems and ICT aspects of e-government. Information systems are a core enabler for e-government/governance in all its dimensions: e-administration, e-democracy, e-participation, and e-voting. EGOVIS brought together experts from academia, public administrations, and industry to discuss e-government and e-democracy from different perspectives and disciplines, i.e. technology, policy and/or governance, and public administration.

The Program Committee accepted 17 papers from recent research fields such as open data and big data analytics, e-identity, e-participation, open government and e-government architectures, blockchain technologies for e-government, intelligent systems, and semantic technologies for services in the public sector. Beyond theoretical contributions, the papers cover e-government practical applications and experiences.

This proceedings volume is organized into five sections according to the conference sessions.

The chairs of the Program Committee wish to thank all the reviewers for their valuable work; the reviews raised several research questions to discuss at the conference. We would like to thank Gabriele Anderst-Kotsis and Ismail Khalil for the administrative support and assisting us in proper scheduling.

We wish pleasant and beneficial learning experiences for the readers. We hope that the discussion will continue between the researchers after the conference and contribute to building a global community in the field of e-government.

August 2019
Enrico Francesconi
Andrea Kő

Organization

General Chair

Roland Traunmüller   University Linz, Austria

Program Committee Chairs

Andrea Kő	Corvinus University Budapest, Hungary
Enrico Francesconi	Italian National Research Council, Publication Office of the EU, Italy

Honorary Chairs

Wichian Chutimaskul	King Mongkut's University of Technology, Thailand
Fernando Galindo	University Zaragoza, Spain

Steering Committee

Gabriele Anderst-Kotsis	Johannes Kepler University Linz, Austria
Ismail Khalil	Johannes Kepler University Linz, Austria
A Min Tjoa	Technical University of Vienna, Austria

Program Committee and Reviewers

Luis Álvarez Sabucedo	Universidade de Vigo, Spain
Alejandra Cechich	Universidad Nacional del Comahue, Argentina
Wojciech Cellary	Poznan University of Economics, Poland
Wichian Chutimaskul	King Mongkut's University of Technology, Thailand
Flavio Corradini	University of Camerino, Italy
Vytautas Cyras	Vilnius University, Lithuania
Joan Francesc Fondevila Gascón	Universitat Pompeu Fabra, Spain
Ivan Futo	National Tax and Customs Administration, Hungary
András Gábor	Corvinus University of Budapest, Hungary
Fernando Galindo	University of Zaragoza, Spain
Francisco Javier García Marco	University of Zaragoza, Spain
Stefanos Gritzalis	University of the Aegean, Greece
Henning Sten Hansen	Aalborg University, Denmark
Christos Kalloniatis	University of the Aegean, Greece
Nikos Karacapilidis	University of Patras, Greece
Evangelia Kavakli	University of the Aegean, Greece

Peter Mambrey	University of Duisburg-Essen, Germany
Javier Nogueras	University of Zaragoza, Spain
Aljosa Pasic	Atos, Spain
Aires J Rover	Federal University of Santa Catarina, Brazil
Erich Schweighofer	University of Vienna, Austria
Julian Valero	iDertec, University of Murcia, Spain
Costas Vassilakis	University of the Peloponnese, Greece
Gianluigi Viscusi	EPFL, CDM, CSI, Switzerland
Roland Wagner	University Linz, Austria
Christopher C. Wills	Caris Research Ltd., UK
Frank Wilson	Interaction Design, UK
Chien-Chih Yu	National ChengChi University, Taiwan

Organizers

Contents

Open Data and Open Innovation

Crowdfunding of Science and Open Data: Opportunities, Challenges, and Policies

Ludovica Paseri[(⊠)]

CIRSFID, University of Bologna, Via Galliera 3, 40121 Bologna, Italy
`ludovica.paseri2@unibo.it`

Abstract. The phenomenon of crowdfunding, in the last two decades, has gained ever increasing success and application, to the point of obtaining the attention of the European institutions, with the proposal of a Regulation aimed at providing a legal framework, in order to promote its growth.

Crowdfunding has also involved the academic world of science, looking for alternative models of research funding. Crowdfunding of science, however, due to its peculiar characteristics, would require specific regulatory provisions that call for further analysis. First and foremost, this is a consequence of the link with the issue of Open Data and the communication to the backers of the research results.

1 Introduction

The digital revolution, promoting the interconnection between people thanks to the dissemination capabilities of digital tools that open up to an infinite number of possibilities, has involved almost all aspects of our lives: it is reshaping not only every form of communication, but also the decision-making process, as well as the relationship between citizens and governments [1]. More and more often, the society wonders: to what extent the data held by governments must be open? With the same question, the scientific community wonders about the opportunity to make open the data produced by research financed with public money. In Zhang et al. [2], a bibliometric analysis of publications produced in the online subscription-based scientific citation indexing service called "Web of Science", show that research on open data has increased rapidly since 2009.

The need to find an answer, and a precise discipline, becomes even more pressing when scientific research is carried out with crowdfunding: this form of financing, on the one hand, identifies a new and alternative fundraising model, but, on the other hand, it necessarily implies that some kind of feedback has to be given to the crowd that has materially participated by providing a micro-financing.

In recent years, universities have not been immune to this trend towards openness: Facebook pages, updated websites and blogs are now considered the practice for an efficient University, up with the times [3]. In recent years, many universities have employed this alternative model of funding in order to support their research: financing their own projects with crowdfunding requires, by its very nature, that, at least, a report of what has been achieved has to be provided to the crowd. Implementing this type of

A. Kő et al. (Eds.): EGOVIS 2019, LNCS 11709, pp. 3–15, 2019.
https://doi.org/10.1007/978-3-030-27523-5_1

feedback can be quite easy for a company that makes known the results of its business project: companies have no constraints on what and how to communicate, especially in relation to the implementation of an entrepreneurial project. On the contrary it can be rather difficult for a team of researchers: opening your own research raises all the problems that are normally related to the issue of Open Science.

Following this introduction, in Sect. 2 the phenomenon of crowdfunding is analyzed in its generality, with closest regard to the different models that have been imposed. In Sect. 3, whereas, the focus is specifically on crowdfunding for scientific research. Then, in Sect. 4, we will summarize opportunities and challenges related to the crowdfunding phenomenon. Subsequently, Sect. 5 analyzes the current policies, with particular attention to the European legal framework. Lastly, final considerations outline the findings of previous sections and draw some conclusions about the possible future of the crowdfunding of science, with regard to the Open Data scenario.

2   Crowdfunding: An Alternative Financing System

Nowadays, crowdfunding is a phenomenon widely known and widespread in our society. The economic impact of crowdfunding is remarkable and affects the whole world. The organization "The Data Crowd Center"[1], in collaboration with the University of Portsmouth, on a sample of projects analyzed from January 1st 2014 to March 29th 2019, has estimated 4.8 billion dollars collected, throughout the world, taking into consideration the main platforms, thanks to the participation of 32.5 billion of backers, for projects that touch a wide range of areas: from technology to art; from business to sport. The famous American platform, Kickstarter[2], launched in 2009, with the mission "to help bring creative projects to life", gathered a total of 4.2 billion, successfully financing 160,301 projects, thanks to the participation of 16 million people.

Furthermore, the data related to crowdfunding for scientific research shows the growth of the phenomenon: the site experiment.com[3], one of the most relevant platforms in this field, boasts 874 funded projects, starting from 2012, the year of its foundation, to date, thanks to the participation of 46,822 backers. After only two years of activity, in 2014, experiment.com exceeded one million of money collected and the large collection of case studies on their site describes the projects that have been successful (success rate 45.83%).

2.1   The Definition of Crowdfunding

Many definitions have been proposed for the phenomenon of crowdfunding. Its roots can be found in the broader crowdsourcing, namely the transposition of ideas, feedback and solutions advanced by the "crowd", to avoid complex problems extremely difficult

---

[1] https://www.thecrowdfundingcenter.com/data/categories#average_raised.

[2] https://www.kickstarter.com/about?ref=about_subnav.

[3] https://experiment.com.

to solve [4, 5]. The crowdfunding has been defined as «an open call, essentially through the Internet, for the provision of financial resources either in form of donation or in exchange for some form of reward and/or voting rights in order to support initiatives for specific purposes», by Schwienbacher and Larralde [6]. Although this definition may seem broad, in literature there are those who have raised the limits, indicating that the same leads to exclude certain types of fundraising that can be classified in the general term crowdfunding [7].

In general, it is possible to identify three related elements that are common to each fundraising definable as crowdfunding: crowds, funding and web 2.0. At the base of a funded project through crowdfunding, in fact, there is an autonomous aggregation of subjects, the crowd, which decides to invest in a specific project. The activity carried out is funding: a group of unrelated and independent subjects contributes to the achievement of an amount of money aimed at the realization of a specific project, of various nature, through the so-called micro-credit. The *trait d'union* between these two elements, the crowd and the funding, was the development of the web: the web 2.0. This expression indicates a development of the web 1.0, that of the origins, in 90 s, namely a participatory web that removed the barriers between the production and consumption of information [1]: therefore, the appropriate instruments are granted to make active participants of an interconnected reality and not just passive users of content[4]. In this large container, crowdfunding platforms find their space: virtual places dedicated to this alternative method of fundraising.

2.2 Crowdfunding Models

Included in the general concept of crowdfunding, many different types of fundraising are grouped together. In the last decade the literature has developed different classifications, basically all-encompassing. Firstly, we can distinguish between the "*ex post facto* crowdfunding" and the "*ex ante facto* crowdfunding". This type of classification is based on the moment in which the fundraising activity is launched: in the first case, the financing campaign takes place after the project, as a sort of recovery of funds, while, in the second, the financing is sought *ex ante*, to say before the project starts. Kappel [8], analyzing the specific case of the American recording industry, defines the *ex post facto* crowdfunding the case «where financial support is offered in exchange for a completed product» and the *ante facto* crowdfunding the one where «financial support is given on the front end to assist in achieving a mutually desired result» .

---

[4] Tim O'Reilley, in a famous post from 2005, defined the phenomenon: «Web 2.0 is the network as platform, spanning all connected devices; Web 2.0 applications are those that make the most of the intrinsic advantages of that platform: delivering software as a continually-updated service that gets better the more people use it, consuming and remixing data from multiple sources, including individual users, while providing their own data and services in a form that allows remixing by others, creating network effects through an "architecture of participation," and going beyond the page metaphor of Web 1.0 to deliver rich user experiences.» http://radar.oreilly.com/2005/10/web-20-compact-definition.html.

A further and commonly accepted classification distinguishes four types of crowdfunding, depending on whether it is based on (a) equity, (b) lending, (c) reward and (d) donation.

Equity-based crowdfunding is one in which «crowdfunders receive a financial compensation (e.g., equity, revenue, and profit-share arrangements)» [9]: as a result, the lender becomes a shareholder of the company through the purchase of shares. This is the model that, generally, is adopted by start-ups and SMEs in order to fund the most innovative projects.

Lending-based crowdfunding is the model that establishes a traditional debtor and lender relationship between donor and crowd-funder [10]: in such a manner, the lender contributes knowing that his reimbursement will consist of the repayment, increased by the interest accrued.

In reward-based crowdfunding, instead, lenders obtain an advantage, in non-monetary terms, in exchange for their economic contribution, such as, for example, pre-ordering of products or services.

Finally, the donation-based model is characterized by giving a grant from donors to the platform, without the first receiving any kind of material reward in return. As claimed by Rijanto [11] «The synergy from socially driven corporate and crowd-funding activities can be a significant source of funding while fulfilling social goals».

After outlining the general characteristics of crowdfunding, we will now analyze the impact of this phenomenon in universities and, in particular, in the world of scientific research.

3   Crowdfunding of Science

Crowdfunding stems from the need to seek alternative financing methods, both in the world of companies and in the public sector and, notably, in universities to fund research projects.

The traditional process for research funding always starts from the assumption that it is possible to draw on a small amount of resources, which must be attributed, following pre-established criteria, to research projects that are considered most deserving: an initial situation characterized by scarcity of resources necessarily implies a selection. To ensure fairness and objectivity in the distribution of grants, projects are evaluated based on a peer review process. In literature, several scholars widely criticize the general structure of these procedures, believing that it ends up making uniformity prevail over innovation [3, 12].

New and alternative forms of funding for research projects makes it possible to bypass the problem of the scarcity of resources that underlies the traditional research funding processes.

Science crowdfunding can, therefore, be seen as an alternative method of funding research, in which a team of researchers proposes its research project to the public, through a crowdfunding platform that allows funds to be raised by interested parties. Backers donate sums of so-called microcredit to support the project presented.

The crowdfunding of science may have been connected to the reward-based crowdfunding model as well as to the donation-based crowdfunding. In the first case, the small financiers will get a good or a service of modest size, as a reward, generally based on their participation, such as the mention of their name in the final paper of the research or a symbolic object, inherent to the same, maybe branded. In the second case, the amount of money given by the lender is by way of a donation, without there being a form of reward: in this case the relationship between researcher and financier is however mutually beneficial, because while the former obtains the funds for his own project, the second will be able to participate in the debate concerning the project itself, thanks to the information provided by the researchers, available online [13].

A recent study [14], based on the analysis of projects funded with crowdfunding from experiment.com[5], the largest of the independent platforms (Table 1), aimed at identifying the factors that most influence funding success, shows that young researchers or PhD students tend to be more successful and in this dynamic the prior publications have much less weight than in traditional processes: it is shown, therefore, that «the crowd may apply different criteria than traditional funders when deciding which projects to support» . The lack of information on why a citizen chooses to participate in a science crowdfunding has so far been placed as a limit to the investigation of this aspect [14, 15].

Table 1. Examples of some of the most used crowdfunding platforms (Doi: https://doi.org/10.1371/journal.pone.0208384.t001)

Name	URL	Opened	Status as of January 2018
Independent platforms			
Experiment	https://www.Experiment.com	2012	Active. 1,820 projects hosted
Petridish	http://blog.petridish.org/	2012	Closed. 32 projects hosted
Davincicrowd	http://www.davincicrowd.com	2012	Active. 92 projects hosted
Consano	http://www.consano.org	2013	Active. 67 projects hosted
Donorscure	http://www.donorscure.org	2013	Active. 16 projects hosted
Wallacea/Crowdscienoe	http://crowd.science	2014	Active. 36 projects hosted
Futsci	http://fiitsci.com	2015	Active. 12 projects hosted
Science Starter	http://www.sciencestarter.de	2015	Active. 122 projects hosted
Institution-specific platforms			
Cancer Research UK	http://myprojects.cancerresearchuk.org	2008	Closed
Georgia Institute of Technology	https://www.gatech.edu/	2013	Closed
UCLA	http://spark.ucla.edu	2014	Active, 15 projects hosted
Virginia Tech	http://crowdfiind.vt.edu	2017	Active. 29 projects hosted

https://doi.org/10.1371/joumal.pone.0208384.t001

3.1   Reporting Requirement: Open Data and Citizen Science

Regardless of the model in which a specific crowdfunding research project is framed, in any case it is necessary for the research team to implement a series of obligations aimed at communicating the phases and results of their research: science crowdfunding necessarily implies that some kind of feedback is given to the "crowd" that participated

---

[5] https://experiment.com.

in it. Communication with citizens-financiers is important at every stage: initially it is essential to attract attention to the project that a researcher intends to subsidize, in order to create your own audience and convince it to participate; subsequently it is relevant because those who have decided to invest an amount of money, even if small, in a scientific research, is consequently interested in the project and therefore also in the realization of the same [16]. To pursue the aforementioned purpose, hence, researchers must keep websites updated, publicize the various phases of their work on social media and respond to the interventions of the financiers [17]: in a research funded by traditional methods, all these tasks are not necessarily required.

Web 2.0 has allowed an evolution in the participation of citizens in the world of research that was unthinkable few decades ago: science crowdfunding makes this participation a pillar. In fact, science crowdfunding involves two other fundamental themes: (i) the public engagement in science and (ii) peer collaboration in science [13].

Public Engagement in Science. The issue of public engagement in science is linked to the very nature of crowdfunding for research: backers get updated information on the state of research and can participate in the debate developed on it. A recent study conducted on the #SciFund Challenge[6], a crowdfunding experiment in which 159 scientists attempted to finance their research [18] showed that high public engagement translates into successful science crowdfunding.

However, the level of interaction between funded researchers and public financiers can increase to take on the role of so-called "Citizen Science" [13, 14]: in such a case, this interconnection is not limited to an exchange of information but, on the contrary, public engagement in science is strengthened with the direct contribution of the public, through the participation of citizens in different tasks, such as collecting, categorizing, transcribing, or even analyzing scientific date [19]. It also aims to enable citizens to develop creative solutions, which becomes particularly effective in certain situations, such as with regard to research projects involving local communities [20].

In this way, multiple, and basically heterogeneous, external skills are put at the service of research, without financial compensation, thus representing a cost savings. If multiple advantages can be identified, many problematic aspects may be singled out: first, the need for a quality check concerning the work carried out by the citizens, as well as the coordination of the volunteers [21].

Peer Collaboration in Science. The issue of peer collaboration in science brings out a further aspect of science crowdfunding: namely, crowdfunding ceases to be seen solely as an alternative method of financing for research projects, to become a useful peer collaboration tool in science [13]. Greater outsourcing of the results of research can foster collaboration with very distant researchers and promote innovation by finding new solutions in order to tackle complex problems.

The impact of collaborative science has been extensively investigated and described by Nielsen [22] who believes that networked science is the path that will lead to the re-invention of scientific discovery. This characteristic of our time will be valued only

---

[6] https://scifundchallenge.org.

if we would be able to exploit its potential, amplifying collective intelligence and restructuring the attention of researchers.

After analyzing the general features of crowdfunding for research, with specific regard to the communication of research data, it is now necessary to pay attention, one the one hand, to the positive aspects and the opportunities and, on the other, the emerging critical issues related to the science crowdfunding.

4   Emerged Issues: Opportunities and Challenges

During the analysis of the phenomenon, in its characteristic elements, advantages and problematic aspects of the issue emerged. In the following paragraphs they will be summarized, in the most general lines.

4.1   Opportunities

The numerous researches funded with crowdfunding projects show that universities increasingly choose this alternative method of funding, taking advantage of that. The attempt to obtain funds in an alternative way is understandable bearing in mind the limited amount of basic resources and the difficulty of obtaining them [18]. There are many who point out that crowdfunding is a way to finance more innovative research, perhaps risky, which might not exceed the traditional selection processes [12, 14].

The true value of this practice does not lie in the ability to collect large sums of money, which are usually rather modest, but in that of creating a community of researchers and financiers, which talks and communicates. The advantages that emerge from this communication are mutual: on the one hand, academics have the opportunity to gain visibility to their research, as well as to fund it, while on the other, backers have the opportunity to become aware of the various steps of the research, with different degrees of involvement, from passive listening to information, to active participation in the case of citizen science, through dialogues and exchanges of opinions by means of blogs and websites. In other words, a crowd-founded research necessarily develops communication skills and, conversely, the dialogue with funders allows a combination of very different skills that, if well channeled, add value to the project.

It is important to focus attention on the concept of community, which is the basis of crowdfunding: the relationship is not only one by one, researcher and backer, because a real network is created, a virtuous circle, which connects a broad variety of researchers who can deal with the same issues, but from different points of view.

4.2   Challenges

As emerged in the course of the dissertation, and summarized in the previous paragraph, the benefits that push researchers to undertake crowdfunding projects to finance their research are wide and varied. On the other hand, there are several problematic aspects of the issue.

Firstly, although crowdfunding allows the financing of riskier research projects, it must be borne in mind that, by proposing a research on a platform, control over the validity of the project itself and on the solidity of research, which is instead implemented in a traditional process of financing at the state or European level, is bypassed. For a complete analysis of the phenomenon, this bias cannot be avoided in the selection of research topics [17].

Secondly, the negative aspects of communication skills cannot be ignored. Communication, in fact, requires both extensive efforts and a lot of time, both the creation of a sort of "marketing of the research", to make it attractive to potential financiers. These tasks are not always easy to carry out by the research team.

Some critical points also emerge in relation to Citizen Science. First of all, it is not always easy to get citizens included and ensure that they are effectively and authentically involved in the project activities. Furthermore, the coordination of a multitude of volunteers [13], having very different backgrounds and therefore also characterized by a different lexicon and without a high and appropriate level of technical expertise, may not be easy to achieve.

The need to keep communication active on the research developments, which we have seen to be a characteristic feature of crowd-funded projects, brings with it, however, some of the typical difficulties linked to the world of Open Science: the risk of theft of one's ideas from other researchers it is still very perceived, from a psychological point of view within the academia, regardless of the fact that, frequently, this perception derives predominantly from the personal attitude of the researcher [23].

Finally, a problematic issue, especially concerning the individual citizen-financier, is the trust to be placed in a platform: it is limited by the lack of transparency in the management of the same, which discourages the contribution of the individual and his participation.

5   The Regulation of Crowdfunding: Policies

5.1   European Policies

Crowdfunding, nowadays, is of considerable importance for the industrial sector, with particular reference to small-medium enterprises and start-ups. The importance acquired by this emerging alternative form of financing has meant that even the European institutions were interested in the phenomenon. In March 2018 a proposal for a regulation on crowdfunding service providers was published by the European Commission[7], which is currently subjected to the co-decision procedure: the aim pursued by the European institutions through this document is to become a relevant source of non-bank financing, through which to pursue the general goals of the European Union, with specific reference to the development of Union Capital Markets. This regulatory proposal is aimed at promoting sustainable financial integration, as an accelerator of economic growth.

The interest of European institutions in developing a legal framework for crowdfunding at European level stems from the fact that the sector is regulated at national level and it is not uncommon for the different disciplines to diverge greatly from one another.

---

[7] https://eur-lex.europa.eu/legal-content/EN/TXT/?uri=CELEX:52018PC0113.

The proposed regulation comes at the end of a project started in 2013, when the European Commission launched a public consultation on crowdfunding in the European Union[8], having the objective of to explore how EU action could promote crowdfunding in Europe. As a result of the survey, in 2014, the European Commission published a communication entitled "Unleashing the potential of crowdfunding in the European Union"[9], which sets out to establish a group of experts to advise the Commission, to pursue policies of raising awareness of the issue, and finally proceeding to map the evolution of national regulations, to assess the need for regulatory action at European level, which has indeed come with the 2018 regulatory proposal.

The European initiatives aimed at regulating the phenomenon of crowdfunding, although well underway, are not specifically provided for crowdfunding for scientific research. In fact, in the European legal framework, science crowdfunding is part of the Open Science movement. In a report produced for the European Commission in 2015 [24] it was, in fact, analyzed how, through crowdfunding projects, the Open Science movement could help Europe to foster Open Innovation, namely «a paradigm that assumes that firms can and should use external ideas as well as internal ideas, and internal and external paths to market, as they look to advance their technology» [25]. Although recognizing that, at the state of the art, there is a lack of incentives for researchers to undertake crowdfunding campaigns, especially considering efforts and time required, the report highlights, however, the possibility of bringing out ideas from multiple stakeholders through crowdfunded projects.

A study conducted in 2017 for the European Commission, carried out in synergy between the stakeholders of the crowdfunding ecosystem in Europe [26], had the purpose of analyzing the potential of crowdfunding and other forms of alternative finance to support research and innovation. Here emerges the fact that, apart from the fragmentation at national level, there are many local well-functioning ecosystems that are disconnected from each other, even within the same Member State. Consequently, in proposing policies to be adopted at European level, an action aimed at strengthening the already existing ecosystems has been suggested by the report, providing models and regulation, generally applicable, as well as standard agreements between research institutions and alternative financing platforms. The need to establish standards at European level is also emphasized with reference to the transparency of the platforms: it is therefore recommended to develop European codes of conduct aimed at increasing user confidence.

Finally, it should be noted that, in the Work Program 2018-2020 of the Horizon 2020 project, in the section entitled "Support to Open Science, Open Access and Open Data"[10], one of the eight action lines is dedicated to Citizen Science which, as seen above, can also be considered an extreme development of the concept of collaborative science that is the basis of crowdfunding for research.

---

[8] http://ec.europa.eu/finance/consultations/2013/crowdfunding/index_en.htm.

[9] https://eur-lex.europa.eu/legal-content/EN/TXT/?uri=CELEX:52014DC0172.

[10] https://ec.europa.eu/research/participants/data/ref/h2020/wp/2018-2020/main/h2020-wp1820-societies_en.pdf.

Ultimately it can be argued that, as far as the legal framework is concerned, at the moment, there are no precise actions aimed at determining a European regulation of research crowdfunding. On the other hand, however, the desire to strengthen the phenomenon would seem to be linked to the European policies for strengthening Open Science. However, the potential to be developed and the challenges to be faced in order to promote the research crowdfunding persist, in light of the fact that there are many examples of projects funded with this alternative funding model.

5.2 Traditional Instrument of Law: The "Ricerca e Talenti" Foundation of the University of Turin

In 2012, from the collaboration between the University of Turin and an Italian banking institution, "Cassa di Risparmio di Torino", a university foundation was set up with the aim of promoting fundraising activities and supporting projects for young researchers University, the foundation "Ricerca e Talenti" (research and talents)[11].

The foundation established its legal basis in law 388/2000[12], which established the so-called "university foundations", namely an instrument for reorganizing the university system, which allows the possibility of privatizing certain activities and services, outsourcing them, such as, for instance, searching for alternative funds from traditional processes. One of the objectives that the foundation set itself was to combine traditional fundraising activities with new fundraising methods, such as crowdfunding. The foundation has also pursued projects to bring citizenship closer to the world of research and to raise awareness about new forms of donation for the university and the public research. Although the experience carried out by the University of Turin was certainly innovative and held great potential, at this moment, the foundation has just started the liquidation process. The case of the "Ricerca e Talenti" foundation is an emblematic attempt to regulate innovative and young phenomena through traditional law institutions, which by their nature require ample flexibility in regulation. The try to enclose innovation in rigid traditional legal instruments inevitably risks reducing its potential and hindering its development.

Provide that the crowdfunding discipline for research is implemented with traditional instruments of national law, on the one hand it raises fragmentation [25], which is disadvantageous to the successful implementation of projects and, on the other, subjects these new and innovative phenomena to the risk of seeing themselves entangled in obligations far removed from their nature. It should be noted, for instance, that in Italy, starting from 2019, with the law 3/2019[13], the foundations have been assimilated to political parties: as a result, a series of heavy obligations regarding transparency have been imposed also for foundations. These bureaucratic burdens do not at all enhance a phenomenon, such as that of crowdfunding for scientific research, whose development comes from online platforms.

---

[11] http://ricercaetalenti.it.

[12] www.gazzettaufficiale.it/eli/id/2000/12/29/000G0441/sg.

[13] Article 1, paragraph 20; www.gazzettaufficiale.it/eli/id/2019/01/16/18G00170/sg.

5.3   Regulatory Gap for Crowdfunding of Science

Between apocalyptic and integrated intellectuals [27], the way to favor the phenomenon of crowdfunding is in the middle: science crowdfunding cannot be thought of as a new method of funding research that will replace the traditional. It is more realistic to think that it can be a method of finding alternative funds, which goes alongside the traditional, becoming not only a complementary fundraising method, but also one of the many training tools available to researchers, young and old, for allow them to interface with new realities, such as communicating directly to citizens.

In order to achieve this result, it is necessary to adopt unitary policies, at least at national level, while remaining within the reference framework provided by European Institutions: the challenges are many and it is necessary on the one hand, tackle the challenges that the issue proposes, and on the other hand, increase the awareness of researchers who already carry out crowdfunding campaigns for the research. If the European institutions are in charge of directly financing the macro-research projects, on the other hand, they could foresee policies that allow the financing of micro-projects through standardized crowdfunding procedures. European institutions are the best place to pursue the balance between the principle of the freedom of science and the need to produce quality and reliable research.

The phenomenon of crowdfunding is receiving substantial acknowledgment: this is demonstrated by the empirical data that shows growth as well as by local attempts to provide a discipline and a legal framework [26]. The interest of the European institutions was such as to provide for the adoption of a regulation for European suppliers of crowdfunding services for companies, following a considerable public consultation process. However, there is a gap of regulation due to the fact that the discipline currently undergoing final approval does not take into account crowdfunding of science in any way.

If the goal of European policies is to foster the development of the phenomenon in its entirety, the means to reach the goal would not seem adequate, considering that the specificity of crowdfunding of science is not taken into account.

In light of the proposed analysis of opportunities and challenges regarding the subject, it emerges, therefore, the need of a specific attention to the phenomenon: it is considered necessary to exclude the analogical application of the discipline realized for companies to crowdfunding for research, since it has a series of peculiarities that must necessarily be evaluated in the definition of a legal discipline.

Bringing the phenomenon of crowdfunding back to the Open Science movement appears to be reasonable (for instance, think about the previously discussed topic of the duties of communicating results of researches to the public), but excluding any reference in the identification of the European discipline seems to involve a weakening of the new discipline.

In light of what has been analyzed previously, in order to ensure the elimination of impediments to the growth of the phenomenon that is a source of great opportunities, the potential should be exploited by policymakers.

Many advantages have emerged from the analysis of the theme of Open Data and collaborative science, resulting from the engagement of all the actors at stake. Providing a discipline at European level, with a strong legislative instrument such as the

Regulation, to promote the phenomenon of crowdfunding, without taking into account crowdfunding of science, requires future works in order to deal with identifying the best policy to be adopted.

6 Conclusions

In a globalized and hyperconnected world, reshaped by ICT, even scientific research inevitably is affected by the change. Universities and research institutes are emblematic spaces of freedom, in which dialogue is fostered to the maximum extent, in order to promote the sharing of ideas and innovation. It must be considered that in a digital university, there is a new category of "people interacting with the University" [28], thanks to the use of ICT, unlike in the past.

The phenomenon of crowdfunding, born mainly in the corporate world, has also affected the research sector, as confirmed by the aforementioned statistics.

It would be advisable for the attention of policymakers to focus on the peculiarities of crowdfunding of science, to fully exploit the potential of the phenomenon, both as an alternative method of financing and as a tool to foster collaborative science, to bridge the regulatory gap created with the regulation in approval phase.

References

1. Floridi, L.: The 4th Revolution How the Infosphere is Reshaping Human Reality. OUP, Oxford (2014)
2. Zhang, Y., Weina, H., Shunbo, Y.: Mapping the scientific research on open data: a bibliometric review. Learn. Publ. **31**(2), 95–106 (2018). https://doi.org/10.1002/leap.1110
3. Eisfeld-Reschke, J., Herb, U., Wenzlaff, K.: Research funding in open science. In: Bartling, S., Friesike, S. (eds.) Opening Science, pp. 237–253. Springer, Cham (2014). https://doi.org/10.1007/978-3-319-00026-8_16
4. Kleemann, F., Günter Voß, G., Rieder, K.: Un(der)paid innovators: the commercial utilization of consumer work through crowdsourcing. STI Stud. **4**(1), 5–26 (2008)
5. Belleflamme, P., Lambert, T., Schwienbacher, A.: Crowdfunding: tapping the right crowd. JBV **29**(5), 585–609 (2014). https://doi.org/10.1016/j.jbusvent.2013.07.003
6. Schwienbacher, A., Larralde, B.: Crowdfunding of small entrepreneurial ventures. In: Cumming, D. (ed.) Handbook of Entrepreneurial Finance, pp. 369–391. OUP, Oxford (2012). https://doi.org/10.2139/ssrn.1699183
7. Mollick, E.: The dynamics of crowdfunding: an exploratory study. JBV **29**(1), 1–16 (2014). https://doi.org/10.1016/j.jbusvent.2013.06.005
8. Kappel, T.: Ex ante crowdfunding and the recording industry: a model for the US. Loy. LA Ent. L. Rev. **29**(3), 375–385 (2008)
9. Belleflamme, P., Lambert, T., Schwienbacher, A.: Individual crowdfunding practices. VC **15**(4), 313–333 (2013). https://doi.org/10.1080/13691066.2013.785151
10. Frydrych, D., Bock, A.J., Kinder, T., Koeck, B.: Exploring entrepreneurial legitimacy in reward-based crowdfunding. VC, **16**(3), 247–269 (2014). https://doi.org/10.1080/13691066.2014.916512
11. Rijanto, A.: Donation-based crowdfunding as corporate social responsibility activities and financing. J. Gen. Manag. **43**(2), 79–88 (2018). https://doi.org/10.1177/0306307017748125

12. Horrobin, D.F.: Peer review of grant applications: a harbinger for mediocrity in clinical research? Lancet **348**(9037), 1293–1295 (1996). https://doi.org/10.1016/s0140-6736(96)08029-4
13. Hui, J.S., Gerber, E.: Crowdfunding science: sharing research with an extended audience. In: Proceedings of the 18th ACM Conference on Computer Supported Cooperative Work & Social Computing, pp. 31–43. ACM, New York (2015). https://doi.org/10.1145/2675133.2675188
14. Sauermann, H., Franzoni, C., Shafi, K.: Crowdfunding scientific research: descriptive insights and correlates of funding success. PLoS ONE **14**(1), e0208384 (2019). https://doi.org/10.1371/journal.pone.0208384
15. McKenny, A.F., et al.: How should crowdfunding research evolve? A survey of the entrepreneurship theory and practice editorial board. ETP **41**(2), 291–304 (2017). https://doi.org/10.1111/etap.12269
16. Vachelard, J., Gambarra-Soares, T., Augustini, G., Riul, P., Maracaja-Coutinho, V.: A guide to scientific crowdfunding. PLoS Biol. **14**(2), e1002373 (2016). https://doi.org/10.1371/journal.pbio.1002373
17. Ikkatai, Y., McKay, E., Yokoyama, H.M.: Science created by crowds: a case study of science crowdfunding in Japan. JCOM, **17**(3), A06, 1–14 (2018). https://doi.org/10.22323/2.17030206
18. Byrnes, J.E.K., Ranganathan, J., Walker, B.L.E., Faulkes, Z.: To crowdfund research, scientists must build an audience for their work. PLoS ONE **9**(12), e110329 (2014). https://doi.org/10.1371/journal.pone.0110329
19. Bonney, R., et al.: Next steps for citizen science. Science **343**(6178), 1436–1437 (2014). https://doi.org/10.1126/science.1251554
20. Petridis, P., Fischer-Kowalski, M., Singh, S.J.: Noll, D: The role of science in sustainability transitions: citizen science, transformative research, and experiences from Samothraki island Greece. ISJ **12**(1), 115–134 (2017). https://doi.org/10.24043/isj.8
21. Sauermann, H., Franzoni, C.: Crowd science user contribution patterns and their implications. Proc. Natl. Acad. Sci. **112**(3), 679–684 (2015). https://doi.org/10.1073/pnas.1408907112
22. Nielsen, M. (ed.): Reinventing Discovery: The New Era of Networked Science. Prince University Press, Princeton (2011)
23. Moksness, L., Olsen, S.O.: Understanding researchers' intention to publish in open access journals. J. Doc. **73**(6), 1149–1166 (2017). https://doi.org/10.1108/jd-02-2017-0019
24. Crouzier, T.: Science Ecosystem 2.0: how will change occur. Publications Office of the European Union, Luxembourg (2015). https://doi.org/10.2777/67279
25. Chesbrough, H., Vanhaverbeke, W., West, J. (eds.): Open Innovation: Researching a New Paradigm. Oxford University Press on Demand, Oxford (2006)
26. Jakimowicz, K., Osimo, D., Gallo, C., Pappalepore, G., Weber, C.: Assessing the potential for Crowdfunding and other forms of alternative finance to support research and innovation. Publications Office of the European Union, Luxembourg (2017). https://doi.org/10.2777/046608
27. Eco, U., Lumley, R. (eds.): Apocalypse Postponed. Flamingo, London (1995)
28. De Martin, J.C. (ed.): Università futura: tra democrazia e bit. Turin, Codice (2017)

Open Data Ecosystems: A Comparison of Visual Models

Csaba Csáki(✉) ⓘD

Corvinus University of Budapest, Budapest, Hungary
Csaki.Csaba@uni-corvinus.hu

Abstract. The practice of open (public) data (OD) is usually interpreted in the context of open government initiatives. Public data may be opened up for the reason of transparency in support of accountability or with the intent to allow for innovative re-use in value added services. To investigate the resulting complex setting of OD researchers often use the ecosystem metaphor. This approach is based on theories of biology and ecology and over the years the ecosystem view of OD has become the dominant model underlying discussions. The research reported in this paper has been set out with the goal of collecting and analysing the various open data visual models that had appeared in relevant literature. Results of a systematic comparison and categorization indicate that while there have been many papers published utilizing ecosystem as a model to investigate the OD phenomena, there is no common way of how to represent entities and relationships of such an ecosystem in a visual model. The final goal is to to prepare the ground for an open data ecosystem model visual notation.

Keywords: Open data · Open data reuse · Open data ecosystem · Open data ecosystem model · Visual modelling notation

1 Introduction

The rise of the open government idea is typically dated around 2009 (or so) but the practice of open (public sector) data is much older than that. In developed countries governmental data was identified as a cornerstone for transparency and thus account-ability as early as the late 50 s. Over time the principle of 'right to information' (RtO) or 'freedom of information' (FoI) has evolved [21]. Later, in the 90 s this was augmented with the possibility of commercially reusing public sector information (PSI) in value added services. With the arrival of the Open Government (OG) movement the picture has become even more complex as transparency goals have become mixed with free availability of government data to be used in innovative services [8, 47].

To explain the open data phenomenon researchers started to apply approaches and models utilized in private sector data management such as the data lifecycle, data supply chain or data value chain. However, in the context of open government (OG) and open government data (OGD or OD for short) such models could not cope with the large number of actors, the complexity of the data flow, and the various relationships of participants present in the data chain. In addition, it was realized that the 'chain' needs to be more like a loop, offering feedback for end users of OD [43]. Furthermore, the final

© Springer Nature Switzerland AG 2019
A. Kő et al. (Eds.): EGOVIS 2019, LNCS 11709, pp. 16–30, 2019.
https://doi.org/10.1007/978-3-030-27523-5_2

goal was not simply the ability to reuse OD in services, but raised questions about the benefits of publishing and reusing public data (especially when data from different government sources are integrated or even combined with private data). Such benefits were investigated at individual, local, community or even at societal level. In order to understand the resulting complex picture of the practice of open government data more and more scholars have started to apply a metaphor rooted in biology and treat participants and their actions and relationships as part of an ecosystem (ES) [33]. With a growing interest in the ecosystem approach several authors presented visual representation of their interpretation of the open data ecosystem (ODE). However, this resulted in a proliferation of various visual models, each using their own notation and focusing on different aspects of the ecosystem or using a unique lens.

In order to establish an acceptable common notation for open data ecosystems this paper proposes a five-phase research aimed at putting forward recommendations for such a visual notation to model open data ecosystems and also presents the outcome of the first phase already executed (other phases have also been completed but all the results would not fit the size of a single conference paper, besides, the logical evolution of the model ought to be presented in sequence). The five phases are as follows:

1. Review existing ODE visual models, categorize them and identify common elements used as well as weaknesses or missing elements;
2. Establish a set of design requirements for ODE visual model (i.e. a baseline for required model elements) – based on the models from the first step;
3. Review potential alternatives for ODE visual notation based on existing (engineering and software, etc.) modelling notations;
4. Design a visual notation for ODE along with a metamodel;
5. Test the notation by comparing it to the models collected during the first step and also by applying it to existing case studies published.

The expected final outcome would have both theoretical and (especially) practical significance. Theoretical contributions include a means of presenting ODE concepts and elements, analyzing actors, their relationships and actions; while for practice it would offer the ability to augment case studies or being able to compare country or area specific ecosystems in a standardized way.

Consequently, the paper would first review definitions of open data and ecosystems before proceeding to show the need for a common notation of ODE visual models. After the methodology section the paper reviews close to three dozen publications that include or offer open date models in some visual format, then these models are evaluated, categorized and compared. Finally, the paper presents key direction for the remaining four steps and thereby prepares the way for collecting requirements for ODE notation.

2 Open (Government) Data Ecosystems

2.1 Open Government Data

Over the last two decades vast amount of data related to the various functions of the public sector (PS) have been made available with various levels of granularity. In most jurisdictions traditional freedom of information legislations have been established first eventually followed by reuse policies [21]. While access for transparency is usually provided for free, reuse has different fee models depending on the country. However, the open data movement has changed this landscape once it reached the public sector [4], because the essence of open data is that it is accessible to everyone, it is available to any user for free, and it may be reproduced with no additional copyright fee to the re-user, provided that credit is given to the source and the results are also shared (albeit not necessarily free anymore, depending on the value added) [31].

Open data initiatives in a narrow sense are treated as a task of making public sector information available by providing access to it in various forms. In a broader view they fall under the umbrella of Electronic Government (eGov - [4]) where the intent is to use information technology (IT) and the World Wide Web to enhance the efficiency, effectiveness, transparency, and accountability of governments. Open data also plays a crucial role in another public administration governance method called open govern-ment (OG), which is aimed at allowing new spaces for transparency through higher openness and continued dialog between governments and citizens. Citizens should have the right to access public sector data, information and documents generated by governments and should be able to participate in related procedures [8]. Even in OG context, one must take note that not all data that is generated, collected, stored, or retrieved by public sector bodies is automatically open data – not even if it is available in digital format. One of the key drivers of open government data is its power to encourage collaboration and a free flow of innovative ideas [22, 47].

However, it appeared, that traditional data modelling frameworks, such as the data supply chain or data value chain approaches had been often inadequate to properly reflect and handle the complexity inherent in the setting surrounding OGD initiatives – with its multitude of actors, their motivations, goals, and values.

2.2 Information Ecology and Ecosystems

In order to understand and explain the issues of organizational and inter-organizational information sharing [30] applied the principles of ecology. Ecology is defined as the "*scientific study of the processes influencing the distribution and abundance of organisms and the transformation and flux of energy and matter*" ([14], p. 74). Therefore, information ecology means "*a system of people, practices, values, and technologies in a particular local environment*" ([30], p. 49). The goal of information ecologies is to understand and describe the elements of information systems – including roles and tasks – and the relationships formed amongst those elements. [6] identified several elements of information ecologies. Their model considers three different environments: outside, organizational, and informational. Within those environments the key elements are: stakeholders, their strategy, culture and behaviour, as well as principles, rules, and processes, with all these relying on a technological architecture. Considering an inter-organizational information ecology model [14] claimed that information sharing between organizations is a disjointed process. Any ecology relies on a few elements or "*keystone species*" ([30], p. 53) to function properly, as they execute or enable crucial functions. For example, to connect elements across institu-tional boundaries an inter-organizational information ecology requires mediators [32].

A biological ecosystem consists of different organisms that form a community and live in a given physical environment that provides resources but also imposes restrictions on them. As an analogy, a business ecosystem is a dynamic structure of interconnected firms and organizations that engage in various interactions and are dependent on each other and their shared environment with each having its own goal [33]. Furthermore, a digital ecosystem is defined as an *"open, loosely coupled, domain clustered, demand-driven, self-organising agent environment, where each agent of each species is proactive and responsive to its own benefit[...] but is also responsible to the system"* ([3], p. 399). Agents may be humans, hardware, software, or autonomous robots that use computer platforms as infrastructure for technical and social sharing. By considering bi-directional relationships between actors, ecosystem models assume (and allow for the analysis of) different types of connections between producers and users. Indeed, one key feature of an ecosystem is a rich set of actor-roles.

2.3 Ecosystem as a Metaphor to Represent Open Data Settings

Open data ecosystem(s) (ODEs) is a specific way of looking at how participating actors and groups create shared meaning and generate value around open data and how the structural properties of their interactions shape this process, which in turn enables or constrains the growth and health of the ecosystem itself. However, there might not always be clear, identifiable boundaries and the structure of an OD ecosystem may constantly change as well.

Open government data ecosystems thus may be defined as dynamic and open systems *"where stakeholders of different sizes and roles find, manage, archive, publish, reuse, integrate, mashup, and consume open government data in connection with online tools, services and societies"* ([13], p. 326). ODEs have several key roles and various authors have proposed a range of additional roles. A comprehensive review of ODE roles is provided by [47], who also names specific participants taking up those roles. Roles include data suppliers, users, developers (building applications), complementors (providing extra services), intermediate data consumers, and facilitators. Typical (actual) participants taking up above roles include not only government actors but private organizations or individuals as well: governmental departments, public sector agencies, civil servants, their partners, citizens, communities at large, and other individual stakeholders.

However, there is no accepted notation how to (visually) model open data ecosystems. Therefore, the following research objective has been formulated: Identify Open Data Ecosystem visual models in relevant literature and analyse how they represent elements and concepts commonly associated with ODE.

3 Methodology: Systematic Review of ODE Models

Under the above objective the following research questions were proposed: (1) What are the existing ODE visual models used in related literature? (2) How such models may be categorized? (3) What commonalities can be identified in such models? To answer these questions a 5 phase research design was created as presented in the Introduction. This paper presents the first step that answers the three questions above.

The research method selected is a systematic literature review based on the combination of the PRISMA method [25] and the approach advocated by [45]. The research framework utilized the first four phases of the five phases of the latter: (1) definition of review scope; (2) conceptualization of topic; (3) literature search; (4) literature analysis and synthesis; (5) research agenda; while the third and fourth steps (literature search and preliminary synthesis) also considered the detailed selection steps of the former: Identification, Screening, Eligibility, and Inclusion.

Under the [45] framework the scope of the review is the open data ecosystems domain. Intended audience includes both scholars and OD practitioners, while the focus is to create a model notation that is able to consider various (existing) ODE model interpretations. Therefore, the conceptualization of topic (aimed at selecting and defining key terms) considered a selection of a short list of broad terms to ensure a wide coverage of potential literature, i.e. this was not a sample selection (as PRISMA was planned to be used to refine and fine-tune a broad selection). The terms were based on the discussions in Sect. 2 above: Open Data Ecosystem, Open Data Ecosystem Model, Open Government Ecosystem, Open Government Data Ecosystem. The search strategy included two rounds conducted in January and February of 2018 and considered all types of English language publications (i.e. not only papers from selected journals, but allowed for white papers, quoted blogs, and research reports as well as Master thesis and PhD dissertations – to be consistent with the principle of wide coverage). The above terms have been searched in both the Scopus database and in Google Scholar and resulted in an integrated set of 583 documents as the input to the *Identification* phase of PRISMA. Then 103 duplicates as well as 65 non-English items, citations and non-scientific reports have been removed leading to 415 identified starting records.

In the first round of *Screening*, articles were assessed by their title and abstract and as a result 3 were eliminated due to errors in the title or author field (as paper could not be identified properly) and an additional 67 was also excluded as the item actually discussed other fields (the paper was from other scientific area – such as physics – and had nothing to do with OD ecosystem). The remaining 345 had a second round of Screening (articles that mentioned open government data or open government along with ecosystem or ecology were included) and 96 had been eliminated due to the fact that they had nothing to do with ecosystem (3 were full conference proceedings, not one item; 2 considered legal aspects of OD or OG; 9 looked at organizational issues only; 7 dealt with policy; while 74 with other, general areas of OG, and 3 with various other irrelevant issues). The *Eligibility* step thus started with 249 items and the full-text of the articles were assessed in two rounds. First studies were paged through to see their relevance regarding ecosystems and those that focused exclusively either on open data or on ecosystem separately were excluded: 124 items were left out, as they had turned out to be not interesting after this review pass. In addition, 24 could not be reviewed as the full paper was not available, and there were 2 additional duplicates found. Then 99 papers were read even deeper for a second *Eligibility* round leading to the exclusion of 58 items as they did not actually have any usable model of ODE. So finally *41 papers* were left to be used in collecting ODE model examples.

The *Inclusion* step of PRISMA is focused on collecting visual models from the remaining documents. During this process 15 items turned out have no usable model. While 4 others had no original model, instead they had referenced models from other papers – if these referenced papers had not been in the mix yet, they now were considered: the result was 11 new papers (all of which had been excluded in one of the earlier steps, mostly during Screening). 4 items had two different visual ODE representations, leading to a total number of 37 visual ODE models from 33 pieces. These models were then all collected and analysed – and this data analyses is discussed in the next section while an overview of the papers and results can be seen in Table 1.

4 Visual Representations of Open Data Ecosystems

The first appearance of a relevant ecosystem model found during the search is in [35]. Although this is not an open data model, its significance lies in the fact that this is the earliest diagram representing the connection between people and data that is later reused by papers analysing open data ecosystems: it depicts a simple process from people to data mitigated by the trio of Policy, Access Network, and Standards (p. 15) – all being part of various ODE models later.

While the concentric shell model of open data supply presented by [1] is not directly connected to the ecosystem approach, it does look at data from the perspective of users and is also referenced by ODE papers. It lists features of open data such as known, attainable and usable – which are all important features in ODE as well, and also presents the steps a user has to follow to assess if data was suitable for the desired purpose.

The model representing the 'Characteristics of business ecosystem' by [33] (p. 64) may also be considered an important pre-cursor to ODE models: while its focus is business ES, the features listed are all important for ODE as well and the model is regularly referenced as a starting point for presenting ODE specific models.

It actually took a while until the above ecosystem visualizations had an impact on ODE representations. In this sense the representation of the infrastructure and ecosystem of artefacts and events of a specific case study by [7] could be considered to be the first real ODE visual model (p. 3). The infrastructure is defined through a list of technical components and processes, while the ecosystem (emerging over the infrastructure) is made up of a series of interrelated tools and services and the relationships formed between these components.

The 'Assemblage of open-data complementarities' by [24] (p. 11) is essentially a data flow in a value chain with three types of components (identified in a legend): physical artefacts, human agency, and material agency. While it is not called an ecosystem, the goal is to represent instances of open-data-use with the intent to identify so called 'complementarities', which later became a key part of ODE as intermediaries. The article also noted on the autonomous emergence of features of an open data 'assemblage' (again an allusion to the ES concept): the physical artefacts 'allow' the human and material agencies to evolve raw (open) data into innovative services.

While the above five early examples may not be definitive cases of ODE visual models, the two models in [10, 11] do state explicitly the intention to provide

Table 1. Overview of papers with open data ecosystem visual model

Y.	Paper	Model type	Shapes/Lines	Legend	Comments
2002–5	[35]	Components	Boxes, arrows	N/A	Mixed types of concepts;
	[1]	Conceptual	Circles	N/A	Open data desired features
	[33]	Conceptual	Boxes, lines	No	Descriptive feature relationships (business ecosystem)
2011	[7]	Technological	Boxes, arrows with text	No	Services, tools, relationships, over Infrastructure (specific)
	[24]	Data flow	Shapes, arrows	Yes	Value chain
2012–3	[10]	Data flow	Circles, arrows	Yes	Actor types, some activities
	[11]	Data flow	Circles, boxes, various arrows	No	Just 3 actor groups/types
	[16]	Conceptual	Overlapping circles	N/A	Context - mixed roles and actors (types)
	[17]	Conceptual	Text, arrows	N/A	Loop – very generic
2014	[15]	Actor	Boxes, arrows	In text	Actor groups and relationship (over OD as platform)
		Technological	Layers	In text	Architectural
	[18]	Actor - role	Text, circles, arrows	No	Role types and relationships
		Conceptual	Ovals	N/A	Conceptual elements of ODE
2015	[26]	Actor – role	Boxes, arrows	No	Value network
	[28]	Attributes	Dots, squares, colours	Yes	Attributes for categorization (of anything, e.g. actors)
	[34]	Actor - role	Text, arrows	No	Actor types
	[40]	Conceptual	Concentric colour circles	N/A	Mixed elements: actors, roles, and abstract concepts
	[41]	Actor-relationship	Icons, boxes, arrows	No	Actors, flow, activities, relationships, contributions
	[42]	Actor-relationship	Circles, text, squares, arrows	No	Capital – simplified

(*continued*)

Table 1. (*continued*)

Y.	Paper	Model type	Shapes/Lines	Legend	Comments
2016	[2]	Actor - role	Text, embedded boxes, arrows	Yes	Roles and contributions
		Activities	Text, arrows	N/A	Feedback; case specific;
	[5]	Conceptual	Boxes, coloured arrows	Yes	Dependencies, logical arrows
	[9]	Components (& influence)	Boxes, text, arrows	In text	Main participants, groups and processes in lifecycle
	[12]	Conceptual	Conc. circles	N/A	Circular (mixed concepts)
	[19]	Mixed	Various shapes, colours, arrows	No	Actors, services, process – over a technical platform
	[43]	Actor/Data flow	Various shapes & arrows, text	Yes	Application area specific
	[46]	Actor – role	Various icons, shapes, arrows	No	Actor categories (role and some action)/specific case
2017	[20]	Service, abstract models	Various shapes, colours, arrows	No	Service as an element of ODE with capabilities
	[23]	Role	Circles	No	Four generic roles
	[27]	Role-relationship	Icons, boxes, arrows	No	New role and its relationships to other (general) roles
	[29]	Data flow	Boxes, arrows	In title	Process with feedback
		Mixed	Boxes, arrows	Partial	Actor, data flow, notation
	[36]	Process	Text, arrows	In text	Org. steps of building ODE
	[37]	Actor-relationship	Icons, lines	No	Specific application; Entities;
	[38]	Mixed	Text, arrows,	No	Rules to mitigate uncertainty
	[39]	Conceptual	Overlap circles	N/A	Only three 'dimensions'
	[44]	Activities (by Actors)	Boxes, arrows, text	No	A few activities & relationships (country specific)

representation(s) of ODE. [10] shows the flow of data in the ecosystem of three actor types (p. 9): government, businesses and citizens each may supply data to another actor type directly, while government and businesses may use either of the three classes of data to deliver additional services. While [11] has some added activity beyond the actor types (where the trio of government, businesses and citizens are now augmented with the actor group of application developers), it still focuses on the data flow (p. 2). However, the goal here is to explain the characteristics of what they call the OD 'marketplace' with the intent to explain emerging business models. Although there is payment from customers to supplies (of data or services), the terminology used (such as 'intermediaries') points towards the idea of an ecosystem.

The model next in chronological order is actually not an open data but an open government ecosystem representation by [16] that presents the domains and environment comprising an OG ecosystem (p. 910). It is important, however, for three reasons: the paper is well received and quoted by not only OG but OD researchers alike; open government is the base for and catalyser of open data as well as OD is key to successful OG programs; finally, the components in this model often reappear in OD models as well (with special attention to the recommendation to consider the environment of an ecosystem). In contrast to the [10, 11] models, the three key actor groups here are Government, Innovators, and Businesses and Citizens together. Beyond context the diagram also alludes to other elements of and activities within an ecosystem (such as policies, practices, expectations, etc.) but instead of events, associated with actor types.

While investigating the evolution of Digital Infrastructures, [17] presents another view (p. 912) that had an influence on ODE models: although its conceptual approach resulted in a very generic loop of socio-technical mechanisms, the consideration of how actions at various levels influence the (shared) infrastructure as well as the idea of generative evolution are central to several ODE models later (see for example the value loop of [22]).

[15] has actually presented two distinct ideas how ODE may be visualized (p. 662 and 663). The first one concentrates on relationships of actor-groups (over OD as a service platform), while the other focuses on the technological architecture needed for ODE. The research originally looked at the need to provide an acceptable (scientific) definition for ODE and their claim is that the key participants above the three discussed by others (i.e. Civil Society, Government and Developers) are Universities and Funding agencies – and the roles they may assume (see also above) are data provider, data consumer, data aggregator and data sponsor. The OD platform (as an additional detail) should consist of several layers of services supporting end-user applications.

[18] also presents two models: one discussing actors, roles and relationships (p. 91) while the other considering conceptual elements within an ODE as business (p. 92). The first one actually focuses on types of roles (and potential subtypes) while the latter's interest is in business models and lists (as well as defines) mixed things (including activities, actor types, and abstract concepts) without an apparent structure.

The model in [26] is another open-data value network (p. 56) that looks at the linkages connecting roles in a 'data-processing chain' that turns raw data into valuable content. The goal is to show how data is enriched to gain information leading to value while the activities executed by the roles lead to an 'open-data community' – which is essentially a synonym for an ecosystem here.

[28] presents several instances (p. 8, 10, etc.) of visually analysing one specific case of an ODE. Their focus is to identify common features displayed by various elements within this ODE case study. These entities cover various (concrete) actors, country, data sources and data types all categorized over specific attributes using a generic notation (of coloured dots and lines between them).

The diagram by [34] (p. 3) is based on [11] and lists four roles with enablers taking a special role to connect suppliers (the usual three actors) to consumers and to also mitigate intermediaries (including aggregators, developers and enrichers) in the ODE.

The online report [40] published on the networkimpact website is actually a presentation of a mixture of conceptual elements including data, actors, roles, tools, and abstract concepts in concentric circles from data in the centre to culture in the outer most layer (with no specific notation).

[41] discusses value exchanges in open data ecosystems and its visual model shows participants (such as Citizens, Public or Private Providers or Developers as well as Aggregator, Enricher or Enabler) and their relationships (including providing data, platform, or service) along with the flow of data and resulting benefits. While this is a rich depiction of ODE, it should be noted that there is no legend provided and the notation applied does not differentiate actor types from the various roles, while the flow of (value) exchanges mixes things at different levels (e.g. data with services or with abstract concepts such as reputation or benefits).

[42] investigates how open data intermediaries connect the supply and use of data (p. 16): the diagrams denote various forms of capital (including data assets) and different specific intermediaries using a combination of shapes and colours.

Through the example of Belgium [2] addresses the question of innovation within an ODE and generates models based on the approach by [24]. His depiction of the Belgian open data ecosystem (p. 14) is a layered structure of roles with specific actors listed in each role group (such as initiators, providers, re-users, infomediaries and end users) along with their contributions to this specific ODE. Using a specific case it also emphasizes the need for feedback (p. 28).

[9] uses the ecosystem approach to explain how to design OGD initiatives. Their model of OGD programs (p. 19 and 25) differentiates three main role groups (Providers, Users and Beneficiaries) with actor types in each group (e.g. political leaders, civic community) and connects them through activities (such as data use or feedback) and other abstract concepts (including motivation, benefits, characteristics, or data products). Similarly to other models, neither the notation nor the use of mixed concepts as relationships is clarified. The model is similar to value chains but the connections are not clean data or value flows as they also represent elements of influences and concepts.

[5] looked at the connection developing between Municipalities and Businesses through open data and comments on the idea of Data Market in the context of aspects of a specific ODE. The model presented is based on the one by [9] and focuses on differentiating various dependencies between mixed types of entities (including actors, abstract concepts and activities): these dependencies (p. 71) may be soft, hard, regulatory, or interest (depicted by arrows of different colours) as well as connections to other parts of the ecosystem. In addition, the various conceptual entities may also be grouped into sub-ecosystems (p. 93).

While addressing the question of generating value from open data [12] composed two circular diagrams of how ODE may grow: his simplified view is centred around OD and circles out towards the citizens with intermediaries (providing services) working with various end users in different order. The four layers contain entities of different types and at different abstraction levels, such as data, services, actor types, roles and groups.

[19] focuses on issues of ecosystem-based service requirements engineering with some attention to open data specifically. Their digital service ecosystem model (p. 156) presents elements of such an ecosystem along phases of developing services all supported by a technical platform – so it represents mixed types of things (technical, process and actors). It also categorizes different types of ecosystems (p. 153) such as Business, Digital Service and Software ES.

[43] investigates the roles of intermediaries in ODE. It presents a model of an application area and country specific ODE (university ODE in South Africa - p. 73) along with its context (such as related regulations, standards, and agreements). The main focus is to depict specific entities (e.g. institutions) who have control over different types of data sources. It also shows some data flow and feedback among actors.

[46] also investigates a specific case of a university OD ecosystem (p. 251): it looks at actor types or categories (such as university, citizens or entrepreneurs) and a few relationships revolving around OD (including some actions as well as value generation and exchange).

[20] looked at the possibility to certify open data and they discussed related issues in the context of digital service ecosystems. The resulting model (p. 1268) focuses on services as elements of an Evolvable Open Data based digital service Ecosystem and shows how various models provide capabilities to form services within this ES.

[23] provide a generic representation of four roles that are key to an ODE forming a simple circle (p. 401): Data providers, Service providers, Application developers and Application users. Need to note, that the authors call these quadruple 'actors', but in comparison to other models they are rather roles.

[27] proposes a new role called the 'stimulator' (function) for the ODE and presents a diagram (p. 61) that shows this new role with its relationships to other roles (including the Citizen/Consumer, Public and Private Providers, and Infomediary roles). The model also shows that relationships may be actions, events, services, data and capabilities, influences or value/benefits – although the notation of the connections is not explained (but uses the same imaging as [41] above).

[29] presents data-flow-like connections among different types of concepts related to open data ecosystems complete with feedbacks (p. 2713), what they call abstract layers of an ODE. The elements included are Data, Applications, Use and Benefits – thus including artefacts, activity, and abstract concept. They have a second type of model summarizing their view of the main sectors and feedback processes present in OGD ecosystems (p. 2716). This is essentially an actor-relationship approach mixed with data flow and conceptual elements, and although it uses what appears to be a dedicated notation, there is no legend provided.

Although they call it an open government ecosystem model, the (circular) organizational process proposed by [36] (p. 92) investigates the (6) steps of building an OGD ecosystem.

The entities represented in the model of [37] are mainly actors and their relationships through concepts and data (p. 114) covering a specific area (e.g. the ecosystem around a given software application). The work provides a few more similar models of ODE over various applications. Their notation uses three figures to denote institutions, data and services, and users (at large).

The study by [38] investigates the uncertainties present in ODE and proposes order-generating rules (p. 24) to control the dynamic relationships in an ODE, where the model covers mixed concepts (artefacts, activities, capacity, etc.) around the data flow, what they call the push-pull trajectory of opening up data. No explanation of the model shapes used is provided.

The conceptual model of [39] only has three elements (p. 134): policy, society, and management. The model (based on [16]) considers these the key dimensions determining an ODE: (government) policy provides the environment in which ecosystem development occurs, society (in general) represent the users of OD, while (organizational) management – and interactions within ODE happen at the intersection of these dimensions – specific to a given country.

[44] presents a diagram of the Nigerian ODE (p. 97) where open data in the center is surrounded by four activities – two on the Government's side (as one actor): Disclosure and Accountability, and two on the Citizens' side (as the other actor): Engagement and Reaction. A fifth activity is associated with the data itself, platform development by various civil society organizations (the third actor type) – and this platform connects the three actors through allowing online access to OD.

5   Categorization of ODE Models and the Need for a Notation

The visual ODE models presented in the papers reviewed interpret ecosystem representation differently and focus on different aspects of an ecosystem or analyse ODE from a wide range of views. Beyond this, there are other factors that make comparing these models difficult. Not all papers provided full explanation of the meaning of shapes, colours and connecting lines used in their model. Some had no legend, while a few had no discussion of the meaning in the text either.

Conceptual models [1, 5, 12, 16–18, 33, 39, 40] focus on contextual factors influencing the ecosystem, factors that typically determine the environment or structure the features of ODEs.

Models focusing on participants in the ODE may be categorized into three main groups: those that look at *Actors* (such as government, NGOs, citizens, business, etc.) [2, 15, 18, 26, 34, 37, 41–43, 46] or the *Roles* they may play in the ODE (in other words the various functions needed) [2, 18, 23, 26, 27, 34, 46] or their *Relationships* [27, 37, 41, 42].

Technological models [7, 9, 15] deal with various aspects of the platform or depict ODE as a platform for other elements and activities – and some of them specifically consider physical *Components* [9] of the platform or system (as different from actors).

Data flow models [10, 11, 24, 29, 43] are mostly based on traditional data lifecycle or value chain models and often place ecosystem actors and roles along the flow.

In addition, one model attempts to analyse *Attributes* [28] of the elements making up the ODE or the *Activities* [2, 44] executed by the actors or, more generally, the *Processes* [29, 36] formed by activities – beyond data flow.

Several models provide integrated view composed of a *Mixture* of elements from the above list [19, 29, 38] – while one model is rooted in the digital *Service* [20] approach.

Table 1 presents an overview of papers offering some form of a visual ODE model. Along the Model type, the table summarizes what types of Shapes and Lines appear in the model and whether there was Legend provided (or some Explanation of the notation in the paper). Finally, short comments are given about the meaning of the model.

Judging from the table the various authors used notations very specific to their own view, approach, background or special topic – often without explanation of the figures in the visual model. Having unique notation not only makes it difficult to understand each model, but leaves the reader with no utility to compare and relate individual models to each other and judge how they each interpret what is key to an ODE.

6 Conclusions and a Call for Standardization

This research paper has demonstrated that most authors of ODE visual models create their own notation and use their own unique interpretation of the shapes, lines, arrows, or colours utilized in their diagram This makes understanding their message all the more difficult and thus comparison of various models or cases is not usually possible. Therefore, this paper argues that a standard notation should be developed where the required elements of an ODE (such as actors, their role, or relationships, etc.) are denoted in a dedicated and commonly acceptable way. The next step for this research is to collect requirements for such a notation (based on the above review of models). After that it would be necessary to generate discussion over the need for a standard notation and create a community of ODE researchers to discuss the soon to be proposed recommended notation.

Acknowledgement. Project no. NKFIH-869-4/2019 has been implemented with the support provided from the National Research, Development and Innovation Fund of Hungary, financed under the 2019 Domain Excellence Fund scheme.

References

1. Backx, M.: Gebouwen redden levens. Toegankelijkheidseisen van gebouwgegevens in het kader van de openbare orde en veiligheid. Unpublished MSc thesis. TU Delft, (2003)
2. Barthélemy, F.: The Belgian open data ecosystem and innovation through open data, MSc Thesis, Université catholique de Louvain (2016)
3. Boley, H., Chang, E.: Digital ecosystems: principles and semantics. In: 2007 Inaugural IEEE-IES Digital EcoSystems and Technologies Conference, pp. 398–403. IEEE (2007)
4. Chun, S.A., Shulman, S., Sandoval, R., Hovy, E.: Government 2.0: making connections between Citizens, data government. Inf. Polity **15**(1–2), 1–9 (2010)

5. Crusoe, J.: Open data ecosystem: the data market between municipalities and businesses. MSc Thesis, Linköping University (2016)
6. Davenport, T.H., Prusak, L.: Information Ecology: Mastering the Information and Knowledge Environment. Oxford University Press on Demand, Oxford (1997)
7. Davies, T.: Open data: infrastructures and ecosystems. Open Data Res. (2011)
8. Dawes, S.S., Helbig, N.: Information Strategies for open government: challenges and prospects for deriving public value from government transparency. In: Wimmer, M.A., Chappelet, J.-L., Janssen, M., Scholl, H.J. (eds.) EGOV 2010. LNCS, vol. 6228, pp. 50–60. Springer, Heidelberg (2010). https://doi.org/10.1007/978-3-642-14799-9_5
9. Dawes, S.S., Vidiasova, L., Parkhimovich, O.: Planning and designing open government data programs: an ecosystem approach. Gov. Inf. Q. 33(1), 15–27 (2016)
10. Deloitte, A.: Open Data – Driving Growth, Ingenuity and Innovation. A Deloitte Analytics White Paper, Deloitte, UK (2012)
11. Deloitte, A.: Open Growth - Stimulating Demand for Open Data in the UK. A Briefing Note from Deloitte Analytics, Deloitte, UK (2012)
12. Dickinson, A.: The pull of Open Data, how easy is to extract value from open data and open gov. data? (2016). https://medium.com/@digidickinson/the-pullof-open-data-ef9c35be922
13. Ding, L., et al.: TWC LOGD: a portal for linked open government data ecosystems. Web Semant.: Sci. Serv. Agents World Wide Web 9(3), 325–333 (2011)
14. Fedorowicz, J., Gogan, J.L., Ray, A.W.: The ecology of interorganizational information sharing. J. Int. Inf. Manag. 13(2), 73–85 (2004)
15. Gama, K., Lóscio, B.F.: Towards ecosystems based on open data as a service. In: ICEIS, no. 2, pp. 659–664 (2014)
16. Harrison, T.M., Pardo, T.A., Cook, M.: Creating open government ecosystems: a research and development agenda. Future Internet 4(4), 900–928 (2012)
17. Henfridsson, O., Bygstad, B.: The generative mechanisms of digital infrastructure evolution. MIS Q. 37(3), 907–931 (2013)
18. Immonen, A., Palviainen, M., Ovaska, E.: Requirements of an open data based business ecosystem. IEEE Access 2, 88–103 (2014)
19. Immonen, A., Ovaska, E., Kalaoja, J., Pakkala, D.: A service requirements engineering method for a digital service ecosystem. Serv. Oriented Comput. Appl. 10(2), 151–172 (2016)
20. Immonen, A., Ovaska, E., Paaso, T.: Towards certified open data in digital service ecosystems. Softw. Qual. J. 26(4), 1257–1297 (2017)
21. Janssen, K.: Open government data and the right to information: opportunities and obstacles. J. Community Inform. 8(2) (2012)
22. Jetzek, T., Avital, M., Bjorn-Andersen, N.: Data-driven innovation through open government data. J. Theor. Appl. Electron. Commer. Res. 9(2), 100–120 (2014)
23. Kitsios, F., Papachristos, N., Kamariotou, M.: Business models for open data ecosystem: challenges and motivations for entrepreneurship and innovation. In: Proceedings of 19th IEEE International Conference on Business Informatics, pp. 398–408 (2017)
24. Kuk, G., Davies, T.: The roles of agency and artifacts in assembling open data complementarities. In: 32nd International Conference on Information Systems, Shanghai (2011)
25. Liberati, A., et al.: The PRISMA statement for reporting systematic reviews and meta-analyses of studies that evaluate health care interventions: explanation and elaboration. PLoS Med. 6(7), e1000100 (2009)
26. Lindman, J., Kinnari, T., Rossi, M.: Business roles in the emerging open-data ecosystem. IEEE Softw. 33(5), 54–59 (2015)

27. Martin, S., Turki, S., Renault, S.: Open Data Ecosystems. In: Kő, A., Francesconi, E. (eds.) EGOVIS 2017. LNCS, vol. 10441, pp. 49–63. Springer, Cham (2017). https://doi.org/10.1007/978-3-319-64248-2_5

28. McLeod, M., McNaughton, M.: A methodological approach for understanding an emergent Caribbean Open Data eco-system. In: Open Data Research Symposium, Paper 54 (2015)

29. Najafabadi, M., Luna-Reyes, L.: Open government data ecosystems: a closed-loop perspective. In: 50th Hawaii International Conference on System Sciences, pp. 2711–2720 (2017)

30. Nardi, B.A., O'day, V.: Information Ecologies – Using Technology with Heart, Chapter 4, pp. 49–57, MIT Press, Cambridge (1999)

31. OKF - Open Knowledge Foundation. Open Knowledge Definition (2006). http://www.opendefinition.org/. Accessed 17 Sept 2017

32. Parsons, M.A., et al.: A conceptual framework for managing very diverse data for complex, interdisciplinary science. J. Inf. Sci. 37(6), 555–569 (2011)

33. Peltoniemi, M.: Business ecosystem: a conceptual model of an organisation population from the perspectives of complexity and evolution. Research Reports 18, Tampere (2005)

34. Ponte, D.: Enabling an open data ecosystem: preliminary findings from the market. In: ECIS 2015 Paper 55 at http://aisel.aisnet.org/ecis2015_rip/55 (2015)

35. Rajabifard, A., Feeney, M.-E.F., Williamson, I.P.: Directions for the future of SDI development. Int. J. Appl. Earth Obs. Geoinformation 4(1), 11–22 (2002)

36. Sandoval-Almazán, R., Luna-Reyes, L.F., Luna-Reyes, D.E., Gil-Garcia, J.R., et al.: Building Digital Government Strategies: Principles and Practices. Springer, Heidelberg (2017). https://doi.org/10.1007/978-3-319-60348-3

37. Sangiambut, S.: Geospatial open data: reshaping citizens and governments, roles and interactions, Ph.D. diss., McGill University (2017)

38. Shehzad, M.: Open data initiatives: understanding management in an uncertain ecosystem, MSc Thesis, Umea Universitet (2017)

39. Styrin, E., Luna-Reyes, L.F., Harrison, T.M.: Open data ecosystems: an international comparison. Transform. Gov.: People Process Policy 11(1), 132–156 (2017)

40. Taylor, M., Welsh, A., Whatley, A.: Leveraging data and tech for healthy, equitable, sustainable communities (2015). http://www.networkimpact.org/leveragingtech/

41. Turki, S., Foulonneau, M.: Valorisation des données ouvertes: acteurs, enjeux et modèles d'affaires. In: Big Data-Open Data: Quelles valeurs? Quels enjeux? pp. 113–125. De Boeck Supérieur (2015)

42. Van Schalkwyk, F., Cañares, M., Chattapadhyay, S., Andrason, A.: Open data intermediaries in developing countries. Step Up Consulting Services, Canada (2015)

43. Van Schalkwyk, F., Willmers, M., McNaughton, M.: Viscous open data: the roles of intermediaries in an open data ecosystem. Inf. Tech. Dev. 22(s1), 68–83 (2016)

44. Van Schalkwyk, F., Verhulst, S.G., Magalhaes, G., Pane, J., Walker, J.: The Social Dynamics of Open Data. African Minds, Cape Town (2017)

45. vom Brocke, J., Simons, A., Niehaves, B., Riemer, K., Plattfaut, R., Cleven, A.: Reconstructing the giant: on the importance of rigour in documenting the literature search process. In: Proceedings of ECIS 2009, Paper 161 (2009)

46. Zubcoff, J.J., Vaquer, L., Mazón, J.-N., Maciá, F., Garrigós, I.: The university as an open data ecosystem. Int. J. Design Nat. Ecodyn. 11(3), 250–257 (2016)

47. Zuiderwijk, A., Janssen, M., Davis, C.: Innovation with open data: essential elements of open data ecosystems. Inf. Polity 19(1, 2), 17–33 (2014)

The Societal Benefits of Open Government Data with Particular Emphasis on Geospatial Information

Henning Sten Hansen[(✉)] and Lise Schrøder

Aalborg University Copenhagen, A.C. Meyers Vænge 15,
2450 Copenhagen, Denmark
hsh@plan.aau.dk

Abstract. During the last decade several initiatives have worked towards open and free data. First, the success by the open and free OpenStreetMap and partly the free use of Google Maps has been an eye opener for many users as well in the public sector as in the private sector including individuals. Besides several legal frameworks like the EU directive on Re-use of Public Sector Information and the INSPIRE Directive on geographic information have in various ways encouraged to opening up free re-use of public sector information. As a consequence, a minor group of European countries have launched their own open government data projects, and the current research focuses on the role of open and free public sector information as a major step towards a digital society by analysing the observed socio-economic impact of the Danish open government data initiative.

Keywords: Open Government Data · Public sector information ·
Spatial data infrastructure · Socio-economic impact

1 Introduction

Open Government Data and particularly open geospatial information has received increasing awareness during the last ten years in parallel with the preparation and implementation of the INSPIRE Directive [1]. Traditionally geographic information in Europe has been financed through the so-called cost recovery principle, where the revenue obtained by selling data is used for updating the data and maintaining the data quality. However, this model has been under pressure from the EU by the PSI [2] and INSPIRE [1] Directives although the cost recovery is not directly in conflict with this legislation.

Data sharing is a fundamental component in the modern digital societies, and easier access to data and information has been a vision since the early days of the information era. Not at least the possibility to avoid duplicate data collection has been emphasised, although this being perhaps even one of the minor advantages of data sharing. However, very little progress has been achieved until about a decade ago, and the success of the free OpenStreetMap is perhaps the most positive example on a worldwide solution on data sharing. Generally, there is a growing tendency to release at least to some

© Springer Nature Switzerland AG 2019
A. Kő et al. (Eds.): EGOVIS 2019, LNCS 11709, pp. 31–44, 2019.
https://doi.org/10.1007/978-3-030-27523-5_3

degree various sorts of public data allowing citizens and businesses to freely re-use public data for their own purposes [3]. The real driver towards free sharing of data and information comes from the government sectors including for example the European Union.

The launch of the so-called Digital Agenda of the European Union [4] has emphasised the need for maximising the economic and social benefits of Information and Communication Technology (ICT) towards a sustainable future. As a follow-up on the PSI and the INSPIRE directives several EU Member States launched open government programmes. For example, back in 2012 the Danish Government decided a new initiative on Basic Data [5], which is considered an essential basis for public authorities to perform tasks properly and efficiently across units and sectors, as outlined in the Danish e-Government Strategy 2011–2015 [6]. Due to this vision, Basic Data is to be the high-quality authoritative common foundation for public sector information – including the private sector. A general principle is, that all basic data should be freely available for all public authorities, private businesses and citizens.

Rather recently (early 2019), the Danish Public Accounts Committee (Rigsrevisionen) carried out a survey, which concluded that at the moment is no comprehensive overview over open government data in Denmark [7]. Therefore, Rigsrevisionen carried out a survey, which shows, that in total 921 open government data sets are available from 88 different agencies and other public organisations. This lack of data overview can imply, that citizens and private enterprises may have difficulties finding the data they need. As a consequence, there is a risk that the expected socio-economic benefits may not be obtained.

The aim of the current research has been to analyse the socio-economic implications of the Danish decision on making government data open and freely available. After this introduction follows a chapter describing the background and theoretical foundation for the tendency towards open government data. The third chapter describes in detail the Danish Open Government programme and chapter four describes and analyses the social and economic implications of open governmental data respectively. The paper ends with a discussion of the current state of play and potential barriers to the widespread adoption of open geospatial data as well as some concluding remarks including perspectives for subsequent research.

2   Background and Theory

Large amounts of data and information are daily produced by the European public authorities being the largest single source of information in Europe. This is even accelerated by the increasing digitisation of the public administrations around Europe.

EU Digital Agenda is the first of seven so-called flagship initiatives included in the Europe 2020 Strategy presented in May 2010 [4]. The aim of the Digital Agenda is to Europe's citizens and businesses to get the most out of the digital technologies. The Digital Agenda contains 101 actions organised into 7 pillars: (1) Digital Single Market, (2) Interoperability and Standards, (3) Trust and security, (4) Fast and Ultra-fast Internet access, (5) Research and innovation, (6) Enhancing digital literacy, skills and inclusion, and (7) ICT-enabled benefits for the EU society. One of the actions (no. 3) within the Pillar 1: Digital Single Market are concerned with opening up public data resources for re-use. Already back in the 2003 the Directive on Re-use of Public Sector Information aimed at regulating and stimulating the reuse of public sector information (PSI). Although the PSI Directive [2] deals with all kinds of public sector information, a majority of this information has a geographical reference. Thus, the focus for public sector is to manage and service people, businesses, real properties, roads and areas, which all are located somewhere on the surface of the earth.

2.1 Open Data in the Digital Society

According to the recently started Open Government Data initiative (http://www.opengovernmentdata.org) 'Open data' means 'data free for anyone to use, re-use and re-distribute', and 'Government data' refers to 'data and information produced or commissioned by government or government-controlled entities'. This initiative has produced a handbook aiming at supporting implementation of open government data around the world, and at the same time building a common framework for assessing existing open government initiatives. The Open Data Handbook [8] points to several areas, where Open Government Data may create additional value including: (a) Transparency and democratic control, (b) Public participation, (c) Self-empowerment, (d) Improved or new private products and services, (e) Innovation, (f) Improved efficiency and effectiveness of government services, (g) Impact measurement of policies, and (h) New knowledge from combined data sources and patterns in large data volumes. These advantages can be organised into two main groups. One group (items a–c) can contribute to enhanced democracy and participation, while the other group (items d–g) primarily focuses on the economic benefits obtained through more efficient public sector and improved innovation and business possibilities in the private sector.

The issue of data sharing is closely related to open data, and the concept goes back to the 1990es, where the book 'Sharing Geographic Information' [9] explored organisational issues in the context of sharing geographic information. Within the UK local governments very little data sharing took place even between departments, and paper maps were still at that time a major source to information [10]. However, during the last 15–20 years the development towards a digital society has really put data sharing on the political agenda. Frequently bottlenecks connected with costs, legal restrictions, and proprietary data formats have hindered real re-use of data for the benefits of the society.

Globally the value of data sharing and free data has been demonstrated by the emergent free map services like Google Maps and not at least the OpenStreetMap, which have put severe pressure on the National Mapping Agencies. Surveys have demonstrated that not only the citizens and smaller private companies are using these map services, but also public organisations like agencies and municipalities. However, the most important reason for the recent focus on Open Government Data is the implementation of digital governance with extended use of self-service solutions. This requires access to data and information across the public sector – from municipalities over regional authorities to the national governments.

2.2   European Legal Frameworks on Open Government Data

The PSI Directive [2] was implemented in July 2005 aiming at regulating and stimulating the reuse of public sector information. The initial intention of the European Commission was to make all public sector information in the Member States available for re-use. However, this caused some Member States and public institutions great concerns, as many of these institutions are expected to provide for at least part of their own funding. Therefore, in the negotiation process between the European Parliament and the Council the general principle was toned down to a mere encouragement for the Member States to make their information available for re-use. Nevertheless, the PSI directive has gained a lot of impacts in the Member States as demonstrated in the next paragraph.

A key objective of INSPIRE was to make more and better spatial information available for Community policy-making and implementation in a wide range of sectors. Initially, it would focus on information needed to monitor and improve the state of the environment - including air, water, soil, and natural landscape - and later extended to other sectors such as agriculture and transport [11]. The INSPIRE Directive was adopted by the European Council and Parliament in spring 2007 and entered into force May 2007 [1]. The INSPIRE Directive is a framework, where the details are defined through a set of so-called implementing rules, where the Member States provide experts for drafting the rules, which are finally adopted by the INSPIRE Committee. Thus, a high degree of Member States involvement is ensured. In a national Danish context, the so-called Geodata Law was a derived effect of the INSPIRE Directive. The INSPIRE Directive relies on a set of basic principles of which the one on data availability and accessibility 'Spatial data needed for good governance should be available on conditions that are not restricting its extensive use' is of major importance regarding open government data. Altogether there were several reasons and encouragements for opening up public sector information in a broader scale among the European countries. As an example, the next section will describe the Danish approach to Open Government Data.

3   The Danish Open Government Data Initiative

E-Government is generally being defined as the use of information and communication technologies (ICT) to improve the activities of public sector organisations and their agents and e-Government has been the key driver for all activities regarding information and communication technology in the public sector[1]. Similar to the other Nordic countries, Denmark has a leading role in digitisation of the society. In the 2018 United Nations E-Government Surveys rankings, Denmark is ranked in the top as number one followed by Australia, the Republic of Korea, the United Kingdom, and Sweden [12].

---

[1] http://www.europarl.europa.eu/RegData/etudes/IDAN/2015/565890/EPRS_IDA(2015)565890_EN.pdf.

Since the mid-1990es various Danish governments have put e-Government on the political agenda with initiatives like "Information Society by the year 2000" [13] and not at least "Project Digital Government" [14], which sat up a so-called Digital Task Force aiming at enhancing e-Government solutions across the public sector. To underline the importance of the Digital Task Force the Ministry of Finance chaired it. The Danish e-Government strategy for 2007–2010, entitled "Towards better digital services, increasing efficiency and stronger cooperation" (Danish Government, Local Government Denmark and Danish Regions, 2007) has three overarching strategic priority areas: (a) better digital service, (b) increased efficiency, and (c) stronger collaboration. The national SDI is one of the prerequisites for fulfilling the strategy and handling the new dependencies. This policy was followed by an updated strategy concerning the period 2011–2015 [6].

The first step towards Open Government Data in Denmark was the decision taken by the Ministry of Environment in the late nineties to make open access to all environmental information. This was a natural consequence of the Aarhus Convention from 1998 [15] emphasising the importance of public participation in all decisions related to the environment, which requires access to data and information. Thus, open access to government data is addressed in Directive 90/313/EEC of 7 June 1990 [16] by stating the aims of 'ensuring freedom of access to, and dissemination of information on the environment held by public authorities and to set out the basic terms and conditions on which such information should be made available'. The stepwise process towards open government data is described in [17].

3.1 The Danish Basic Data Concept

By using a common geographic basis for administration, it is possible for example to link relevant data about the environment, traffic, health, property, companies and people. Basic data constitutes the core information needed by public authorities in their daily work, and contains information about *Persons*, *Businesses*, *Real properties*, *Addresses*, *Roads* and *Areas*. All these data have a spatial reference, and accordingly geography and maps are important elements in the Basic data concept (Fig. 1). Therefore, the Digital Task Force has stated that geographic information is a backbone in e-Government [18].

This Fig. 1 illustrates clearly the interconnection between the different components of the Basic Data set. Each person, business unit, property, house and road has for decades been provided with unique identifiers, and a cross-reference register has ensured the interconnection between the different objects in the infrastructure. Besides, all persons and business units are assigned an address. Finally, the addresses, properties (parcels) and buildings are assigned a geographic reference, ensuring its connection with geography (maps). Thus, the Basic Data set constitutes an integrated system facilitating the core functions in public administrations.

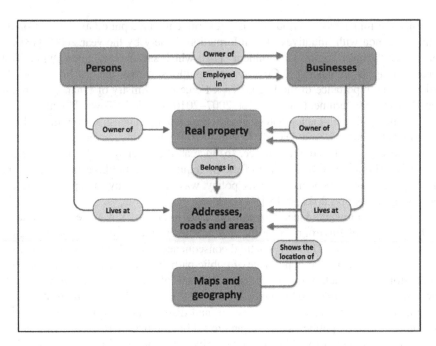

Fig. 1. The basic data concept in the Danish Open Government Data strategy [5].

At a later stage in the process it is expected to expand the Basic Data set to include personal data, income data, business financial statements, and road infrastructures. Recently, meteorological data from the Danish Meteorological Institute have been added to the list of open government data. In order to maintain the authoritative status required for public administration, management and decision-making, the Basic Data needs to comply with the following principles: (1) Basic Data needs to be as correct, complete, and up-to-data as possible; (2) All public authorities must use the Basic Data in their daily work; (3) As far as possible Basic Data must be made freely available to businesses as well as the public (sensitive personal data excluded); (4) Basic Data must be distributed efficiently and accommodate the needs of the users.

In order to produce, maintain, and ensure data quality a specific business model has been developed. The Danish National Government and the organisation of local authorities – Local Government Denmark – have agreed to share the costs of Basic Data through a mutual agreement. Particularly in the first phase of the implementation additional costs for setting up facilities for data distribution, the costs may balance the benefits, but based on previous experiences from making address data freely available, the Danish Ministry of Finance has estimated that a revenue of more than 100 million Euro is expected when the Basic Data initiative is fully implemented by 2020. One third of this is expected from a more efficient public sector, and two-thirds from the private sector through enhanced innovation and competitiveness.

4   The Socio-Economic Implications of Open Government Data

During the last twenty years major discussions have taken place regarding the benefits versus costs of various initiatives on the digitisation of the society based on establishing spatial data infrastructures and providing public data open and freely available. Few studies have tried to estimate the costs and benefits connected with such initiatives but rather few really cost-benefit analyses. However, a survey carried out in the Netherlands estimate the economic value of the Dutch geoinformation sector to be 1.4 billion Euros – corresponding to 0.25% of the national Dutch GNP [19]. During the 1990es the national Danish Address Register went through a major harmonisation and quality upgrade, and from 2002 the Address Register including addresses coordinates was made open and free to use for everybody [20]. An analysis from 2010 concluded that the direct benefits from the open and free access to the Address Register in the five years period from 2005–2009 were more than 60 million € [21]. The analysis assumes that the economic value of the open and free addresses corresponds to the price paid by the users of addresses before the new open policy on address data, which is equivalent to 78 million €. These figures may even represent an underestimation due to the wider scope for use in the new agreement, where everyone may add value to the data and sell them for profit aims.

On the other side you may claim that the general movements towards the digital society, inevitably would have led to lower prices on address data. In order to reduce the uncertainty in the analysis the value of address data is reduced with 25% - i.e. (75% × 78 million €) = 59 million €. Contrary, the authorities as well as the users have saved thousands of person hours earlier spend on negotiations, agreements, and data delivery, and in the calculations these savings are estimated to be 5 million €. This adds to 64 million € for the years 2005–2009 – and 13 million € yearly. However, these figures do not include indirect and derived benefits obtained from: (a) no need for alternative address data sets; (b) higher security for police, ambulances, fire brigades etc. due the same and accurate address data set.

Based on these figures, the Danish Ministry of Finance tried to estimate the costs and benefits from the new initiative on open and free public data at the broader scale. When the new Open Government Data policy is completely in operation in 2020, it is expected that the public sector yearly will save about 36 million € (Table 1), and for the private sector the yearly benefits will be more than 65 million €. Thus, the total yearly economic benefits for the Danish society will be about 100 million €.

Although Basic Data is freely available for everyone, the cost of producing the data is still there. As mentioned above the funding of the open government data project is based on shared costs between the different administrative layers in the Danish public sector. The expected benefits are more uncertain, but the calculations carried out by the Ministry of Finance are based on recent cost/benefit studies from Finland and Australia, and generally the estimates are conservative. Based on experiences from Australia, Houghton [22] concludes that 'the direct and measurable benefits of making PSI available freely and without restrictions on use typically outweigh the costs. The framework   for   estimating   cost-benefits   he   used   the   following   formula:

Table 1. Expected net profit for the Danish public sector in millions € [5].

	2013	2014	2015	2016	2017	2018	2019	2020
The ministries	−14	−11	−7	−3	1	1	4	6
The municipalities	−3	3	11	19	22	23	23	24
The region	0	1	3	4	6	6	6	6
Net effect	−17	−7	7	20	29	30	33	36

'Benefit/Cost' = ('Agency & User Savings' + Increased Returns to Expenditure on PSI production')/'Agency & Users Cost'. This formula was also applied in the cost-benefit analysis carried out by the Ministry of Finance. The Research Institute of Finnish Economy carried a major analysis on the impact of the pricing of public sector information on performance in the business sector, and based on data from 15 countries during the years 2000–2007 it was found that pricing of PSI really had an effect on company growth - particularly for small and medium sized enterprises [23]. Although the figures vary from country to country it was found that for example free access to geographic information contributes to a 15% higher growth rate (on average) compared with traditional pricing based on the cost recovery principle.

4.1   Case Study of the National Danish Basic Data Programme

In connection with the launch of the Basic Data Programme in 2012, the Geodata Agency asked the international consultant enterprise Deloitte to carry out a pre-assessment aiming at defining a reference level by assessing the value of the geospatial data in the Basic Data programme before the data became free [24]. A similar analysis was carried out by Price Waterhouse Coopers (PWC) in 2017 in order to demonstrate the effect of the open and free geospatial data three years after launch [25].

PWC defines three effects, which contributes to societal benefits: (a) streamlining effect, (b) market impact, and (c) value added. The streamlining effect refers benefits obtained by doing internal working processes in a more efficient way and hereby reduced costs. For private companies, more efficient production can result in cheaper products or higher profit, whereas the public sector can provide more services for the same amount of money. The market impact is only relevant for the private sector but is the effect of free government data to the value added. One example could be new products or services being possible through the free geospatial data. Nearly all municipalities answering the survey reply that geospatial information is applied within the technical and environmental administrations, but many municipalities report about use of geospatial information within the school administration and rescue [25].

PWC [25] mentions the potential for additional welfare benefits like better health among the citizens or improved state of the environment but neglects those effects due to uncertainties.

Table 2 shows the overall estimates of the efficiency effect in the three sectors, where the public sector is subdivided into government agencies, municipalities, regions, and independent institutions for the 2016 figures. It is evident that the private enterprises have experienced a huge effect due to streamlining internal working processes during the first three years with open and free government data, while the utility sector has had more moderate effect, but nevertheless more than doubled the effect within that period. It may seem surprising that the effect among the public authorities has more or less been at the same level and even experienced a little decline between 2012 and 2016. This is mainly due to the fact that the Danish public sector has had free access to all public sector information since early in this century.

Table 2. Estimated efficiency effects of free geospatial data for various sectors in million € [25]. The grey area in the 2012 column means that the 6.7 million € are for the four greyed sectors.

	2012	2016
Private enterprises	5.4	97.4
Utility companies	13.4	30.7
Government agencies	-	3.0
Municipalities	6.7	2.4
Regions	-	0.3
Independent institutions	-	0.3
Total	**25.5**	**134.1**

Table 3 shows the estimated production effects of free geospatial data. For 2012 the data regarding municipalities, regions and independent institutions are combined into one number.

Table 3. Estimated production effects of free geospatial data for various sectors in million € [25]. The grey area in the 2012 column means that the 129.5 million € are for the three greyed sectors

	2012	2016
Private enterprises	15.6	59.9
Government agencies	43.1	50.1
Municipalities	-	184.7
Regions	129.5	20.3
Independent institutions	-	26.3
Total	**188.2**	**341.3**

Thus, the total societal value of the open data programme regarding geospatial information is estimated to 0.47 billion € of which the production effect accounts for 0.34 billion € and the efficiency effects accounts for 0.13 billion €.

The effect of open geospatial data on employment may seem surprising. Within the private enterprises the number of employees working with geospatial data were reduced from 840 in 2012 to 225 in 2016. This may mainly be caused by the fact that

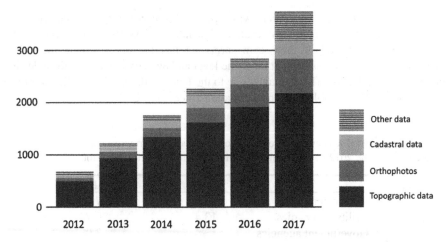

Fig. 2. The number of requests to the national map supply in millions during the period 2012–2017 (adapted from Damvad Analytics [26]).

the open geospatial data has reduced the need specific maps leading to fewer people involved in the production of geospatial data. Contrary, the free geodata are now in higher degree than earlier being applied to create newer innovative products, and integrated systems solutions, where it can be more difficult exactly to identify the work with geospatial data.

As shown above the benefits of using the open geospatial data is most noticeable among the private enterprises. A recent survey carried out by Damvad Analytics [26] provides more details about the business use of open geospatial data delivered through the national Danish Map Supply. As pointed out by the Damvad analysis, the number of requests to the Map Supply obtained, demonstrates a steady increase in the use of open geospatial data since January 2013, were the data became open (see Fig. 2.). This indicates a five-fold increase from the pre-open data year 2012 to 2017.

The different colours in Fig. 2 relate to different data sets: the dark grey refer to topographic maps, the medium grey refer to orthophotos, while the light grey refer to cadastral data. The heavy use of the topographic data is not surprising, as this is the most commonly used map to show elements on the Earth's surface. Likewise, orthophotos and cadastral data is utilised in many applications. Included in the category "Other data", is the new detailed digital elevation model, which is the data set showing the highest growth rate. This can be seen in the light of the past decades increased focus on flooding due to heavy rainfall. Municipalities and property owners are very concerned about their values, so the digital elevation model and the derived flood risk maps fulfil a need due to this purpose.

By using log data for the Danish map Supply, 1177 business users where identified, but only 422 of these were actually active users. 201 of the users accounted for about 90% of the use (calls). The main business users are the engineering consultants with 54 enterprises, and IT consultants with 41 enterprises. This indicates that the business use of open geospatial data is focused on ad-hoc project use and less use for more strategic operational tasks.

5   Discussion

The Danish programme for open government data – the Basic Data Programme – aims to support efficiency improvements, drive economic growth, and identify new business opportunities. Thus, the decision to launch the Basic Data programme was based on a positive business case expecting a revenue of more than 100 million € is expected when the Basic Data initiative is fully implemented by 2020. One third of this amount is expected from a more efficient public sector, and two-thirds from the private sector through enhanced innovation and competitiveness.

As demonstrated by several analyses and assessments [24, 25], the development during the first three years with open government data seem to be in accordance with the original expectations. Following PWC [24] the socio-economic value of the open geospatial data is estimated to about 0.47 billion €. Hereof the production effects account for 340 million € and the efficiency effects accounts for 130 million €.

Although the preliminary results seem convincing some uncertainty in the numbers is inevitable and barriers on the growth potential may appear in the near future.

First, the results of the analysis are in some degree subject to uncertainty – primarily due to the fact that the estimates are based on respondents' individual assessments. In addition, the organisations actively answering the questionnaires may be biased, although we cannot know in which direction. However, it is a fact that for example only 22% of the private enterprises (incl. utilities) participated in the survey, and 19% of the potential public authorities answered the questionnaires.

Second, the efficiency effect cannot continue with same speed in the future, although nearly 80% of the public authorities answered that open geospatial data will have some importance to the efficiency in their operational work. We have already observed problems related to the rapid digitisation, where the replacement of human based assessments was replaced by IT based assessments – for example in the taxation of houses and properties.

Third, the main distribution channel for geospatial data in Denmark is the national Map Supply maintained by the Agency for Data Supply and Efficiency. This portal is easy to use and provided access to data in shape files, standard raster files and various web services like WMS and WFS. From 2019 most (or all) of the geospatial data will be available from a new national portal – the Data Distributor – where all open government data will be accessed. This may be a challenge for geospatial data, including huge data sets like the topographic map, the cadastral map and orthophotos. The general format at the new Data Distributor will be XML, which can be difficult to handle for SME's and other minor users without the expertise to manage and decode the data into appropriate formats for their GIS software packages.

Fourth, private enterprises developing software may find it a barrier for the business potential in new innovations that similar free data are not available across Europe limiting the market possibilities. The INSPIRE directive [1] is only one step into common European solutions by defining rules for exchange standards, data models, etc., but keeping the free availability as a barrier.

Finally, the General Data Protection Regulation (GDPR) Regulation [27] which entered into force in all member states by 1. May 2018 may have negative consequences for the use of open government data. Geospatial data are very personal but also valuable in many respects and considering complexities in geospatial data, it is difficult to foresee in how many ways location data could be used and misused in the future. According to GDPR location data is considered as "personal data" in Article 4 of the Regulation. Under this clause personal data are granted extended rights, including a right to access and a right to erasure. Thus, the GDPR regulation is a new barrier to the use of free open government data, and it will take some time to find new ways of operating sensitive geospatial data like for example addresses, which are among the most important database keys in as well public administration as private enterprises.

6   Conclusion

When the Danish Ministry of Finance in 2012 launched the initiative *Good Basic Data for Everyone – a driver for growth and efficiency* it was received with positive feedback from most stakeholders related to the geospatial community – not at least in the public sector. However, the reaction was less unambiguous in the private sector, where some private enterprises saw new possibilities while others anticipated new challenges. The positive reaction came from the consulting and software industry while the more sceptic reaction came form the rather large industry producing geospatial data.

All investments in the Basic Data programme should be paid by the public sector, which afterwards should save money from a more efficient public sector, but the biggest return from the investments should come from the private sector.

The current research has used different sources to analyse the benefits due to the Basic Data programme in various sectors. The total socio-economic benefits during the first three years with open geospatial data is estimated to about 470 million € of which 340 million € comes from the production effect and 130 million € from the improved efficiency. It is evident from Tables 2 and 3 that the private enterprises have experienced the largest percentage benefits from the Basic Data initiative. Regarding the efficiency effect, the benefits from geospatial data is nearly twenty times as high after three years with open data compared to the situation before the Basic Data launch in 2013. Considering the production effect, a fourfold increase can be observed between 2013 and 2017 for the private enterprises. Thus, the expected advantages from open geospatial data on the private sector can be confirmed. On the other hand, the paper has shown, that some changing policies and market behaviours may raise obstacles for realising the full potential of open government data. Thus, it is evident that the recent adoption of GDPR will inevitably have consequences for data handling and use.

The next steps in our research will compare the Danish experiences with similar open data programmes in Europe to identify similarities and differences regarding the socio-economic implications and to provide an overview concerning implementation strategies and best practises.

References

1. European Commission: Directive 2007/2/EC of the European Parliament and of the Council of 14 March 2007 Establishing an Infrastructure for Spatial Information in the European Community (INSPIRE). Official Journal of the European Union (2007)
2. European Commission: The Reuse of Public Sector Information, Directive 2003/98/EC of the European Parliament and of the Council. Official Journal of the European Union, L345, pp. 90–96 (2003)
3. Kulk, S., van Loenen, B.: Brave new open data world? Int. J. Spat. Data Infrastruct. Res. 7, 196–206 (2012)
4. European Commission: A Digital Agenda for Europe. Communication from the Commission to the European Parliament, the Council, the European Economic and Social Committee and the Committee of the Regions. COM (2010) 245 (2011)
5. The Danish Government & Local Government Denmark: Good Basic Data for Everyone – A Driver for Growth and Efficiency. The eGovernment Strategy 2011–2015 (2012)
6. The Danish Government, Danish Regions & Local Government Denmark: The Digital Path to Future Welfare – eGovernment Strategy 2011–2015, August 2011 (2012)
7. Rigsrevisionen: Open Data – Rigsrevisionen's report submitted to the Danish Parliament, Copenhagen (2019). (in Danish)
8. Open Knowledge Foundation: Open Data Handbook Documentation, Release 1.0.0., 14 November 2012
9. Onsrud, H.J., Rushton, G.: Sharing Geographic Information. Center for Urban Policy Research, New Brunswick (1995)
10. Harvey, F., Tulloch, D.: Local-government data sharing: evaluating the foundations of spatial data infrastructures. Int. J. Geog. Inf. Sci. 20, 743–768 (2006)
11. Vanderhaegen, M., Muro, E.: Contribution of a European spatial data infrastructure to the effectiveness of EIA and SEA studies. Environ. Impact Assess. Rev. 25, 123–142 (2005)
12. United Nations: E-Government Survey 2012: E-Government to the People, p. 2012. United Nations, New York (2012)
13. Ministry of Research: Information Society by the Year 2000. Danish Government, Copenhagen (1994). (in Danish)
14. Ministry of Finance: Digitalisation and efficiency in National Government. Danish Government, Copenhagen (2002) (in Danish)
15. UN ECE: Convention on Access to Information, Public Participation in Decision-Making and Access to Justice in Environmental Matters. ECE Committee on Environmental Policy, Aarhus (1998)
16. European Commission: Council Directive 90/313/EEC of 7 June 1990 on the freedom of access to information on the environment, EuroLex (1990)
17. Hansen, H.S., Schröder, L., Hvingel, L., Christensen, J.S.: Towards spatially enabled e-governance – a case study on SDI implementation. Int. J. Spat. Data Infrastruct. Res. 6, 73–96 (2010)
18. Larsen, B.C.: Geodata – The Backbone of Effective e-Government. The Digital Task Force. Ministry of Finance, Copenhagen (2006)
19. Castelein, W.T., Bregt, A.K., Pluijmers, Y.: The economic value of the Dutch geo-information sector. Int. J. Spat. Data Infrastruct. Res. 5, 58–76 (2010)
20. Lind, M.: Addresses as an infrastructure component - Danish experiences and perspectives. In: Proceedings from ISO Workshop on Address Standards, Copenhagen, 25 May 2008, pp. 94–105 (2008)

21. Danish Business Authority: The Value of the Danish Address Data. Societal Benefits of the Free Access of Address Data in 2002. The Danish Business Authority, July 2002 (2010). (in Danish). https://docplayer.dk/11214689-Vaerdien-af-danske-adressedata.html
22. Houghton, J.: Costs and Benefits of Data Provision. Report to the Australian National Data Service. Centre for Strategic Economic Studies, Victoria University, Melbourne (2011)
23. Koski, H.: Does Marginal Cost Pricing of Public Sector Information Spur Firm Growth. ETLA – The Research Institute of Finnish Economy, Report no. 1260, Helsinki (2011)
24. Deloitte: The Effect of the Free Geographic Basic Data (2014). (in Danish). https://sdfe.dk/media/gst/2618970/Effekten%20af%20de%20frie%20geografiske%20data%20Deloitte%20Rapport.pdf
25. PWC: The impact of the open geographical data – follow up study. Agency for Data Supply and Efficiency, March 2017. (in Danish but an English summary is available). https://sdfe.dk/media/2917052/20170317-the-impact-of-the-open-geographical-data-management-summary-version-13-pwc-qrvkvdr.pdf
26. Damvad Analytics: Business Use of the Map Supply – A Socio-Economic Analysis, March 2019. (in Danish). https://efkm.dk/media/12689/erhvervslivets-brug-af-kortforsyningen.pdf
27. European Commission: Regulation (EU) 2016/679 of the European parliament and of the council of 27 April 2016 on the protection of natural persons with regard to the processing of personal data and on the free movement of such data, and repealing Directive 95/46/EC (general data protection regulation). Official Journal of the European Union (2016)

Data-Driven Approaches
in e-Government

Big Data Analytics
for Tax Administration

Priya Mehta[1], Jithin Mathews[1], Sandeep Kumar[3], K. Suryamukhi[1],
Ch. Sobhan Babu[1(✉)], S. V. Kasi Visweswara Rao[2], Vishal Shivapujimath[1],
and Dikshant Bisht[1]

[1] Indian Institute of Technology Hyderabad, Sangareddy, India
{cs15resch11007,cs15resch11004,cs17mtech01002,sobhan,
cs18mtech11027,cs17mtech11027}@iith.ac.in
[2] Department of Commercial Taxes, Government of Telangana, Hyderabad, India
svkasivrao@gmail.com
[3] Plianto Technologies, Sangareddy, India
cs15mtech11017@iith.ac.in

Abstract. The problem of tax evasion is as old as taxes itself. Tax evasion causes several problems that affects the growth of a nation. In this paper, we present our work in controlling tax evasion by using big data analytics, Android applications, and information technology. We implemented this work for the commercial taxes department, government of Telangana, India. Here we developed a complete software framework for scrutiny of suspicious accounts. This system detects suspicious dealers using certain sensitive parameters and standardizes the process of scrutiny of accounts. We used sophisticated statistical and machine learning tools to predict suspicious dealers. To increase the compliance levels, we developed a regression model for identifying return defaulters and user-friendly Android applications to assist the officers in collecting the tax. The other aspect we explored is the detection and analysis of a tax evasion mechanism, known as *circular trading*, using advanced algorithmic and social-network analytic techniques.

Keywords: Tax evasion · Big-data analytics · Data mining ·
Social network analysis · Forensic accounting

1 Introduction

Paying tax is the duty of every law abiding citizen of a country. Taxes are generally divided into two types: direct tax and indirect tax. Here we work by focusing towards the indirect taxes. Indirect taxes are given to the state by the person or business entity who uses the goods. This tax paid by the consumer is collected by a third party business vendor and then paid to the government. Two examples for indirect taxation system are Value added tax (VAT) and Goods and services tax (GST) [5, 21]. Both VAT and GST are collected at every stage of the production on the amount of value added to the goods. Figure 1, shows how the tax is collected incrementally in the GST system.

© Springer Nature Switzerland AG 2019
A. Kő et al. (Eds.): EGOVIS 2019, LNCS 11709, pp. 47–57, 2019.
https://doi.org/10.1007/978-3-030-27523-5_4

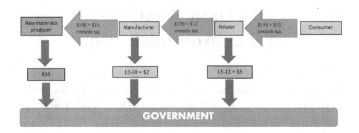

Fig. 1. Tax flow diagram of GST

(i) The manufacturer purchases raw material worth 100\$ by paying tax @10% on it i.e., 10\$. The raw material is processed by the manufacturer, and the finished goods are sold for 120\$ to a retailer with tax @10% i.e., 12\$. Finally, the retailer sells his goods to the consumer for 150\$ with tax @10% i.e., 15\$.

(ii) At each stage in the chain, the tax payer reduces his liability by the amount of tax he paid at the earlier stage which is called Input Tax Credit (ITC). Thus, the manufacturer is liable to pay 12\$ but reduces his liability by the ITC of 10\$ paid by him at the time of purchasing raw material. Thus, he pays only 2\$ to the government. The retailer at his end pays only 3\$ after reducing 12\$ paid to the manufacturer from 15\$ payable by him. Thus, the total tax which enters the government treasury will be 15\$ i.e., 10\$ + 2\$ + 3\$ at each stage. However, the entire amount of 15\$ is collected from the consumer. Thus, there is no burden of tax on any of the businessman involved in the chain.

A businessman may reduce the tax burden by resorting to the following practices to increase their business profit:

(i) Tax evasion, where the tax is avoided by illegitimate means like hiding factual information, manipulating the records, presenting falsified information on tax return statements, *etc.*

(ii) Tax avoidance, where the business vendor actually manages to dodge their tax liability without breaking the law. It is done by taking undue advantage of the loopholes existing in the taxation system like by twisting the words in the law.

(iii) Tax planning, where, the legitimate concessions and exemptions provided in the tax law are used to reduce the tax liability. Here when two methods are possible to achieve any objective, one of them is selected that guarantees a lower tax liability.

1.1 Tax Evasion

Tax evasion is as old as the taxation itself. Tax evasion causes severe damage to the functioning of government and hampers the growth of an economy [22]. This leads to serious inequality in society. The present work is on the study of tax evasion, which may be resorted to by any of the following methods.

(i) The dealer will not remit the tax collected from the customer or collecting a higher rate from the customer and remitting to Government at a lower rate.

(ii) The dealer does not report all the transactions made by him, though he may record the same.

(iii) The dealer will arrive at lower taxable turnover by wrongly applying prescribed calculations.

(iv) The dealer creates a fictitious transaction where there is no movement of goods, but only the bills are floated in order to claim Input Tax Credit (ITC) and escape payment of tax. This is also called as bill trading.

1.2 Overview of This Work

We divide our work into three parts.

(i) *Part 1 Scrutiny System:* This system detects suspicious dealers using certain sensitive parameters and standardizes the process of scrutiny of accounts. We used sophisticated statistical and machine learning tools to predict the possibility of tax evasion. We designed a detailed dossier about each suspicious dealer, which enabled tax officials to pinpoint the evasion easily.

(ii) *Part 2 Regression model to predict return defaulters:*
The Indian taxation system experienced some issues during its inception stages of transitioning from the previous taxation system to GST. The tax payer who understood these issues planned his tax filings that resulted in low tax return filings. We build regression models to predict possible return defaulters. Along with this, we developed Android applications to track the return filing and provide real-time information to tax officials.

(iii) *Part 3 Algorithms to detect circular trading:* This part of our work is regarding the detection and analysis of a tax evasion mechanism, known as circular trading, using advanced algorithmic and social-network analytic techniques.

2 Related Work

In [23], Stankevicius and Leonas have shown the usefulness of big data processing ability in identifying the tax evaders. In [24], Wu et al., used various data mining and data science techniques for detection of the tax evaders. Using the data mining tool they designed a system which can identify possible noncomplaint tax returns. In [13], Lin et al., have used data mining techniques along with expert questionnaires in order to collocate various fraud facets and then grade them according to their importance. In [7], Frunza quantified the market exploitation effect caused by performing VAT fraud. In [8], González et al., have used various data mining technique along with dealers tax payment and their historical performance to detect potential users of false invoices. In [3,16], the authors have shown a case study of tax evasion which they have detected through data mining techniques for Kazakhstan and Minnesota respectively. In

[14], Liu et at., have presented clustering based data mining algorithms to identify tax evasion. In [2,9,19,20], the authors have mentioned various problems as well as their solutions about tax compliance. In [17], Prat-Pérez et al., have used K- means clustering algorithm to detect fraudulent activities on telecommunication company with the purpose of identifying malicious refunds. In [11], Khadivi et al., designed a novel flow-based anomaly detection technique which is based on the K-means clustering algorithm. In [12], Klymko et al., developed various analytical models to predict the amount of tax-defaulted by firms. They built a social network of firms connected via shared membership. In [6], Durak et al., showed that the clients who get associated with better-connected individual auditors have lower effective tax rates as compared with the other clients. Their study suggest that an environment encouraging individual cross-appointments over multiple engagements can open the door for the transfer of expertise between the members of professional teams.

3   Scrutiny System

In this section, we present the flow in which the anti-evasion operation is facilitated by our scrutiny software system. We used big data analytics to identify suspicious dealers and developed a software system for scrutiny of accounts of suspicious dealers.

3.1   Identification of Suspicious Dealers

Potential tax evaders are identified based on the parameters such as comparison of the turnovers declared at different level i.e., way bills vs. monthly returns, the ratio of purchases to sales, the ratio of exempt sales to taxable sales, etc. We also used the data from third parties like online market places, other government agencies, and banks. We applied sophisticated statistical and machine learning techniques like Benford's analysis [15], ratio-analysis, data clustering, time series analysis [4], etc., to identify suspicious dealers.

Returns Database. Figure 2, shows a sample of the database we used for identifying tax evaders. Our database contains millions of rows, and the size of the database is 1.5 Terabytes. The actual database contains many more details like type of goods, the rate of tax, the quantity of goods, vehicle used for transporting the goods, vehicle number, transporter name, invoice number, UOM (unit-of-measure), inserted date, etc.

Feature Extraction and Clustering. We designed clustering models to identify the dealers who are doing tax evasion by using the following methods:

(i) Suppression of sales.
(ii) Under valuation of goods.

Id	GSTIN	Name	Month	Sales Turn Over	Output Tax	Purchase Turn Over	Input Tax	Cash Paid	Non Taxable Turnover
1	2	3	4	5	6	7	8	9	10
1	5OOOG52M	AAA	72017	6865443.57	736030	15481.4	14074	920444	5986633
2	5OOOV5009	BBB	82017	3989375	844402	81455	74050	794694	4372111
3	5OODS383K	CCC	92017	4326558	1045836	153453.3	139503	944320	4464955
4	5OOOH6481	DDD	102017	2511480	496036	142865.8	129878	405938	6710456
5	5OOOM8132	EEE	72017	12084844	709278	115623.2	105112	709898	9214619
6	5OOODO21	FFF	82017	15092839	854368	52869.3	48063	850722	9698020
7	5OOOKH891	GGG	92017	13199148	789028	132882.2	120802	769253	9924345

Fig. 2. Returns database

(iii) Showing excessive input tax credit (ITC) through showing fake purchases.
(iv) Applying the incorrect tax rate.

To cluster the dealers, we derived the following features based on the data explained in Fig. 2.

- Percentage of value addition (PVA). $PVA = Total\ sales/Total\ purchases$
- Effective tax rate ratio (TRR), $TRR = Effective\ rate\ of\ tax\ of\ sales/Effective\ rate\ of\ tax\ of\ purchases$
- Liability to input tax credit (ITC) ratio (LIR). Lower ILR means low cash payment. $LIR = Liability\ on\ sales/ITC\ on\ purchase$

Clustering is an unsupervised data mining technique which can be used for detecting fraud [1,18]. Clustering algorithms can learn from data and detect fraud. In clustering-based fraud detection, the model is trained using unlabelled data that consists of both normal as well as fraudulent data points. The motivation behind this technique is that anomalous data points form a small percentage of the total data. Anomalous data points can be detected based on the distribution of dealers in each cluster and cluster size [8,10,14]. We used the spectral clustering algorithm on three-dimensional data (TRR, LIR, and PVA) and taken those dealers, who are at the boundary of each cluster as possible tax evaders. Cluster boundaries are defined based on the assumption that the distribution of points in a cluster follows Gaussian distribution.

3.2 Module for Scrutiny of Accounts of Dealers by the Tax Authorities

This module provides a summary of inconsistency in the accounts of the dealer, calculators for arriving at exact taxable turnover and matching systems for verifying invoices, payment details such as tax deducted at source (TDS) etc., exemption details which identify unmatched and irregular claims. A detailed dossier about the dealer is provided in the system through which the officers can identify the tax evasion in an easy and transparent manner. This avoids the human biases in identifying the tax evasion. Figure 3a and b are screen shots from the scrutiny system. From this module, officers can pass penalty orders and track the payments and legal issues related to these orders.

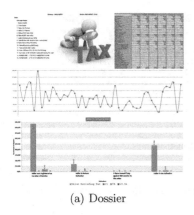

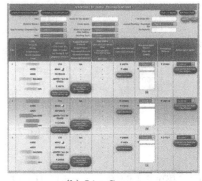

(a) Dossier   (b) List Screen

Fig. 3. Scrutiny system

4   Tax Enforcement

In GST, the business entities or dealers are supposed to file their tax returns
on a monthly basis. However, if an entity is unable to file them due to some
concern, they can file them in the coming month by incurring some penalty. The
commercial tax department of India experienced some problems while transitioning from the previous taxation system (VAT) to GST in the initial stages.
The tax payers sensed these issues and they employed plans packed with financial chicanery which resulted in low tax return filing and poor compliance. For
the same, we developed a logistic regression model to detect possible non-filers of
returns, and Android mobile applications to assist the tax officers for enforcing
crystallized demand.

4.1   Identifying Return Defaulters Using Logistic Regression

Here our aim is to devise a machine learning model that predicts whether a
business entity will file their GST returns or not in the upcoming month. The
model is built based on the following attributes.

(i) The previous tax filing behavior of the business entity
(ii) Quantity of business
(iii) The interactions of a dealer with other dealers
(iv) *Mean Absolute Deviation* value of the first digit Benford's law on the sales
transactions of the firm

Training accuracy of the constructed model at the cutoff equal to 0.5 is
86.38%, and testing accuracy equal to 86.33%. The Precision of the model is
85.5%. Recall of the model is 97.97%. The confusion matrices for the model are
given in Fig. 4a and b. By observing them, one can conclude that almost all the
class 1 records and 54% of the class 0 records are correctly classified.

	Predicted 0	Predicted 1
Actual 0	5953	4933
Actual 1	612	29209

(a) Training Confusion Matrix

	Predicted 0	Predicted 1
Actual 0	2514	2125
Actual 1	260	12548

(b) Testing Confusion Matrix

Fig. 4. Confusion matrices

Concordance and Discordance tests also performed. Concordance value for the model is 0.8119749 and discordance value is 0.1880251. As given in Fig. 5a and b, the area under the training ROC curve is 0.814, and the testing ROC curve is 0.812. One can conclude that the model is not over fitting as the area under both the curves is almost same. Also, the model is not under fitting as the area under the training ROC curve is more than 0.7.

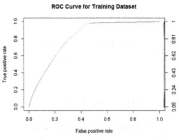

(a) Training Confusion Matrix

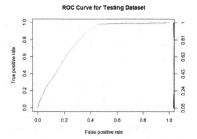

(b) Testing Confusion Matrix

Fig. 5. ROC curves

4.2 OIC Android Application

We developed an Officer In-charge (OIC) Android application and back-end software systems to assist the tax officers for enforcing crystallized demand. This mobile application provides detailed information about the return defaulters and real-time filing statistics. It helps the tax officials in optimizing their travel time by grouping defaulters by their physical location. In addition to this, Officials can also send legal notices to defaulters from this mobile application. Figures 6, 7, 8 are few screen shots of Android application.

5   Circular Trading

Circular trading is rampant financial fraud. The motivation for circular trading is to hide illegitimate transactions, which are performed to minimize the tax liability. They hide these illegitimate transactions by super imposing several

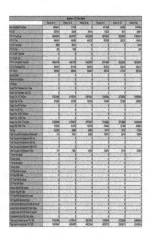

Fig. 6. Login screen   **Fig. 7.** List screen   **Fig. 8.** Dossier

fraudulent (fake) transactions without any value-add. In this manner, they create confusion to tax officials. There are two patterns that generally arises in circular trading

- Goods circles around without any value add.
- The fraudulent transactions are performed in a short span of time.

As the actual value-added is nil in any fraudulent transaction, dealers are not actually paying taxes on the transactions available in a circular trade. In fact, in a circular trade, some malicious business vendors are created by fraudulent traders. In Fig. 9, dubious transactions are the ones in red color. To escape from the investigations of taxation authorities, dealers overlap malicious transactions on the dubious transaction, as shown using gray lines. As one can observe, the tax liability of business traders did not change by the overlapping of thin gray lines. Note that the superimposition of the thin lined transactions did not change the tax liability of any dealer. The major challenge lies in identifying dubious sales transaction, composite sequences of malicious sales transactions in circular trading.

Advanced social network analysis techniques are used where we build a model as a graph with dealers as vertices and transactions as directed edges. We designed and implemented algorithms to identify and remove fraudulent transactions that are created to hide the illegitimate transactions. This allows for easier identification of the manipulated transactions by tax enforcement officers. Figure 10a, shows a complex sequence of sales and purchase and Fig. 10b, shows the result after applying our algorithm.

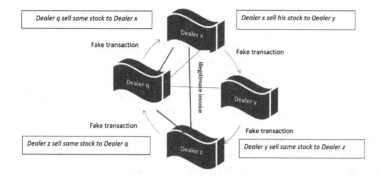

Fig. 9. Circular flow of sales/purchases

(a) Complex Network of Sales and Purchases   (b) Experimental Result

Fig. 10. Circular trading

6   Impact of This Work

Before our initiative, there was a huge tax evasion which went unchecked in various components of the commercial taxation system. There was no system that would automate the process of scrutinizing the tax return statements. In fact, there was a lack of technical expertise to develop the same.

Due to this work compliance levels are increased significantly, and tax collection is increased by 16%. Through OIC Android application tax collection responsibility is given to all levels of tax officials from junior officials to senior most officials. This increased the sense of belongingness in the department, which indirectly contributed to the revenue collection. This empowered the officials by providing 360° of information about tax payers.

7   Conclusion

In this article, we outline the work that we performed towards controlling tax evasion for the state of Telangana, India. This is the first initiative in India of its kind that developed a system to monitor the amount of tax paid by business entities for potential tax evasion. The system is highly scalable across the nation to different states after the advent of GST. We described all the three phases that we have worked so far, starting from the process of scrutiny, then, towards controlling tax-leakages and finally on the sophisticated tax evasion technique called circular trading. In the future, we wish to work towards identifying complex tax-evasion techniques arising in the Goods and Services Taxing system.

Acknowledgment. We offer our sincere thanks to the government of Telangana, India for graciously sharing the Commercial tax data set and giving us consistent motivation and financial support. This work has been supported by Visvesvaraya Ph.D. Scheme for Electronics and IT, Media Lab Asia, grant number EE/2015-16/023/MLB/MZAK/0176.

References

1. Jain, A.K., Murty, M.N., Flynn, P.J.: Data clustering: a review. ACM Comput. Surv. (CSUR) **31**(3), 264–323 (1999)
2. Andreoni, J., Erard, B., Feinstein, J.: Tax compliance. J. Econ. Lit. **36**, 818–860 (1998)
3. Assylbekov, Z., Melnykov, I., Bekishev, R., Baltabayeva, A., Bissengaliyeva, D., Mamlin, E.: Detecting value-added tax evasion by business entities of Kazakhstan. In: Czarnowski, I., Caballero, A.M., Howlett, R.J., Jain, L.C. (eds.) Intelligent Decision Technologies 2016. SIST, vol. 56, pp. 37–49. Springer, Cham (2016). https://doi.org/10.1007/978-3-319-39630-9_4
4. Baesens, B., Vlasselaer, V., Verbeke, W. (eds.): Fraud Analytics Using Descriptive, Predictive, and Social Network Techniques: A Guide to Data Science for Fraud Detection. Wiley, Hoboken (2015). ISBN 978-1-119-13312-4
5. Dani, S.: A research paper on an impact of goods and service tax (GST) on Indian economy. Bus. Econ. J. **7**, 264 (2016). ISSN 2151–6219
6. Durak, N., Pinar, A., Kolda, T.G., Seshadhri, C.: Degree relations of triangles in real-world networks and graph models. In: CIKM 2012 Proceedings of the 21st ACM International Conference on Information and Knowledge Management, pp. 1712–1716. ACM (2012). ISBN: 978-1-4503-1156-4
7. Frunza, M.: Aftermath of the VAT Fraud on Carbon Emissions Markets, 30 May 2012. https://ssrn.com/abstract=2070927 or http://dx.doi.org/10.2139/ssrn.2070927
8. González, P.C., Velásquez, J.D.: Characterization and detection of taxpayers with false invoices using data mining techniques. Expert Syst. Appl. **40**(5), 1427–1436 (2013)
9. Graetz, M.J., Wilde, L.L.: The economics of tax compliance: fact and fantasy. Nat. Tax J. **38**(3), 355–363 (1985)
10. Huang, S.Y., Tsaih, R.H., Yu, F.: Topological pattern discovery and feature extraction for fraudulent financial reporting. Expert Syst. Appl. **41**(9), 4360–4372 (2014)
11. Khadivi, A., Ajdari Rad, A., Hasler, M.: Network community-detection enhancement by proper weighting. Phys. Rev. E **83**, 046104 (2011). https://doi.org/10.1103/PhysRevE.83.046104

12. Klymko, C., Gleich, D.F., Kolda, T.G.: Using triangles to improve community detection in directed networks. In: ASE BIGDATA/SOCIALCOM/CYBERSECURITY Conference, Stanford University abs/1404.5874 (2014)
13. Lin, C.C., Chiu, A.A., Huang, S.Y., Yen, D.C.: Detecting the financial statement fraud: the analysis of the differences between data mining techniques and experts' judgments. Knowl.-Based Syst. **89**, 459–470 (2015)
14. Liu, B., Xu, G., Xu, Q., Zhang, N.: Outlier detection data mining of tax based on cluster. Phys. Procedia **33**(44), 1689–1694 (2012)
15. Mark Nigrini, J.T.W. (ed.): Benford's Law: Applications for Forensic Accounting, Auditing, and Fraud Detection. Wiley, Hoboken (2012). ISBN 978-1-118-15285-0
16. Hsu, K.-W., Pathak, N., Srivastava, J., Tschida, G., Bjorklund, E.: Data mining based tax audit selection: a case study of a pilot project at the Minnesota department of revenue. In: Abou-Nasr, M., Lessmann, S., Stahlbock, R., Weiss, G.M. (eds.) Real World Data Mining Applications. AIS, vol. 17, pp. 221–245. Springer, Cham (2015). https://doi.org/10.1007/978-3-319-07812-0_12. ISBN 978-3-319-07811-3
17. Prat-Pérez, A., Dominguez-Sal, D., Brunat, J.M., Larriba-Pey, J.L.: Shaping communities out of triangles. ACM International Conference Proceeding Series, July 2012
18. Jarvis, R.A., Patrick, E.A.: Clustering using a similarity measure based on shared nearest neighbors. IEEE Trans. Comput. **C–22**(11), 1025–1034 (1973)
19. Riahi-Belkaoui, A.: Relationship between tax compliance internationally and selected determinants of tax morale. J. Int. Acc. Audit. Tax. **13**, 135–143 (2004)
20. Saad, N.: Tax knowledge, tax complexity and tax compliance: taxpayers' view. Procedia - Soc. Behav. Sci. **109**, 1069–1075 (2014)
21. Schenk, A., Oldman, O. (eds.): Value Added Tax: A Comparative Approach. Cambridge University Press, Cambridge (2007). ISBN 978-1107617629
22. Slemrod, J.: Cheating ourselves: the economics of tax evasion. J. Econ. Perspect. **21**(1), 25–48 (2007)
23. Stankevicius, E., Leonas, L.: Hybrid approach model for prevention of tax evasion and fraud. Procedia - Soc. Behav. Sci. **213**, 383–389 (2015)
24. Wu, R.S., Ou, C., Lin, H.Y., Chang, S.I., Yen, D.C.: Using data mining technique to enhance tax evasion detection performance. Expert Syst. Appl. **39**, 8769–8777 (2012)

Vacancy Mining to Design Personalized Learning Analytics for Future Employees

Ildikó Szabó$^{(\boxtimes)}$ and Réka Vas

Department of Information Systems, Corvinus University of Budapest,
Fővám tér 13-15, Budapest 1093, Hungary
{ildiko.szabo2, reka.vas}@uni-corvinus.hu

Abstract. Educational institutions have responsibilities to train future employees meanwhile labor market needs are continually changing due to the new technological innovations. Students must prepare themselves for these changes and monitor their progress in learning process to evaluate their position on the labor market. This paper presents a method which connects competence gap analysis or vacancy mining to learning analytics for providing students an integrated toolset to facilitate their self-development.

Keywords: Digital transformation · Competence · Learning analytics · Data mining

1 Introduction

In the era of the fourth industrial revolution, there is a permanent need for access to high-level knowledge and skills. Increasing knowledge expectations pose challenges on higher education institutions who have the responsibility to educate future employees. Institutions should have a clear understanding concerning knowledge and competence expectations of the labor market to be able to modify, update curricula in time and provide better learning services to their students.

Employees use both skills and knowledge to execute tasks or solve problems. At the same time attitudes and sense of responsibility also have an influence on what extent they are applied in work settings. In summary, skills, knowledge, attitude and responsibility are all needed to make an employee competent. Competences should be acquired during studies conducted at higher educational institutions, while they are required for executing tasks in work settings. Hence competences can serve as a basis to compare the two sides of labor market with each other and to determine if an education program is appropriate for training future employees. There is not a common consensus about the competence concept. In cases, skill, competency, knowledge have the same meaning as competence has.

Hecklau et al. [1] analyzed macro-environmental challenges with using framework. Consequences were drawn about future competencies based on this analysis. They classified these competencies into four categories. Technical competences are knowledge, skills and abilities related to work. Personal competences are motivations and attitudes of people. Social competences are abilities to cooperate, communicate with

A. Kő et al. (Eds.): EGOVIS 2019, LNCS 11709, pp. 58–69, 2019.
https://doi.org/10.1007/978-3-030-27523-5_5

other people. Methodological competences are to support decision making and problem solving. Nowadays competence concept is transforming into hard and soft skill categories. Authors study the same human feature as competence or skill which is required to execute tasks, but they categorize and name it differently. Lippman et al. [2 pp. 4] classified skills, competencies, behaviors and attitudes as soft skills which enhance effective cooperation, collaboration and work performance. Wikle and Fagin [3] identified hard skills or technical competences derived from professional backgrounds and soft skills governed by human instincts. In summary, professional and technical competences cover the same meaning, meanwhile personal, social and methodological competences derive from the personality of people, hence it constitutes a group of soft skills determined by Lippman et al. This paper follows this categorization hereinafter.

Competence or skill gap analysis is a hot topic for decades on the table of European government. OECD, CEDEFOP, European Commission and others support studies and projects in this domain to enhance decision making processes. OECD [4] highlighted the importance of ICT foundation skills to get better jobs and higher wages. Social skills, a solid level of information processing skills, information sharing, giving presentations, providing advice, working autonomously, managing, influencing and solving problems and the ability to collaborate are all enumerated in their report as skills to be improved. The study also draws attention to the deepening inequality among different age groups. At the same time CEDEFOP considers women, older-aged and lower-educated workers as highly risked groups and emphasizes the importance of complementary ICT skills, like foundation skills (literacy, numeracy), soft skills (planning and organization) and behavioral skills (communication and teamwork) [5]. The study of the World Economic Forum makes a step forward and predicates skills that will be required by 2020 (Fig. 1). On this list complex problem solving is the most important one. But critical thinking and creativity will also be more required by 2020 than in 2015 [6].

in 2020	in 2015
1. Complex Problem Solving	1. Complex Problem Solving
2. Critical Thinking	2. Coordinating with Others
3. Creativity	3. People Management
4. People Management	4. Critical Thinking
5. Coordinating with Others	5. Negotiation
6. Emotional Intelligence	6. Quality Control
7. Judgment and Decision Making	7. Service Orientation
8. Service Orientation	8. Judgment and Decision Making
9. Negotiation	9. Active Listening
10. Cognitive Flexibility	10. Creativity

Fig. 1. Predicated skills by Word Economic Forum

The Institute for the Future run a research for the University of Phoenix Research Institute that has discovered ten new skills based on six key drivers of change: sense-making, novel and adaptive thinking, transdisciplinary, new media literacy, computational thinking, social intelligence, cognitive load management, cross cultural competency, design mindset and virtual collaboration [7]. In summary, the ability to collaborate and share knowledge, processes thinking and creativity must be all possessed by future employees. This is not so surprising, because these skills are crucial to apply new technologies for business purposes.

However, these skills are mainly rooted in tacit, not formalized knowledge. This way these studies only provide partial information on how curricula should be modified or updated. A method for identifying profession specific explicit knowledge that can be expressed on formal ways also have to be worked out. Few studies deal with connecting competence gap analysis or vacancy mining to learning analytics.

Edison project focused on developing competencies classification service architecture "to determine to what extent courses in its curriculum cover the identified competence group" in the field of Data Science. Students can select training programs to develop their competences instead of checking their own capabilities in this field [8]. Smart Plus system provides a report to educational institutions about actual skill market gap analysis and a self-assessment tool for students to improve their skills required by the labor market in tourism. But these two modules of this system are independent and skills in self-assessment tool are not refreshed by the report [9]. These solutions are lack of personalized learning analytics functionality to enhance students' own progress monitoring. Section 2 presents our method which uses data mining to analyze job vacancies published in ads and learning analytics to monitor student progress against labor market needs detected by data mining. Section 3 reveals which data mining process was used to. Sections 4 and 5 prove how students can use this method to detect in what extent they can meet the requirements of a Data Scientist position. Conclusion and future work is showed in Sect. 6.

2 From Vacancy Mining to Personalized Learning Analytics

Job vacancies can provide the most comprehensive and up-to-date view on what kind of competences are currently required by the labor market. Job ads published on Indeed.com provide us continually available data source reflecting these needs. Indeed is a job portal widely used in several countries, hence it is appropriate to study this topic. Data mining provides opportunities to extract and structure most required competence needs and classify job ads into clusters for highlighting co-occurrences. Competence model resulted from the data mining process is the input of the personalized learning analytics. Competence gap analysis validates the knowledge network originated from learning outcomes of a training program by comparing the competence model [10]. An integrated toolset for learning analytics is created to monitor progress of future employees against these needs. This method is presented by Fig. 2.

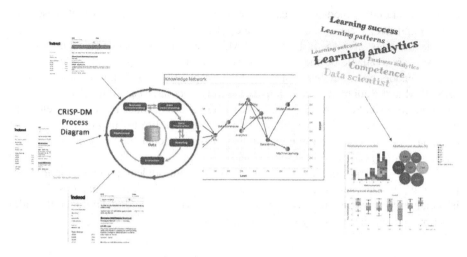

Fig. 2. Method for designing personal learning analytics

3   Data Mining Methodologies

Data mining aims at revealing hidden patterns, correlations behind data sets. This transformation is executed within the data mining processes of different methodologies. Crisp-DM (CRoss Industry Standard Process for Data Mining) is a data mining methodology elaborated by IBM SPSS.

Turbulent environment generates decision situations for companies continually. Business understanding phase is to understand these situations and result an organizational objective realized by data mining process. Data Preparation is to identify relevant data sources and methods used to collect them. Meanwhile problems in data consistency are handled in this stage. Data Understanding is to select data fit to purpose and Modeling phase is responsible for executing iterative processes of selecting and refining modeling techniques. Initial models are evaluated based on their performance and data mining success criteria determined previously. Final models fitting to business success criteria are chosen in Evaluation phase. Deployment is about using new insights provided by previous stages to improve the business operations [11].

SAS Institute created a data mining process called SEMMA. This is the acronym of Sample, Explore, Modify, Model and Assess words. SEMMA is quite similar with Crisp-DM, but business context is less important within it than within Crisp-DM. Sample phase contains techniques to get statistically representative sample of large full detail data sources without losing any significant information. It assumes that patterns, if they exist, are inherited by sample data as well, hence this phase spare data mining experts some processing time. Explore stage is to explore datasets graphically and statistically to detect missing, extreme data or connected variables. Association analysis, descriptive statistics, plots are used to do it. Modify is to transform, refine datasets or extend it with new variables to prepare them for the Modeling phase to build different data mining models. Assess phase contains steps to compare models based on their compliance, accuracy and performance [12].

The products of SAS Institute or IBM are commercial ones, but open source programs are available on the market as well. Gartner magic quadrant evaluates data mining vendors based on their visions and their capabilities for fulfilling these visions. SAS, IBM and Rapidminer were considered as leaders last year in the Gartner Magic Quadrant for Data Science Platforms [13]. IBM® SPSS® Modeler aims at developing predictive models and deploying them into the business life to support and improve decision making. It offers a variety of new and traditional modeling methods like machine learning, artificial intelligence, and statistics.

Dynamic vacancy mining is required to facilitate student progress monitoring frequently, hence understanding of actual and future business situations has an important role in our research. Hence, we opted for IBM SPSS Modeler due to its wide functionality and its capability of following Crisp-DM.

4   Vacancy Mining

The context of *Business Understanding* is given by the mechanisms of the fourth industrial revolution. Nowadays' turbulent environment is resulted from the symptom in what extent technological innovations are applied to restructure, create and modify business processes or business models. These changes also entail modification of human cognitive processes. Improved or new competences are needed to perform modified or new tasks. The role of data science in controlling digital transformation processes is getting important because data management, business analytics, business intelligence etc. provide humans a wide spectrum palette to monitor and manage operations of robots, machine learning algorithms or IoT tools. Growing number of job vacancies in Data scientist position reflect such labor market need that educational institutions and students have to take into their considerations. Our business objective is to detect and monitor changes in competence needs of Data Scientist position for planning future learning activities by students. The goal of this data mining project is to create a competence model facilitating these activities. UK labor market as an emerging an turbulent market was selected in the *Data preparation* phase. A python crawler downloaded 670 Data scientist job ads published this year from Indeed UK. Competence needs reside in only job descriptions which were chosen as relevant data source in *Data understanding* stage. *Modeling phase* consisted of two steps (see Fig. 3). First of all, a competence model – including soft skills and knowing of artificial intelligence, machine learning, big data, business analytics, business problem, data cleansing, data mining, modeling, software vendors in this field, statistics, visualization as hard skills – was created to measure in what extent its competence elements are needed by companies in a given time period. A general text mining method was selected to validate this model based on job descriptions, but a process-based text mining method could have been applied as well [14]. The dataset downloaded by the crawler was extended with new columns representing each competence. They hold 1 if a position in row required a competence in column and 0 if it did not. Only 11% of job vacancies needed other competences.

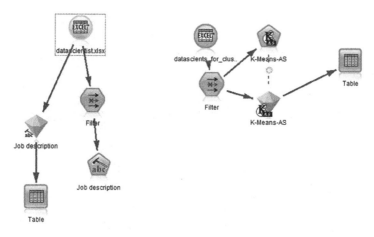

Fig. 3. *Modeling phase in IBM SPSS Modeler*

This extended dataset served as the input of the K-means clustering algorithm. Data mining of binary datasets were handled by determining frequent closures [15] or by analyzing clusters [16]. Cluster analysis is an unsupervised machine learning method in that no goal variable exists. The number of clusters must be defined at the beginning of this procedure. Having calculated the centrums of these clusters randomly, it counts the distance of points from them and recalculate new cluster centers. This iterative process is repeating till the end of a given time or until finding the appropriate cluster centers [17]. In SPSS Modeler three clusters were created and all job ads were inserted into only one cluster at the end of this phase. During the *Evaluation*, clusters were presented in Tableau software. Tableau is a market leader in the Gartner magic quadrant among analytics and business intelligence platforms for six years in row. It provides users rich functionalities e.g. informative charts, dashboards, story maker to execute descriptive or predictive analytical procedures [18]. Figure 4 presents that Cluster 0 has Data scientist positions focusing on processing big data with using AI, ML methods or algorithms. The least published job vacancies belonged to this cluster. Positions in Cluster 1 required knowledge about AI methods and programs but not in the field of big data. Positions in Cluster 2 needed to know statistics, mathematics, programming, data cleansing, products of software vendors, business analytics and big data. It contained the most job vacancies. Some of these competences are taught in Management Information System bachelor training program of our university. In the *Deployment* phase, the result of this data mining was used to design personalized learning analytics tool for students.

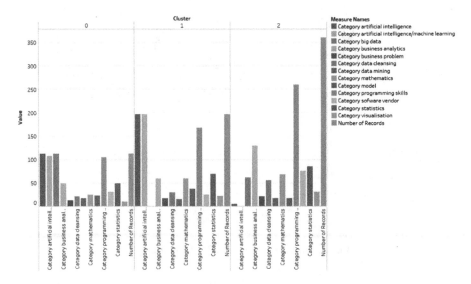

Fig. 4. Clusters of published positions

5 Learning Analytics

Even though results of vacancy mining provide a clear view of labor market expectations, it is still not evident how students or new entrants to the labor market should adjust their learning processes to acquire the required knowledge and competencies. As the last element of our approach the role of learning analytics in evaluating actual learning performance and in supporting preparation will be discussed. Learning analytics includes the measurement of learning activities and the collection and analysis of related data for the purpose of understanding learning patterns, optimizing learning outcomes and improving learning success [19]. As a result, learners can have better information concerning their progress in learning and deeper insight into those factors that contribute to success on the job market.

Job vacancies provide comprehensive and up-to-date view on what kind of competencies are currently required by the labor market. Three clusters of data science related jobs have been identified as the result of vacancy mining. Each cluster is characterized by a specific set of job roles and/or skills (that are listed on Fig. 4). Cluster 2 is used here as an example to represent how information extracted from vacancies can be applied to set learning goals and guide the learning process. The following job role and skill expectations dominate Cluster 2: data cleansing and business analytics.

In the followings it will be described how students of a Management Information System bachelor training program can follow how well they proceed in acquiring knowledge and skills required by positions in Cluster 2. In the first step knowledge taught in data science related courses of this training program has been represented as a network of relations (See Fig. 5). Circles represent major knowledge areas taught in the related courses, while in-coming arrows represent the prerequisites for the given knowledge area. This knowledge network enables the mapping of labor market expectations and learning outcomes and serve as a basis to model students' competences.

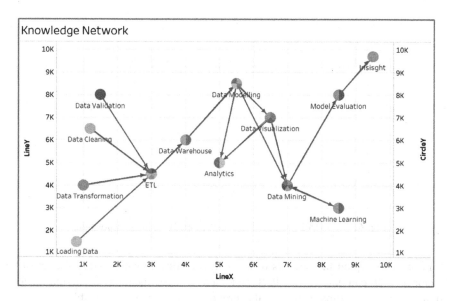

Fig. 5. Data science knowledge network

Concerning expectations in Cluster 2, both data cleansing (as "Data Cleaning") and business analytics (as "Analytics") are part of the knowledge network of courses (see also Fig. 6). Once key knowledge requirements are identified on the network representation of the curriculum, students should be advised which other knowledge elements are relevant concerning their carrier goals. In order to ensure solid, high level performance concerning the key knowledge areas (analytics and data cleaning) students are also suggested to monitor their progress concerning the prerequisites for these knowledge areas. Figure 6 highlights all of those knowledge areas that students must efficiently acquire in support of successfully applying for positions in Cluster 2. The directed network representation of required knowledge areas also serves to guide learning activities since it is advisable to pick up prerequisites first and move on to more complex knowledge areas only afterwards.

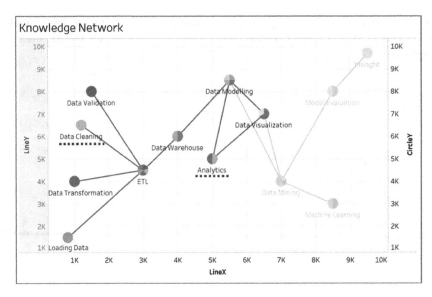

Fig. 6. Knowledge required in business analytics related positions

In order to exploit the benefits of learning analytics an integrated toolset must be developed that can identify, collect and then process data based on the various requirements. The primary aim of the proposed solution is to be able to monitor progress against labor market needs. This way data from learning management systems and from test engines must be incorporated first in the toolset to enable multiple ways of analytics on student related datasets. The goal is to provide a lens on learning progress in such a way that adds more insight on how to get the desired position.

In the frames of the proposed solution all students will have access to a dashboard of analytics which provides them feedback on their progress concerning each knowledge areas in the network (see Fig. 6). The "Individual Scores" dashboard image represents their last test results concerning the different knowledge areas (see Fig. 7). As analytics has high relevance in Cluster 2, the rest of the images provide further details concerning this area.

The "Group Results" image provides details concerning the overall performance of each seminar group. This allows students to spot and switch to those groups where it is more likely to reach better performance or where they are more likely to find inspiring, challenging environment of student interactions.

The "Analytics Result" image of the dashboard gives additional details concerning the analytics exam and its results. The distribution of points reached by different students on the exam will explain to the students what the typical results were.

Finally, the "Ranking by Analytics Results" describes who are the top 10 students, what their actual and average performance is and where each student is located in the rank. This way students can clearly see how much they must improve to be amongst the best ones.

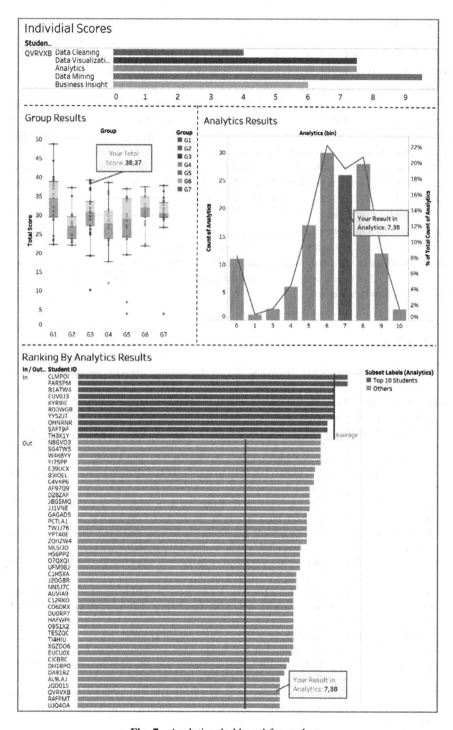

Fig. 7. Analytics dashboard for students

6 Conclusion

This paper presented a solution how a student can monitor its progress against labor market needs in a turbulent environment conducted by digital transformation. This method connects vacancy mining as competence gap analysis to a learning analytics tool which is a new approach in this field. Data mining process of Crisp-DM was used to analyze labor market needs in Data Scientist position and its result was adopted in developing an integrated toolset for students. Competence gap was studied on the Data Science Knowledge Network. Data cleansing and business analytics were discovered as required and taught competences. Analytics dashboard for students was created to highlight how a student performed in tasks required these competences among other students who will be its competitors on the labor market.

This method is repeatable. It can be executed on a new dataset downloaded by the crawler and new student performance historical data. But it can be extended with new aspects of learning analytics such as analyzing collaborative skills, social networks of students with network analytics. A data warehouse from job vacancies can facilitate trend analysis of competences required by different positions to study not just actual but future labor market needs.

References

1. Hecklau, F., Galeitzke, M., Flachs, S., Kohl, H.: Holistic approach for human resource management in industry 4.0. Procedia CIRP **54**, 1–6 (2016)
2. Lippman, L.H., Ryberg, R., Carney, R., Moore, K.: Workforce connections: key "soft skills" that foster youth workforce success: toward a consensus across fields—VOCEDplus, the international tertiary education and research database. Child Trends Publication (2015)
3. Wikle, T.A., Fagin, T.D.: Hard and soft skills in preparing gis professionals: comparing perceptions of employers and educators. Trans. GIS **19**, 641–652 (2015)
4. OECD: Skill for a Digital World. http://www.oecd.org/els/emp/Skills-for-a-Digital-World.pdf. Accessed 07 May 2018
5. Cedefop: Briefing note - People, machines, robots and skills. http://www.cedefop.europa.eu/en/publications-and-resources/publications/9121. Accessed 07 May 2018
6. World Economic Forum: The jobs of the future – and two skills you need to get them. https://www.weforum.org/agenda/2016/09/jobs-of-future-and-skills-you-need/
7. Davies, A., Fidler, D., Gorbis, M.: Future work skills 2020. Institute for the Future for the University of Phoenix Research Center (2011)
8. Belloum, A.S.Z., Koulouzis, S., Wiktorski, T., Manieri, A.: Bridging the demand and the offer in data science. Concurrency Comput.: Practice Exp. e5200 (2019). https://doi.org/10.1002/cpe.5200
9. Smart Plus Project – Official Website. http://smartplus-project.org/
10. Szabó, I., Neusch, G.: Dynamic skill gap analysis using ontology matching. In: Kő, A., Francesconi, E. (eds.) EGOVIS 2015. LNCS, vol. 9265, pp. 231–242. Springer, Cham (2015). https://doi.org/10.1007/978-3-319-22389-6_17
11. IBM Knowledge Center - IBM SPSS Modeler CRISP-DM Guide. https://www.ibm.com/support/knowledgecenter/de/SS3RA7_17.1.0/modeler_crispdm_ddita/modeler_crispdm_ddita-gentopic1.html

12. Data Mining and SEMMA :: Data Mining Using SAS(R) Enterprise Miner(TM): A Case Study Approach, Third Edn. http://support.sas.com/documentation/cdl/en/emcs/66392/HTML/default/viewer.htm#n0pejm83csbja4n1xueveo2uoujy.htm
13. Gartner Magic Quadrant - Data Science. https://www.ibm.com/analytics/data-science/gartner-mq
14. Ternai, K.: Semi-automatic methodology for compliance checking on business processes. In: Kő, A., Francesconi, E. (eds.) EGOVIS 2015. LNCS, vol. 9265, pp. 243–256. Springer, Cham (2015). https://doi.org/10.1007/978-3-319-22389-6_18
15. Boulicaut, J.-F., Bykowski, A.: Frequent closures as a concise representation for binary data mining. In: Terano, T., Liu, H., Chen, A.L.P. (eds.) Knowledge Discovery and Data Mining. Current Issues and New Applications. LNCS, pp. 62–73. Springer, Heidelberg (2000). https://doi.org/10.1007/3-540-45571-X_9
16. Li, T.: A general model for clustering binary data. In: Proceedings of the Eleventh ACM SIGKDD International Conference on Knowledge Discovery in Data Mining, KDD 2005, pp. 188–197. ACM, New York (2005). https://doi.org/10.1145/1081870.1081894
17. Turban, E., King, D., Sharda, R., Delen, D.: Business Intelligence: A Managerial Perspective on Analytics. Prentice Hall, New York (2013)
18. Tableau Software. https://www.tableau.com/
19. Siemens, G., Long, P.: Penetrating the fog: analytics in learning and education. EDUCAUSE Rev. **46**, 30 (2011)

Towards a Data-Driven Approach for Fraud Detection in the Social Insurance Field: A Case Study in Upper Austria

Johannes Himmelbauer[1]([⊠]), Jorge Martinez-Gil[1], Michael Ksen[2], Katharina Linner[2], and Sieglinde Plakolm[2]

[1] Software Competence Center Hagenberg GmbH,
Softwarepark 21, 4232 Hagenberg, Austria
`Johannes.Himmelbauer@scch.at`
[2] Oberösterreichische Gebietskrankenkasse, Gruberstrasse 77, 4020 Linz, Austria

Abstract. The Social Insurance industry can be considered as a basic pillar of the welfare state in many countries around the world. However, there is not much public research work on how to prevent social fraud. And the few published works are oriented towards detecting fraud on the side of the employees or providers. In this work, our aim is to describe our experience when designing and implementing a data-driven approach for fraud detection but in relation to employers not meeting their obligations. In fact, we present here a case study in Upper Austria but from which interesting lessons can be drawn to be applied in a wide range of different situations.

Keywords: Data mining · Health insurance · Social insurance · Fraud detection

1 Introduction

In many countries of the world, social insurance plays a crucial role according to the social security and welfare of a state. The Austrian health system is based on the principles of solidarity, affordability and universality. Many of its responsibilities have been delegated to self-governing bodies, although most of the regulations are defined by law. Therefore the Austrian health system is complex, fragmented, and because of its high standards it is relatively costly [3]. The Austrian health insurance is mainly financed by income-related periodic contributions the employers have to pay.

This system has proven to work very well and high levels of well-being and safety for workers have been achieved. However, the rigorous supervision of the whole system is necessary so that degradation does not occur. In this context, fraud control is of great importance as a means of keeping down the costs for employers who fulfill their obligations properly. The major problem here is that

A. Kő et al. (Eds.): EGOVIS 2019, LNCS 11709, pp. 70–84, 2019.
https://doi.org/10.1007/978-3-030-27523-5_6

fraud is intended to be processed as normal, which means that fraud has to be looked for to be discovered, and this task is far from being trivial. Moreover, most fraud control activities are often performed manually, this means that unexplored automatic fraud detection techniques have an enormous potential to make an impact on this context. For these reasons, this research intends to shed light on the design of a data-driven strategy to help to detect fraudulent behaviors. Therefore, the major contributions of this work can be summarized as follows:

- We introduce our data-driven approaches for fraud detection in the context of employers that do not follow the rules for hiring workers.
- We present a use case in the context of the Upper Austrian health insurance, whereby our approaches have shown to provide useful support to control fraudulent activities.

The remainder of this work is organized as follows: Sect. 2 outlines the State-of-the-Art in relation to fraud detection for Social Insurance industry. Section 3 introduces a real-world case study for fraud detection in the area of employment settled at the Austrian social insurance system. Section 4 presents the data-driven procedure that we have designed and implemented in order to facilitate and support fraud monitoring. Section 5 summarizes the achieved results with respect to the presented case study and how our approach have had an impact on the regional health insurances in Austria. Finally, we highlight the conclusions and future research lines that could be derived from this work.

2   State-of-the-Art

There is a large body of literature in relation to fraud detection in the context of the Social Insurance industry, but in the vast majority of cases it is either in relation to workers who use dishonest tactics to get benefits that are not theirs, or it deals with service providers (e.g. doctors, hospitals) that make false claims by charging the insurance for unnecessary or even not done treatments. In general, it is widely assumed that the Social Insurance industry consists of the following stakeholders:

- Insurance carriers (governmental health departments, private insurance companies)
- Service providers (hospitals, doctors, laboratories,...)
- Insurance subscribers (employees and patients)
- Insurance payers (employers)
- External providers (pharma industry).

With this vast amount of actors in mind, it is not difficult to envision that there are multiple variants to commit fraud. In fact, Thornton et al. [11] have identified many different kinds of fraud, among which the following stand out: *identity theft*, i.e. stealing confidential information from stakeholders and using that information to prepare false bills, *phantom billing*, i.e. billing for good or services that are not actually performed, *unbundling*, i.e. billing different phases of a procedure as if it was a different treatment, *upcoding*, i.e. billing services more expensives than the ones performed, *bill padding*, i.e. providing unnecessary services to a patient, *kickbacks*, i.e. a negotiated bribery in which some money is paid to do something in return, and many more.

In order to fight against frauds of this kind, some remarkable techniques have been already proposed. For example, Rawte et al. built a novel hybrid approach making use of supervised and unsupervised learning for detecting fraudulent claims [8], Diaz-Granados et al. have proposed a solution to extract and analyze social media data in pursuit of identifying insurance fraud [1], or Dua and Bais have worked towards novel data mining fraud detection models [2]. Slightly different is the proposal of Tsai et al., who have proposed a knowledge model along with the existing database applications using the popular CommonKADS methodology [12].

However, the case that we address here is of different nature, since we focus in companies that do not register (some of) their employees appropriately in order to reduce the labor costs, so we mean a situation shared by insurance payers, insurance subscribers, and insurance carriers. Therefore, this fraud directly harms both the employee (insurance subscriber), who cannot make use of his or her right to appropriate medical treatment and the insurance company (insurance carrier) that does not receive the proper contributions that all employers are obligated to pay for having people working for them.

When analyzing the literature in this context, it is possible to see that most of the works belong to one of these two large groups: those that focus on issues such as causes, consequences, statistics, impact on society, etc. and those that describe techniques that can be useful to help to detect fraudulent cases. In addition, recent breakthroughs in computational paradigms such as artificial intelligence, data mining, and machine learning allow many of these techniques to be implemented (and even improved) by means of computer systems. In our particular case, we are interested in describing our experience in relation to the research and development of some of these fraud detection techniques by means of computer systems.

In relation to the existing literature in this field, interesting works have been carried by Van Vlasselaer et al. whereby the goal is to identify those companies that intentionally go bankrupt in to avoid paying their contributions [13]. Widder et al. proposed a fraud detection by using a combination of discriminant analysis and techniques based on artificial neural networks [14]. To do that, they propose an event processing engine for detecting known patterns and aggregating them as complex events at a higher level of analysis in real-time. Finally, Konijn and Kowalczyk propose a method that consists of analyzing the historical records and aggregating these results in order to detect outliers [4]. The work that we present here is, to the best of our knowledge, the first attempt to build up data models that can support the generation of recommendation lists based on current data so that fraudulent behavior can be inspected according to a ranking of priorities.

3   A Case Study - Social Fraud Detection in the Area of Employment

The Austrian social insurance system is based on the principles of solidarity, affordability, and universality. It is primarily funded through insurance contributions. It includes the branches of accident, health and pension insurance, and it is formed by a number of institutions existing under the Main Association of Austrian Social Security (HVB) as their umbrella organization.

In this context, the Austrian social insurance system constantly has to face the most diverse amount of attempted frauds. One major type of fraud is related to employers not meeting their obligations, i.e. they do not pay the proper amount of contributions for their employees. More concretely, either they do not register worker(s) at all (classical black labor), or - more often and also more difficult to discover - they specify a wrong, too low assessment basis for their payments.

Consequently, there is continuous work on measures against social fraud in that area. Over the years a steadily growing base of knowledge and experience has been build up by the financial in-house experts at the Austrian health insurance. This available expert knowledge is commonly used as follows to detect or even prevent social fraud in the area of employment: in-house experts manually examine the available data of selected companies and if according to the expert there are found reasonable suspicious circumstances in the data of a certain company it might ask the proper authority for inspections at site. For this purpose, the expert usually either searches for already known specific suspected patterns (e.g. in the construction sector a high rate of marginal part-time employees is suspicious) or checks if in general there can be found larger deviations from average behavior.

In the course of this process, during last years a dashboard tool has been developed at the Upper Austrian Health Insurance[1] whose aim is to support in-house experts in their work towards social fraud detection. More concretely, the RAD-Tool (German abbr. for risk conspicuousness of employers) enables the user to visualize and compare relevant historical and current data of each employer. Figure 1 contains a screenshot of the tool. Utilizing this dashboard in daily work facilitates and improves the examination of companies based on their data. However, one major issue remains: considering the available personal resources (usually only a few in-house experts per federal region) it is impossible to check a larger part of existing employers (up to 100.000 per region). Therefore selecting randomly companies for examination remains somehow like looking for the needle in the haystack. This is where our work intends to tie in and great potential with respect to automatic data analysis is seen. Basically, the motivation for the data-driven strategy that is presented in the following section is to provide the dashboard user with automatic recommendations (based on current and historical data) of which companies are considered worthy to give a closer look.

---

[1] Oberösterreichische Gebietskrankenkasse (short OÖGKK).

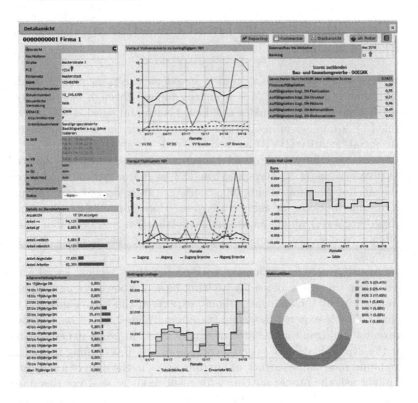

Fig. 1. Screenshot of the dashboard tool RAD (German abbr. for risk conspicuousness of employers)

We have chosen a semi-automatic, multi-step approach for building up models that automatically generate recommendation lists based on current data. *Semi-automatic* means that besides data-driven steps manual interventions (like final model selection) are necessary. The reasons why we have refrained from trying to install a fully automatic approach are manifold:

Use of prior knowledge: We want to incorporate the extensive expert knowledge that is available.

Legal conditions: The mere suspicion of fraud is not enough to act as legal proof, so a computer system cannot determine by itself what is a fraud or what is not.

Soft requirements for model valuation: We need to take into account that the model is not intended to be used as a black box, but serves as a decision making support for human experts. A necessary condition that the system can be helpful is that the user finds basic confidence in its decisions. Therefore interpretable, comprehensible models that at least partially represent the existing knowledge and intention of the user are preferable to non-transparent, complex systems; even if the later show slightly better performance with respect to statistical performance measures.

In the following, we describe a procedure that takes into account the above conditions by combining heuristic strategies and statistical evaluations.

4 Procedure for Knowledge Discovery in the Area of Social Fraud Detection

A starting point of our work was data regarding over 60,000 companies in Upper Austria and that is accessible for the Upper Austrian health insurance. The database consists of more than 200 entries per company and month (columns) ranging from basic information about each company (e.g. location, economic sector) to financial information (payments, payment default, financial problems like past insolvency) and development (company size, monthly fluctuations) and structure (e.g. sex, age, mode of employment) of the employer's staff. Additionally, the experts of OÖGKK have compiled (and are continuously maintaining) a list of "suspicious" companies at which social fraud has already been detected in history. This list of about 750 firms helps the in-house experts to focus on companies that - based on historical experience - are expected to present a higher risk level with respect to social fraud than the average.

To summarize, from the data analyst's perspective, the data available for our case study consists in a multivariate time series (usually we considered a history of 24 to 30 months) for each of the over 60,000 companies. About 750 of these (i.e. 1.2%) contain the flag *suspicious*, the rest remains unlabeled. The basic idea of our data-driven approach is as follows: we aim to build up a model that gives, as a result, a recommendation list which contains at the top the - according to the data-driven model - most suspicious company, followed by the second most suspicious company, and so on.

The model basically should fulfill the following two conditions: The majority of the companies that are ranked in the top part of the scoring list should be firms labeled as *suspicious*. Calculating the proportion of already *suspicious* employers for the top part of the scoring list gives the possibility to measure and compare the models' performance from a statistical point of view. But beyond, the decisions of the model should be easily comprehensible and need to represent a good, useful basis for final judgment by the expert. Amongst other things, this requires that the in-house experts get recommended companies from unlabeled data (i.e. still *unsuspicious* companies) that turn out to be interesting to be given a closer look. The following three subsections describe our way towards such a model.

4.1 Feature Generation

When starting this work in-house experts have already been using over years the available data to manually search for suspicious patterns indicating possible fraud. For this, they do not look exclusively on data at single points of time, but they investigate the behavior and development of figures over a long past time period (usually one up to two years). There are basically two different approaches to build up a data-driven model in such a setting. Either the raw multivariate time series serve as input itself (e.g. cluster algorithms based on measuring the distances between time series), or aggregated features calculated from the time-series are used as input, instead. In the latter case, extracting potentially useful features prior to the training of a model usually turns out to be a crucial task. For our case study, we tried to make use of existing expert knowledge for doing so. Based on the documentation, explanations, and examples from the side of the experts we tried to come up with mathematical or rather statistical formulations to describe known suspicious patterns. In this way, a large set of potentially interesting features (several hundred) could be generated from the time-series data.

In the following, we show with a concrete example how the feature generation process was typically conducted: In-house experts can say from their experience that an unusually high fluctuation of staff over a longer period potentially indicates a committed fraud. Therefore, when examining a company, amongst other things, experts usually give a closer look at the development of the companies' staff. Figure 2 shows plots of the - in this regard - relevant time series for two different companies. On the left side, for *company A*, the monthly company size (red solid line) remains fairly stable over the whole observation period from January 2017 to December 2018 (with the maximum value of 20 employees). Only in 9 out of 24 months minor changes of the staff (i.e. registrations (turquoise dash-dotted line) and/or deregistrations (green dashed line)) were conducted. There is no odd behavior with respect to the staff's development observable. On the contrary, the plot on the right-hand exhibits major changes. Considering only the time series of the company size (red solid line) with its rapid increase during the first observation year and a relatively stable number of employees during 2018 the behavior of *company B* could be explained as typical for a dynamically growing enterprise. Even the temporary reduction of employees during winter 2017/2018 is comprehensible due to the seasonality of the construction sector. However, a more detailed look to the monthly registrations and deregistrations statistics reveal that over the whole observation period a high proportion of the staff is continuously exchanged. For example, there is only a minor increase of the size of *company B* from 21 to 22 employees in November 2018, but, actually, a high number of change requests, namely 13 (7 registrations and 6 deregistrations), are recorded at the side of the social insurance. According to the experts' opinion, such behavior is abnormal and suspicious.

In summary, according to the experts, the available monthly data about the development of the staff (as shown in Fig. 2) contains useful information to estimate a company's fraud risk. The example above suggests that rather than simply considering the development of the company size itself it is preferable to use the monthly numbers of both the registrations and deregistrations. A first statistical check whether the available data really confirms the above assumption

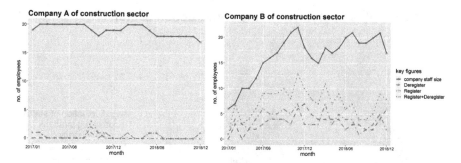

Fig. 2. Development of staff for two companies of the economic sector of construction (January 17–December 18) (Color figure online)

is to compare the average behavior of the already suspected cases with the - up to now - unsuspected ones. In order to obtain more comparable numbers among companies of all sizes it was decided to not use the absolute numbers of the monthly registrations and deregistrations, but to normalize them with respect to the current company size. Therefore, for each company c and month m the current fluctuation of staff is calculated by

$$Fluct(c, m) = \frac{nReg(c, m) + nDereg(c, m)}{company\_size(c, m)}, \tag{1}$$

with $nReg(c, m)$ and $nDereg(c, m)$ as the number of registrations and deregistrations at company c in month m and $company\_size(c, m)$ as the number of currently registered employees, accordingly. Figure 3 shows the monthly fluctuation averaged over all already suspected employers (red thick dash-dotted line) as well as averaged over all the other (unlabeled) companies (blue thick solid line). Hence, the blue line so to speak represents the normal behavior of a company within the construction sector.

Throughout the whole observation period, the average fluctuation of the *suspicious* cases is significantly higher than for the unlabeled companies (about double as high!). This means that the statistical evaluation strongly substantiates the existing experts' view described above. However, we want to point out that due to the high distributional variance of both groups (suspected versus still unsuspected companies) a distinct classification solely based on the staff's fluctuation (1) will not be possible (see the highly overlapping standard deviations shown in Fig. 3). In other words there exist also other reasons than fraud why a company might exhibit a high fluctuation rate of employees, and vice versa.

In order to use the information that is contained in the time series of Fig. 3 with respect to fraud risk for the model generation process we need to calculate aggregated features from the time series data. To sum up, in this situation we are in search for indicators that have high values in the case that a company's data exhibit a suspicious behavior like e.g. *company B* in Fig. 2, and a low value otherwise. Obvious feature candidates for such indicators are standard statistics

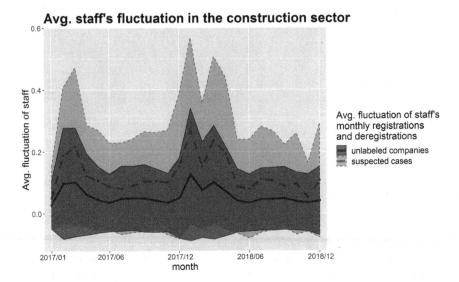

Fig. 3. Comparison of the average fluctuation within the economic sector of construction (January 17–December 18): suspicious companies (red dash-dotted) vs. unlabeled companies (blue solid) (Color figure online)

(like average or extremal values) extracted from the corresponding time series data.

In practice, during our case study the feature generation process was typically conducted in the following way: First, we try to deduce a proper time series (by transformation and/or combination of time series available in the raw data) that lets reveal best a certain suspicious pattern described by the expert (like the staff's fluctuation (1) for the example described above). Next, we extract a set of standard statistics (typically *mean*, *median*, *max*, *min*, and *stddev* for numeric time series, and existence and number of occurrences for binary variables, respectively) over the whole observation period. In some cases, when considered meaningful, we additionally focused also on sub-periods like for example the winter season in case of the gastronomic sector in regions with ski areas. Such decisions were always resulted of taking into account both the expert's view as well as statistical indications.

4.2   Feature Selection

The result of the feature generation process described in the preceding subsection was a diverse set of possible input candidates for generating a model that estimates the risk level for each company. Instead of passing all these several hundred features directly to a learning algorithm it was decided to conduct the first preselection with respect to statistical significance and (visual) interpretability of the features. This was motivated by our aim to finally achieve the highest possible comprehensibility for our model.

As already mentioned above, we tried to define the features in a way that they possibly exhibit high values in case of suspicious behavior and lower values otherwise. In this way, when used later on as input for the model, each input feature can directly be interpreted as a key figure for the riskiness of a company with respect to fraud. Hence, this strategy again facilitates our aim to finally achieve an interpretable model that gives the expert the possibility to easily analyze the reasons for specific risk estimations. Because of those considerations during the feature preselection process, we focused on checking the features' suitability as such risk indicators. One major assistance to do so was a histogram visualization as shown in Fig. 4 for the example of the average value of the staff's fluctuation over the whole observation period. Besides the usual histogram display with the bin counts, Fig. 4 contains additional, distributional information about the target value for each bin. More precisely, the background of each bin is colored with respect of its proportion of unlabeled and suspected companies. Considering all companies belonging to the bin under investigation, the proportion of unlabeled companies is colored in blue, the proportion of suspected companies is colored in red. For example, in Fig. 4, 270 companies fall in the second bin which includes the very low indicator values of the interval [0.005, 0.015], only one company thereof (i.e. only 0.37%) is already suspicious. Hence, the background bar is almost completely colored in blue. On the other hand, 5 out of 11 companies of the interval [0.22, 0.23] with high indicator values are on the list of suspicious enterprises, the proportion of 45.45% is displayed with the red part in the background of the bin.

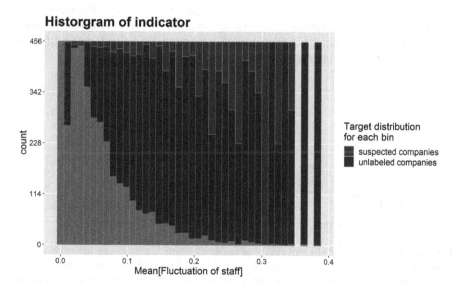

Fig. 4. Histogram of indicator *Mean[Fluctuation of staff]*: colored background shows the target distribution within each bin (Color figure online)

If such a plot, for increasing indicator values, shows a positive trend in the proportion of *suspected companies* (like in Fig. 4), the feature can be considered as useful for a subsequent model generation.

Figure 5 shows two additional plots that can help to judge a feature's potential as an indicator. On the left side, there is a box plot that describes the feature's distribution for each target class. For the staff's fluctuation, this box plot clearly exhibits that the mean value of the class *suspected companies* is far higher than for the *unlabeled companies*, even if the two distributions overlap. Hence there is significant potential of the feature for the use as indicator.

The plot on the right side displays how a simple scoring model that uses only the observed single feature would perform. More precisely, first, the feature is sorted with the highest value at the top and the resulting ordered list of the according companies is taken as recommendation list. As mentioned before we aim at obtaining a scoring list that contains "as many suspicious companies as possible" at the top. Therefore, in our case study, a major performance measure for our models was the proportion of already labeled *suspected companies* for any given length of scoring list $ntop$ (i.e. taking the top $ntop$ entries of the scoring list). The right hand plot of Fig. 5 shows the performance curve (blue line) over an increasing list length (starting with $ntop = 1$) for the recommendation list based on $Mean(Fluct)$ evaluated for companies of the construction sector. The red line represents the base line, i.e. the overall proportion of *suspected companies* in the considered data set (for the given example this is 2.76%). During our evaluations, a typical choice for $ntop$ has been 40, as this is a reasonable amount of companies that in-house experts consider manageable to handle (for closer investigations per month). For the given example, 11 of the top 40 companies are already *suspected*, that makes 27.5%. Hence, compared to selecting companies by chance (2.76%), choosing the companies according to the indicator $Mean(Fluct)$ (27.5%) results in an information gain by a factor of 10.

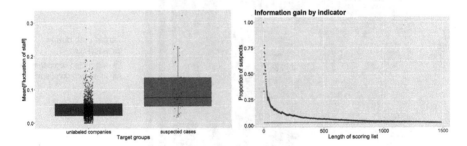

Fig. 5. Plots illustrating the suitability of feature $Mean(Fluct)$ as key figure: a box plot describing the feature's distribution for each target class (left side) and a performance plot of the recommendation list solely based on the feature $Mean(Fluct)$ (right side) (Color figure online))

4.3   Model Generation and Selection

As mentioned before, when working on a recommendation model, our focus was on providing the end user, i.e. the in-house experts of the federal health insurances in Austria, with an easily comprehensible model. The set of feature candidates was generated with the intention that each feature is positively correlated with the riskiness of fraud. However, instead of directly taking the features as they are, we rather want to make use of their inherent ranking. More precisely, for each feature the following preprocessing step is conducted: First the feature is sorted with the highest value at the top and from the resulting ordered list the first 500 entries are selected. To these 500 companies there is assigned a linearly decreasing score value from 1 to 0, i.e. the company with the highest feature value is assigned the score 1 (i.e. 500/500), the second highest takes 499/500, and so on; up to the 500th company with 1/500. Finally, all the other companies with even lower feature values obtain score 0. The in this way calculated scoring variables are eventually the figures that are used for the subsequent model generation.

The motivation for this kind of feature preprocessing was twofold: First, aiming for a recommendation list, we are rather interested in predicting the correct inherent ranking of the companies' risk for fraud than estimating the exact risk for every single company. Therefore we expect that using the ranking information instead of the features' absolute values is the more appropriate way to go. The second benefit we see is that with this feature treatment every single indicator automatically has the same distribution. Hence, all the feature values are directly comparable what will significantly ease the generation of a well-balanced model as well as its interpretability.

At least in the first stage, we decided to stick to linear models. Together with the properties of the deduced features, linear models allow that its coefficients can directly be interpreted as the corresponding feature's contribution to the risk estimation. However, first modeling attempts demonstrated that regression models trained on the available data including the whole generated feature set tend to focus on only a few, dominant subgroups of the known suspicious patterns covered by the available features. However, an important requirement from the experts' side has been the broadness of the resulting model, i.e. the recommendation list shall contain cases that preferably cover multiple (as many as possible) aspects of suspiciousness at the same time.

Therefore, the following two-step approach was realized: First of all, all available indicator variables are manually divided up into six different context groups. For example, all indicators dealing with the payment history of an employer were put together to the indicator group *financial abnormalities*, all the features referring to the development of the staff (like $Mean[Fluct]$ from the previous subsections) form the indicator group *abnormalities of staff's fluctuation*. Based on this additional context information we are aiming for a model that contains reasonable contributions from all indicator groups.

To ensure this, in a first step, models are generated for each indicator group individually. That means that, for each specific indicator group, an extensive grid search is conducted trying out all possible combinations of features. Considering a maximum length of 10 features for a single indicator group, we end up with up to 1023 different models per group ($2^{10} - 1 = 1023$ is the total number of subsets for a set of 10 features). Next, all these models are evaluated by calculating the proportion of *suspected companies* in the according recommendation lists. Additional to the set of all companies of the economic sector under investigation this performance evaluation is always repeated twice on subsets of the data restricted by the company size. The reason for this is that the in-house experts sometimes want to focus their search on enterprises with comparable company size. Thus, the chosen model needs to perform well also in these settings. Finally, based on performance figures as well as other fuzzy criteria (like interpretability, number of used features, ...), up to 5 possible feature combinations are chosen for each indicator groups.

In a second step, a further grid search is conducted to achieve final model candidates, this time combining the in step one identified feature combinations from the different indicator groups. In this way we can guarantee that all indicator groups are represented in our final model and reducing the model with respect to a specific aspect (i.e. measuring the contribution of a certain indicator group) will still result in an optimal model for the according restricted setting. The evaluation and final selection of the model were done equivalently to step one.

5   Results and Experiences

The approaches presented in the previous sections were developed in collaboration with the Upper Austrian health insurance where, in a first stage, we worked on models for the economic sectors of construction and gastronomy based on data of the federal region of Upper Austria. The differentiation of the economic context was motivated by the well-known fact that between the sectors relevant characteristics may differ a lot. Highly suspicious patterns in one sector might express totally normal behavior for another sector. Even when focusing on single economic sectors, we eventually had to deal still with a high heterogeneity of the data, like different economic subsectors or differing scales of company size, to name two major sources.

We had to make the same experiences when we tried to directly transfer the models for Upper Austria to the other 8 federal regions of Austria. Even if one can expect that all in all most of the suspicious patterns somehow exist in all the regions, the differences (be it occasional regionally isolated patterns and/or different local expressions of general patterns) apparently were too big to achieve satisfactory results when simply applying the models developed based on the data of Upper Austria. Thus, we ended up in carrying out the same procedure as described in Sect. 4 for each region and both the economic sectors. That means that we have developed and included to the RAD-Tool altogether 18 recommendation models that are currently in use at the regional health insurances.

With respect to the models' performance, we can make the qualitative statement that "from a statistical point of view the models perform well", in the sense that the proportion of suspicious companies in the resulting recommendation lists is significantly higher than the chance levels. Furthermore, the feedback of the in-house experts that are using the outcomes of the models is mostly promising. However, evaluating our results in a quantitative manner remains a pending task. The reasons for it are manifold, most based on the fact that the output of the models is not directly processed, but only supports the further decision-making process of the human expert:

- The benefit of the model is not only defined by the prediction accuracy, but many fuzzy, difficult to measure criteria (like interpretability of found cases or possibilities of legal prosecution) play a role.
- The financial benefit, eventually the crucial, most interesting figure, is extremely difficult to measure. Effective financial results can often be realized only after a long legal process (months or even years). And even then a quantitative estimation is not always doable.
- Moreover, it is difficult to estimate the exact contribution of the recommendation lists as there are many different factors that lead to a specific financial result.
- Finally, the available amount and quality of target data (i.e. the list of *suspected companies*), at the moment, is not good enough to perform a thorough evaluation.

6   Conclusions and Future Work

In the context of social insurance, it is very important that the available resources might be devoted, and to a greater extent, to those who really need them and pursue any situation in which public funds are used for an unintended purpose. With the aim of providing methods and tools to do that, we have presented here our data-driven approaches for fraud detection in the context of employers that do not follow the rules for hiring workers focusing the competition on the lowest price.

In the future, we want to work towards a fully automated, comprehensive model that is applicable to all of Austria and different economic sectors simultaneously. Benefits of such an all-in-one model would be

- comparability over regions and economic sectors,
- lower costs for quality assurance, and
- exploitation of useful information over multiple related tasks.

We plan to go in this direction by the use of multi-task learning, possibly in combination with learning to rank as well as methods that fit well for partially unlabeled data (to address further particular characteristics of this use case's data).

Still another promising direction will be the use of unsupervised learning methods. For example, clustering of the data and subsequent proper description of the interesting clusters could lead to interpretable models. Additional advantages could be better manageability of the data's heterogeneity as well as the potentiality of discovering even unknown suspicious patterns.

Acknowledgments. The research reported in this paper has been supported by the Austrian Ministry for Transport, Innovation and Technology, the Federal Ministry of Science, Research and Economy, and the Province of Upper Austria in the frame of the COMET center SCCH.

References

1. Diaz-Granados, M., Diaz Montes, J., Parashar, M.: Investigating insurance fraud using social media. In: BigData 2015, pp. 1344–1349 (2015)
2. Dua, P., Bais, S.: Supervised learning methods for fraud detection in healthcare insurance. In: Dua, S., Acharya, U.R., Dua, P. (eds.) Machine Learning in Healthcare Informatics. ISRL, vol. 56, pp. 261–285. Springer, Heidelberg (2014). https://doi.org/10.1007/978-3-642-40017-9_12
3. Hofmarcher, M.M., Quentin, W.: Austria: health system review. Health Syst. Trans. **15**(7), 1–292 (2013)
4. Konijn, R.M., Kowalczyk, W.: Finding fraud in health insurance data with two-layer outlier detection approach. In: Cuzzocrea, A., Dayal, U. (eds.) DaWaK 2011. LNCS, vol. 6862, pp. 394–405. Springer, Heidelberg (2011). https://doi.org/10.1007/978-3-642-23544-3_30
5. Kose, I., Gokturk, M., Kilic, K.: An interactive machine-learning-based electronic fraud and abuse detection system in healthcare insurance. Appl. Soft Comput. **36**, 283–299 (2015)
6. Lu, F., Boritz, J.E.: Detecting fraud in health insurance data: learning to model incomplete Benford's law distributions. In: Gama, J., Camacho, R., Brazdil, P.B., Jorge, A.M., Torgo, L. (eds.) ECML 2005. LNCS (LNAI), vol. 3720, pp. 633–640. Springer, Heidelberg (2005). https://doi.org/10.1007/11564096_63
7. Rao, B.: The role of medical data analytics in reducing health fraud and improving clinical and financial outcomes. In: CBMS 2013, p. 3 (2013)
8. Rawte, V., Anuradha, G.: Fraud detection in health insurance using data mining techniques. In: 2015 International Conference on Communication, Information and Computing Technology (ICCICT), Mumbai, pp. 1–5 (2015)
9. Shi, Y., Tian, Y., Kou, G., Peng, Y., Li, J.: Health insurance fraud detection. In: Shi, Y., Tian, Y., Kou, G., Peng, Y., Li, J. (eds.) Optimization Based Data Mining: Theory and Applications. AI&KP. Springer, London (2011). https://doi.org/10.1007/978-0-85729-504-0_14
10. Sun, C., Li, Q., Li, H., Shi, Y., Zhang, S., Guo, W.: Patient cluster divergence based healthcare insurance fraudster detection. IEEE Access **7**, 14162–14170 (2019)
11. Thornton, D., van Capelleveen, G., Poel, M., van Hillegersberg, J., Müller, R.M.: Outlier-based health insurance fraud detection for U.S. medicaid data. In: ICEIS, no. 2, pp. 684–694 (2014)
12. Tsai, Y., Ko, C., Lin, K.: Using CommonKADS method to build prototype system in medical insurance fraud detection. JNW **9**(7), 1798–1802 (2014)
13. Van Vlasselaer, V., Eliassi-Rad, T., Akoglu, L., Snoeck, M., Baesens, B.: GOTCHA! network-based fraud detection for social security fraud. Manag. Sci. **63**(9), 3090–3110 (2017)
14. Widder, A., von Ammon, R., Hagemann, G., Schoenfeld, D.: An approach for automatic fraud detection in the insurance domain. In: AAAI Spring Symposium Intelligent Event Processing, pp. 98–100 (2009)
15. Yang, W.-S., Hwang, S.-Y.: A process-mining framework for the detection of healthcare fraud and abuse. Expert Syst. Appl. **31**(1), 56–68 (2006)

A Reverse Data-Centric Process Design Methodology for Public Administration Processes

Péter József Kiss$^{(\boxtimes)}$ and Gábor Klimkó

MTA Information Technology Foundation, Budapest, Hungary
mtaita@t-online.hu

Abstract. There were two major bureaucracy reduction programs in Hungary that aimed at the digitization of public administration. The expected benefits of digitization are operations that are more efficient and of a higher level of services. Results of these programs are limited, partly due to the simple support of the existing processes with information technology. The paper proposes a data-centric process design methodology that builds on artifacts as a modeling concept. It is argued and shown based on an example that starting from the expected final artifact of a process and applying a systematic approach, better results can be achieved than with the traditional process-based modelling approach.

Keywords: Business process reengineering ·
Information modelling and integration · Workflow management

1 Introduction

Digital transformation (or digitization) is considered to be of prime importance for Hungarian society. Total digitization of public administration is amongst the long-term objectives [1], besides the implementation of the necessary infrastructural elements (e.g., a high-speed countrywide network) [2]. The expected general benefits of digitization are operations that are more efficient and of higher level of services. Digitization does not mean purely supporting an existing process with information technology but it might also change the process itself. In public administration, there has always been a temptation to simplify the digitization process to the mechanical transcription (imitation) of traditional paper processes. That was exactly the approach taken in Hungary. Today, a number of formerly paper-based applications can now be also submitted by electronic means (the general-purpose form filling program ÁNYK[1], and the "*e-paper*"[2]) but this enhancement did not lead to significant changes in the way how our society operates. There are now about 8.3 million citizens[3] who are entitled to conduct business with the public administration authorities in Hungary. In order to

---

[1] http://en.nav.gov.hu/e_services/E_guidelines/ANYK_guidelines.html .

[2] http://epapir.gov.hu/.

[3] http://www.valasztas.hu/valasztopolgarok-szama.

© Springer Nature Switzerland AG 2019
A. Kő et al. (Eds.): EGOVIS 2019, LNCS 11709, pp. 85–99, 2019.
https://doi.org/10.1007/978-3-030-27523-5_7

contact the authorities, one needs a so-called Client Gate. The Client Gate is a free service provided by the state that authenticates its owner and provides storage for the owner's electronic documents [3, 4]. A citizen should register by personal appearance to get his Client Gate. The number of registered persons peaked at 3.8 million in 2019 January, which is significantly less than the number of entitled citizens.

Hungarian enterprises are obliged by law to conduct their affairs with the public authorities almost exclusively by electronic means, that is, the person who acts on behalf of the enterprises is expected to use his Client Gate for that purpose [5]. The number of Hungarian enterprises fluctuated around 1.7 million[4] in 2016–2018. If we compare this number to the number of individual Client Gate visitors[5] (see Fig. 1), however, it becomes clear that the Client Gate is used much less than it could have been in principle. This indicates that the implementation of digital transformation is not a success story and we believe that one of the potential impediments is the formal digitization approach pursued in Hungary. We are going to support this statement with examples in the next section.

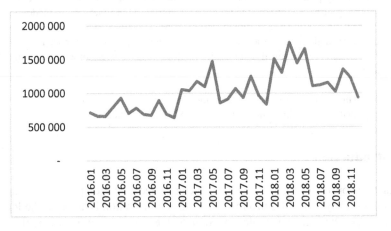

Fig. 1. Number of individual Client Gate visits

There has been a permanent on-going reorganization within the Hungarian public administration since 2010, too [3, 4, 6]. The previously used guiding principle was sectorial affiliation, which was replaced by a county-based approach. The reorganization resulted in 20 Government Offices, one for each county [7, 8]. Due to this reorganization, financial data from different years of the public administration authorities is not comparable, and it not possible to measure the direct financial effect of digitization.

An increase in efficiency - which could be measured by the costs of operations - is often expected from digitization as well. Personnel costs is the largest item in the

---

[4] http://www.ksh.hu/docs/hun/xstadat/xstadat_evkozi/e_qvd021.html.

[5] https://ugyintezes.magyarorszag.hu/dokumentumok/mohustat.xls.

operational costs of Hungarian public administration[6], and because of the fixed salary rules, the fluctuation in the total number of civil servants is a proper indicator for changes in efficiency as no major new public administration tasks were initiated in this period. The time line of the total number of civil servants until the end of 2018 shows a significant decrease at the end of 2017 (see Fig. 2). At that time, however, there was no significant digitization action, but a reorganization process took place. Central sectorial offices were dismissed, all the administrative procedures were integrated into the County Offices [8]. This led to considerable cuts in central and functional (finance, procurement etc.) staff.

We conclude that the use of information technology (that was equated to digitization) plays a limited and formal role in the development of the Hungarian public administration and it did not significantly contribute to the improvement in efficiency. We need more profound actions for a quality change.

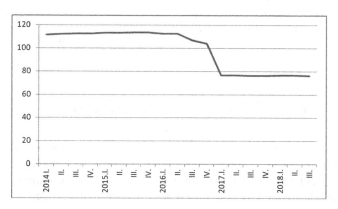

Fig. 2. Total number of Hungarian civil servants (http://www.ksh.hu/docs/hun/xstadat/xstadat_evkozi/e_qli006.html)

2   Problem Statement and Literature Overview

The fact, that public administration in its current form is an excessive burden on Hungarian society, which must be reduced for the sake of competitiveness, was already recognized a long time ago in the Hungarian government. In the course of the reform of Hungarian public administration, two major bureaucracy reduction programs have been implemented since 2010 [3, 4]. In these programs the ongoing administrative processes were reviewed and reorganized. A typical public administration process now looks as depicted in Fig. 3, which should be interpreted for each individual case type. Specific detailed rules are defined by the type of the case concerning the scope of the data to be provided in the application, the documents to be submitted and the required

---

[6] Act L. of 2018 on the 2019 Central Budget of Hungary, Chap. XI. Prime Ministry, Title 12.

certificates. It is simpler, for instance, when no decision has to be made (e.g. handling of notices of data).

The quint-essential elements in Fig. 3 from the point of processing are

1. what the client is expected to prove and
2. whether the application requires a decision made by the authority (e.g. authorization or granting permission) or it is simply an official acknowledgment (acceptance of a notification).

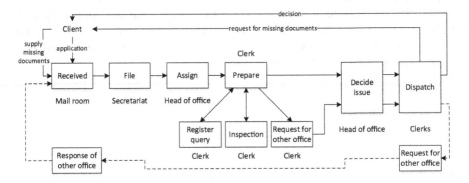

Fig. 3. A typical Hungarian public administration process

In the above mentioned bureaucracy reduction programs, jurists reviewed public administration processes. Their review focused primarily on reducing the types and numbers of required authorizations, shifting towards acknowledgment. In addition, instead of an official proof for data submitted by the client, a mere declaration of proof became often enough in the revised process.

By doing so, the workload of the clients was reduced but the efficiency improvement on the social level is at least debatable. Even though the length of time since the introduction of the new system is still too short to draw conclusions, some problems can already be perceived in the absence of missed preparatory impact assessments. We would like to present the process of a construction permit for a family house [9] as an example.

Right now, there is essentially no need for a construction permit for a family house in Hungary. The administrative (legal) procedure – even for the occupancy permit - is a mere notification, which means that the former professional control of the state essentially ceased to exist. This is a significant relief for the construction authority. However, construction rules still do exist, so compliance checks and responsibility for potential problems related to the family house were devolved to the architect of the house: This responsibility is obviously reflected in the payment for the architect, which means that the financial burden on the client has significantly increased.

In addition, litigation (for example with neighbors) could have been dealt with during the permission phase of the original process. Now, disputes have been transferred to the judiciary system, resulting in greater costs for all parties. In order to avoid litigation, the proportion of informal consultations, for example, with local governments has increased significantly.

In summary, the reviewed and reorganized process of obtaining a construction permit resulted in more of an overload rather than a reduction in the tasks of construction authorities. Similar problems may occur due to lifting of the requirement of proof for the correctness of the submitted data. The costs incurred due to the control, abuse and the ex-post sanctioning procedures may even exceed the work saved in the filing.

The review did not take into consideration the possibilities of simplification and support provided by information technology, so it did not result in a substantial change in the administrative services provided. All these indicate the need for a more systematic, methodologically sound review that takes into consideration the existing and possible IT-support of sub-processes, instead of having ad-hoc reviews that are carried out from a purely legal point of view, so as to have a positive impact of digitization on public administration. Our research objective was to contrive an improved process design approach that might provide better results in terms of efficiency.

However, any approach should consider the specialties of public administration. The controversial result of the previous bureaucracy reduction programs shows that a process-focused review itself is not sufficient to optimize the complex system of public administration. The reason for the mistake is that the development of the public administration was "stuck" to the process-based approach (which dominated the Hungarian public administration from the beginning of the 20th century). The process-based approach starts with the established types of cases, which does not allow for revealing their broader connections and for reaching higher abstraction levels.

Different methods of reviewing (improving) processes in the literature have been discussed in detail for a long time [10–13]. Most methods start from an existing process and focus on their redesign, using simpler processes.

The process centricity of current public administration development approaches can be perceived not only in practice, but in the literature, too. A typical example is the work of Punia and Saxena who focus on advancing with the retention of the traditional administrative institutional structure [14].

The process-based approach makes it difficult not only to improve efficiency but also to implement a "one-stop-shop" service model that is now widely accepted in public administration as an improvement. The importance of the one-stop-shop is pointed out in the literature [15]; the EU has made it mandatory for cross-border services in the 2006/123/EC Directive (the Internal Market Directive).

It should be noted that there is a significant difference between the client-side and the core-public administration interpretation of the "one-stop shop" concept. In the practice of the profit-oriented sector (primarily in financial institutions) single-window administration is actually a "transactional" administrative action, such as cash withdrawal or depositing, or even opening an account with the agent (or electronic interface) immediately. On the other hand, the Hungarian public administration (and the one-stop administration) has stalled at the launching of the processing of a case. While the profit-oriented sector focuses on the one stop service, and the literature even deals with the conditions for a "no-stop shop" service [16], in the Hungarian public administration only the beginning of the process is to be integrated - due to its process-centered attitude. This also indicates that the review of the processes should be different in the future.

The need for re-thinking the process of switching to digitized operations was discussed in the literature under the term of Business Process Reengineering (BPR). Stemberger and Jaklic review and propose methodological approaches to change processes in eGovernment development [12]. They examine business process change (BPC) methodological issues and build on the seven-stage phase-activity framework model proposed by Kettinger, Theng and Guha [17]. The stages of their framework are (1) Envision, (2) Initiate, (3) Diagnose – as-is model, (4) Redesign – to-be model, (5) Reconstruct and (6) Evaluate.

This approach is in line with the process-based approach of review and at the substantive step it relies on the use of "creative" methods, but the original process still limits the scope for action.

Process description techniques have also evolved meanwhile. The enhanced models typically use a more formalized technique (for example "hypergraphs", [18, 19]). The new techniques can support automation better, but they are hardly suitable for understanding and modelling the complex legal, sociological, social policy, information technology and economic aspects. Still these techniques put the process into focus, and in public administration, the closeness of the concept of 'case type' delimits the opportunities for redesign. One must find such a design methodology that goes beyond the process review of the current case type (higher abstraction level) and, at the same time, is capable of accommodating the concepts of different fields of expertise.

3   The Reverse Data-Centric Process Design Approach

The limitations of the process-based approach and the related review methods were recognized in the literature and the so-called data-centric approach was proposed as an alternative. This methodological approach, suggested by IBM researchers, allows for the introduction of new concepts and looks at the process from another perspective [21, 22]. It builds on the concept of "business artifact". An artifact corresponds to key (real or conceptual) business entities that should be managed. It can be an object or a set of information in the context. Cohn and Hull argued that *"the artifact abstraction provides a vehicle for understanding the interplay between data and process in ways not supported by previous Computer Science abstractions"*. ([20] pp. 7) Cohn and Hull also claim that the artifact-centric approach makes the separation of the logical and the physical design concerns possible.

Bhattacharya, Hull-and Su propose a four-step data-centered model design methodology that is based on two principles, as

1. *"data first"*, which requires that at each step, data consideration, specification, and design should precede that of any other component; and
2. *"data centered"*, which means that the specification and design of tasks and workflow should be formulated using the data design obtained at each step.

In the first step of this methodology, one should identify the artifacts, which means that it does not start with mapping activities. Having done that, the life cycles of the artifacts should be discovered. The second step is to develop a detailed logical specification of the data needed about the artifacts, the services that will operate on the artifacts and the linkages (associations) between the services and the artifacts. Services and associations should be described using pre-conditions and conditional effects for the services as well as Event-Condition-Action (ECA) rules for the associations. The third step is to map this description into a more procedural specification, and in the final fourth step the workflow may be realized [21]. The methodology is summarized in Table 1.

Table 1. Data-centric design methodology [21], pp. 6.

STEP 1: *Business Artifacts Discovery*
  (a)   Identify critical artifacts for the business process
  (b)   Discover key stages of artifacts' life cycles from the scenario-based requirements
STEP 2: *Design of Business Operations Model (BOM)*
  (a)   Logical design of artifact schemas
  (b)   Specify services for artifacts needed for moving artifacts through the life-cycles
  (c)   Develop ECA rules that enable artifacts progress in their life cycles
STEP 3: *Design of Conceptual Flow Diagram*
STEP 4: *Workflow Realization*

The data-centric design seems to be an applicable method for optimizing public administration processes, but the differences between the problems of profit-oriented activities and the problems of public administration have to be taken into account. In the profit-oriented world, both processes and related data have little hidden connections (buyer, vendor, contract, etc.). They are simpler, so they can be handled more individually from the point of digitization.

Both in the process-based and in the data-centric process design proceed in time order, which means, starting at the initial state. The forward-proceeding data centric methodology applied in the context of public administration would not mean a qualitative change. It would start at the initial artifact, that is, at the application and by the end of its processing, it would reach the final artifact, the decision. This approach cannot go beyond the limitations stemming from the logic of the existing case type.

We propose to start the design of a process at the final state, that is, to begin at the final state or the artifact of a case type. Grove also proposed starting from the output in a general sense, but he did not use the artifact concept [22]. We call this the *"reverse data centric process design"* approach and we shall show how to do it with help of an example in the next section. We are going to demonstrate that this approach may provide a higher abstraction level that can be interpreted by all actors involved in public administration.

Some examples of final artifacts are tax that has been collected; an inhabited family house or a family that was given social benefit. Having identified an artifact, you also need to determine whether it is of active or passive nature. An active artifact may be an actor to whom tasks can be assigned (for example, a client who submitted an application), whereas there are passive (purely data) artifacts where only processing bears meaning (for example, property records where we can add data or query and no further function is defined). We want to promote digitization; therefore we should also define the data characteristics of artifacts, including where they are handled (for example, already registered somewhere, customer data in the state personal records, etc.).

We will examine the final (and the further) state with the question *"what do we need to achieve it?"*, and from the answer given, we will deduce what actors should be involved and what steps are needed. We shall repeat this process until we arrive at the initial artifact (state). Note that alternatives may arise during the reverse design. For example, in the case a construction permit the possibility of formal involvement of the local government can be raised (there are advantages and disadvantages).

In reverse data-centric process design, you need to determine how to handle the descriptive data of the artifacts. In this respect, the traditional systems analysis approach differs from the existing practice used in public administration. Though a design methodology may prescribe the unified management of an object (by describing its "attributes"), in practice, the descriptive data of an artifact may be stored in already existing separate registers due to regulatory requirements and in many cases, there is no way to change these registers.

In the course of reverse data-centric process design, the traditional systems analysis techniques can be used for description. Such technique is the artifact lifecycle description used by Bhattacharya, Hull and Su [21], the Business Process Modelling Notation description and the Unified Modelling Language figures. Even techniques, such as using hypergraphs that are on a higher level of abstraction, can be used.

Our practical experience shows that the acceptance and understanding of a technique by participants in the design process is more important than the actual descriptive power of that technique. It is often the case that a highly abstract technique is understandable only for its creator. When a system is implemented based on such abstract description its users might be shocked with the outcome.

4 An Example of Using the Proposed Methodology

We are going to look at the management of a local tax on real estate paid by natural persons. In Hungary, a local government may levy local tax on real estate and houses (within their territory). Tax liability is determined by a municipal decree; the affected clients (owners) should prepare their declaration and pay the tax. If we use the traditional process-based modeling approach on this taxation process, on the basis of the current "case type" we would model the following elements

1. The client prepares and submits his tax declaration.
2. The tax authorities levy the tax to be paid (in the traditional model this might require the participation of several clerks) and send (by mail) a check to the client.
3. The client pays the check in the post office or sends the money via bank transfer.

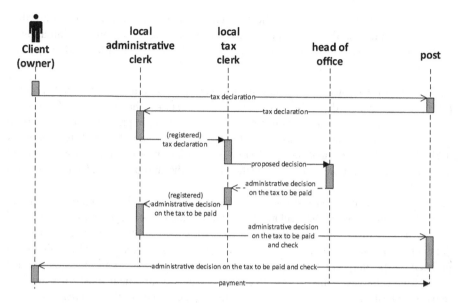

Fig. 4. The real estate tax collection process

Using the traditional process-based approach, this looks like a simple procedure as shown in the sequence diagram on Fig. 4.

In the traditional modelling approach, digitization of the real estate tax collection process would be limited to the automation of case management (automatic filing) and the direct registration of the declaration.

It is easy to see that certain foregoing activities, like the acceptance and publication of the actual rules of taxation by local government, are also part of the process but these are typically overlooked during traditional modelling. The taxation rules provide unequivocally procedures and could well change every year, but the procedure on Fig. 4 does not even indicate this as part of the case.

Activities that follow the payment are also part of the process, these are typically not included into the review either, as they are not described in the concerned local decree, but they are prescribed by other regulations. Such activities are:

1. The concerned staff books the amount of the received money. It is simple in the case of the traditional check-based payments, when the tax authorities created the checks. If payment by bank transfer is also allowed, then a transfer could be made by a third party from a different bank account, therefore reconciling the payment with the identifier (registration number) of the specific case might be difficult or even impossible.
2. The concerned staff (typically another organizational unit of the local government) checks the payment with the participation of several clerks and administrators. It differs for from organization to organization whether this is part of the previous process or it is an entirely separate process.

3. There is another process for collecting unpaid taxes. In the previously described processing model, this is not an organic part of the case either, and the initiation of the collection can be delayed for years (typically, if there is a labor shortage and processing is done manually).

Leaving out actions before and after in time, the taxation process is not the only problem with the model on Fig. 4. This model assumes that the client knows the decrees on local taxation, but this is not a valid assumption. In practice, some clients do not follow these regulations, thus, even if they remember their obligation to submit tax declarations, these declarations are based on earlier information! Thus, additional activities, the correction of the tax declaration by the authorities and the client also belong to the process.

According to the previous model, the client has to provide the data of his/her real estate for completing the tax declaration, including the classification based on the type of use. It is assumed here that the client has at his disposal the evidence of property deed where the necessary data is available (and he knows where to look for them). In practice – especially in the case of less educated older persons who inherited the real estate from relatives – this is not always the case, and the client must visit the land registry and ask for the required data. Apparently, the *"booking the payment received"* part of the process seems to be simple, but with the introduction of the possibility of bank transfers very often linking a payment to the proper taxpayer causes significant extra work for the authorities (e.g., the payer might be a different person, the file number was not entered in the comment field). Thus, starting from a case type (*"real estate tax collection"*) we have not detected either the process as a whole or the actual problems. The recognition of the problem depends to a great extent on the "creativity" of the reviewer.

Let us now model according to the proposed reverse data-centric process design methodology. Starting from a higher abstraction level, we should identify the artifact that the authorities need in the course of the whole taxation process. It is the tax payment received (collectable). The next question is what the descriptive data of this artifact is, which is needed for the taxation authority; and the answer is the tax that was paid and is on the proper account of the local authority, more precisely of the local government. This is what must be achieved, this is the final state. Thus, we have two artifacts: the *paid (individual) tax* and the *local government* to which the money belongs. Since the base of the tax is real estate, the concerned *property* (real estate) itself can also be identified as an artifact already at this level.

The data of the real estate are available in the Real Estate Register[7], where the type of use, the owner (ownership share) and its extent can be found. The tax is to be paid by the owner, thus the *owner* (or client) is also an artifact. Address data of the owner is available in the Personal Data and Address of Citizens Register, including his official and electronic address (if the natural person voluntarily accepts being approached by electronic means and has registered for their client gateway).

We model (design) the taxation process starting from final artifact, *"paid (individual) tax"*, and we arrive at a completely different result from that of the process-

---

[7] Act CXLI of 1997 on Real Estate Registration.

based approach. Whereas traditional analysis starts from the *"what happens?"* question to explore the related elements, the data-centered approach starts from the problems and at each step poses the question *"what do we need to achieve it?"*

In the taxation example, the client who wants to pay the tax needs to know, that

- he has the obligation to pay,
- to whom he should pay and
- how much he should pay.

The client must receive the necessary information to fulfil his obligation. To determine the tax liability of an individual, the rules of taxation must be laid down in regulations (local government decrees; this is a precondition outside the scope of this review). Thus, we have discovered another artifact, *regulation*. The regulation must (also) be published according to the law as an unstructured text in a Central Register, therefore it has an assigned data part. Note that this discovery perfectly illustrates the difference between the traditional process-based and the reverse data-centric approach. In time, the issue of the regulation precedes the payment of the individual tax; but the objective of taxation is to collect the payments and the regulation is required only to achieve this goal. The existence of the regulation is only a necessary condition.

Though our starting point is the *paid (individual) tax*, it is clearly necessary to handle the case when a tax is not paid. At this point we have arrived to the introduction of an intermediate artifact, namely to the concept of *tax liability* of the individual taxpayer. It is important to stress that this intermediate artifact can appear in different objectified (tangible) forms. One form is when the taxpayer himself formulates the declaration (tax return) and the authorities perform only a random check. Another form is when the tax authorities determine the tax liability and the taxpayer is notified on his obligation. Note here that previously in Hungary personal income tax was paid on the basis of tax returns submitted by the taxpayers, but with the advent of digital transformation now the tax authority computes the tax to be paid (based on all known personal income).

The initially discovered artifacts are shown on Fig. 5, where different symbols indicate the active elements (owner, local government) and the passive, data elements. During analysis, we have to categorize (group) the elements to separate those that would be included in the review and those that are external elements. In our example, we focus on the individual real estate tax liability artifact. At this level, mapping the data of individual tax liability is not determined yet, while for the other artifacts it is possible to identify the mapping of their data (e.g. Personal Data and Address of Citizens, Real Estate Register). Here we have arrived at alternative solutions. We can link *"tax declaration"* either to *"tax statement"* where the client is expected to declare his tax; or to *"notice on tax liability"* issued by the local tax authority. In the first case, the failure to establish tax liability should be also examined; in the second case there is no such activity. The only element that must be examined is the case of non-payment.

A local authority has all the necessary data to determine individual tax liability therefore (since the aim of digitization to achieve more efficient operations) here we have chosen sending a notice to the taxpayer. On this basis, the process of determining the individual tax liability is shown in Fig. 6.

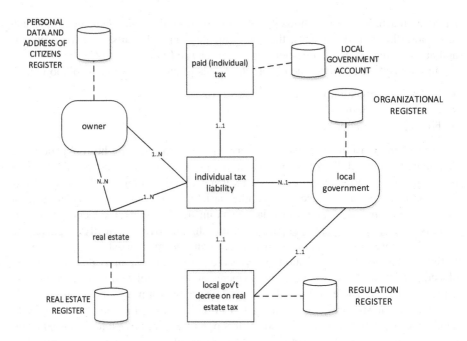

Fig. 5. Initially discovered artifacts for real estate taxation

It was necessary to introduce a parametrization step to correlate the "*regulation*" artifact to the "*individual tax liability*" artifact because a regulation text is not suitable for direct automation. Furthermore, as the chosen alternative was sending a tax notice, it became necessary to ensure the possibility of querying the electronic accessibility of the client. This makes the use of electronic communication as much as possible. Data required for this can be retrieved from the Personal Data and Address of Citizens. For the purpose of simplicity, Fig. 6 does not show the steps involved in the acceptance of the payment but a deeper analysis should include these steps, too in order to ensure that all the steps of the process fit, all the necessary data are created and can be transferred/received.

The activities of the actors of the process (including a possible non-payment) is shown on Fig. 7. The digitized process is substantially automated; supervision by clerks is essentially required only at the problematic branch. The problems caused by erroneous returns and mistaken payments will also decrease.

The actual IT support for the above process should be built on such document formats that can be processed by both man and machine (for instance the notice should be this kind of electronic document), because at the connections of the process (collection, controversies) this will support electronic, and if possible automated processing. Kiss and Klimkó [23] discussed this issue in detail.

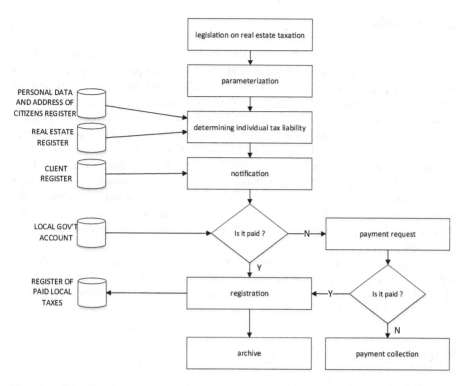

Fig. 6. The process resulted by using the reverse data-centric design methodology

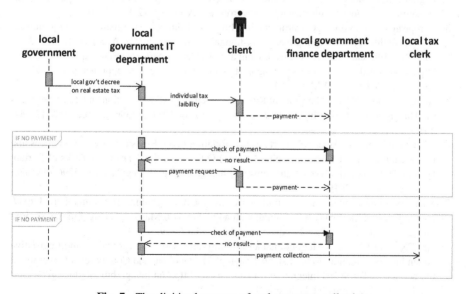

Fig. 7. The digitized process of real estate tax collection

5 Conclusions

Due to the complexity of public administration processes and the alignment of the "case types" with the paper-based operation, the traditional process design that starts from the existing processes *a priori* limits the possible outcomes of any development that aims at the implementation of one-stop-shop, automated administration or "life-situation" based services. In order to eliminate these barriers, we have proposed a modelling approach in which the review or analysis should be carried out in reverse order, starting from the final state (or the required artifact). During the design process one should scrutinize the artifact step by step by posing the question *"what do we need to achieve it?"* with consistent follow-ups. The reverse data-centric process design approach enables the communication with the other professionals involved in the review and makes it possible to design a process by revealing its abstraction levels, and therefore it reduces the implementation risks of the supporting information systems for the review process.

Taking into account the compromise in the level of abstraction, our proposed approach also eases the communication with those who are involved in this area of the administration, reducing the risks of implementing the systems redesigned backed by information technology.

References

1. National Infocommunication Strategy 2014–2020. https://joinup.ec.europa.eu/sites/default/files/document/2016-11/nis_en_clear.pdf. Accessed 12 Mar 2019
2. Digital Single Market, Policy: Country information – Hungary. https://ec.europa.eu/digital-single-market/en/orszaginformaciok-magyarorszag. Accessed 12 Mar 2019
3. European Commission: eGovernment in Hungary, Edition 16.0 (2014). https://joinup.ec.europa.eu/elibrary/factsheet/egovernment-hungary-april-2014-v160. Accessed 12 Mar 2019
4. OECD: Public Governance Reviews. Hungary: Towards a Strategic State Approach (2015). http://www.oecd.org/publications/hungary-towards-a-strategic-state-approach-9789264213555-en.htm. Accessed 12 Mar 2019
5. Act CCXXII of 2015 on the General Rules for Electronic Administration and Trust Ser-vices (in Hungarian). http://njt.hu/cgi_bin/njt_doc.cgi?docid=193173.338642. Accessed 12 Mar 2019
6. Act CIV of 2016 on Amending Certain Acts Relating to the Revision Of Central Offices and the Strengthening Of District (Capital District) Offices and the Transfer of Tasks of Certain Budgetary Bodies (in Hungarian). http://njt.hu/cgi_bin/njt_doc.cgi?docid=197962.338820. Accessed 11 Mar 2019
7. Magyary Zoltán Public Administration Development Programme (in Hungarian). https://magyaryprogram.kormany.hu/admin/download/a/15/50000/Magyary_kozig_fejlesztesi_program_2012_A4_eng_%283%29.pdf. Accessed 11 Mar 2019
8. Act CXXVI of 2010 on Metropolitan and County-level Government Offices and Legislative Amendments Pertaining to the Establishment of Metropolitan and County-level Government Offices and to Territorial Integration (in Hungarian). http://njt.hu/cgi_bin/njt_doc.cgi?docid=132734.362760. Accessed 11 Mar 2019

9. 155/2016. (VI. 13.) Government Decree on the simple announcement of the construction of a residential building. http://njt.hu/cgi_bin/njt_doc.cgi?docid=195876.364610. Accessed 11 Mar 2019
10. Radnor, Z.J.: Review of Business Process Improvement Methodologies in Public Services, pp. 1–94. Aim Research, London (2010)
11. Zellner, G.: A structured evaluation of business process improvement approaches. Bus. Process Manag. J. **17**(2), 203–237 (2011)
12. Stemberger, M.I., Jaklic, J.: Towards E-government by business process change—a methodology for public sector. Int. J. Inf. Manag. **27**(4), 221–232 (2007)
13. Weerakkody, V., Janssen, M., Dwivedi, Y.K.: Transformational change and business process reengineering (BPR): lessons from the British and Dutch public sector. Gov. Inf. Q. **28**(3), 320–328 (2011)
14. Punia, D.K., Saxena, K.B.C.: Managing inter-organisational workflows in eGovernment services. In: Proceedings of the 6th International Conference on Electronic Commerce, pp. 500–505. ACM, March 2004
15. Wimmer, M.A., Tambouris, E.: Online one-stop government. In: Traunmüller, R. (ed.) Information Systems. ITIFIP, vol. 95, pp. 117–130. Springer, Boston, MA (2002). https://doi.org/10.1007/978-0-387-35604-4_9
16. Scholta, H., Mertens, W., Reeve, A., Kowalkiewicz, M.: From one-stop-shop to no-stopshop: an e-government stage model. In: Proceedings of the 25th European Conference on Information Systems (ECIS), Guimarães, Portugal, 5–10 June 2017, pp. 918–934 (2017)
17. Kettinger, W.J., Teng, T.C., Guha, S.: Business process change: a study of methodologies, techniques, and tools. MIS Q. **21**(1), 55–81 (1997)
18. Polyvyanyy, A., Weske, M.: Hypergraph-based modeling of ad-hoc business processes. In: Ardagna, D., Mecella, M., Yang, J. (eds.) BPM 2008. LNBIP, vol. 17, pp. 278–289. Springer, Heidelberg (2009). https://doi.org/10.1007/978-3-642-00328-8_27
19. Molnár, B., Őri, D.: Towards a hypergraph-based formalism for enterprise architecture representation to lead digital transformation. In: Benczúr, A., et al. (eds.) ADBIS 2018. CCIS, vol. 909, pp. 364–376. Springer, Cham (2018). https://doi.org/10.1007/978-3-030-00063-9_34
20. Cohn, D., Hull, R.: Business artifacts: a data-centric approach to modeling business operations and processes. Bull. IEEE Comput. Soc. Tech. Comm. Data Eng. **32**(3), 3–9 (2009)
21. Bhattacharya, K., Hull, R., Su, J.: A data-centric design methodology for business processes. In: Handbook of Research on Business Process Modeling. IGI Global (2009)
22. Grove, A.S.: High output management. Vintage (2015)
23. Kiss, P.J., Klimkó, G.: Electronic forms-based model of public administration operations. In: Kő, A., Francesconi, E. (eds.) EGOVIS 2017. LNCS, vol. 10441, pp. 19–31. Springer, Cham (2017). https://doi.org/10.1007/978-3-319-64248-2_3

E-Government Cases - Data and Knowledge Management

e-Participation in the Exploration of Innovations: Confronting *Aedes aegypti* and Microcephaly in Brazil

Thaísa Barcellos Pinheiro do Nascimento[1]([⊠])(iD),
Everton Leonardo de Almeida[1](iD), André Grützmann[2](iD),
André Luiz Zambalde[2](iD), Paulo Henrique de Souza Bermejo[3](iD),
Alyce Cardoso Campos[1](iD), and Teresa Cristina Monteiro Martins[1](iD)

[1] Departamento de Administração e Economia, UFLA, Lavras, Brazil
thaisapinheiro35@gmail.com, evtufla@gmail.com,
alycecardosoc@yahoo.com.br, teresacristina.ufla@gmail.com
[2] Departamento de Ciência da Computação, UFLA, Lavras, Brazil
andregrutzmann@gmail.com, zambaufla@gmail.com
[3] Departamento de Administração e Economia, UNB, Brasilia, Brazil
paulobermejo@next.unb.br

Abstract. The Zika virus infection occurred as an outbreak of unprecedented magnitude in the Americas. Brazil was the most-affected country, with estimates ranging from 440,000 to 1.3 million cases reported as of December 2015. In response, the Ministry of Education launched a national campaign for popular mobilization, encouraging people to send proposals for innovative actions to combat the *Aedes aegypti* mosquito through a technological platform. Analyses showed that the four-stage crowdstorming lifecycle can serve as a basis for the use of idea management platforms with the aim of gaining social participation. In addition, a highly significant relationship exists between the incidence of Zika virus cases and participation in the challenge of ideas, and no relationship exists between socioeconomic data and participation. Once positive proposals and experiences submitted for public consultation stemming from the population itself have been obtained, managers and others involved may show less resistance to implementation.

Keywords: e-participation · Crowdsourcing · ZikV

1 Introduction

Organizations and government agencies have used Web 2.0 to promote a more open dialogue with society [5]. This collaboration increases government effectiveness, facilitates the articulation of opinions among citizens, and broadens the acceptance and quality of public decisions [51]. However, some governing authorities have used eParticipation only to improve communication rather than to

A. Kő et al. (Eds.): EGOVIS 2019, LNCS 11709, pp. 103–118, 2019.
https://doi.org/10.1007/978-3-030-27523-5_8

promote social innovation [50]. New research is needed to understand the methods and practices of open innovation in government [28], as well as the forms, strategies, arrangements, and results of intelligent government in different local contexts [27].

Citizens want to influence public policies [38]. Therefore, modern initiatives to formulate these policies should include them, with crowdsourcing being one of the tools suggested for doing so [24]. Crowdsourcing can be used for decision-making [49] and to facilitate data collection on high-risk populations [11].

In early 2016, the World Health Organization (WHO) declared the Zika virus (ZIKV) a public health emergency of international concern [47]. At that time, Rio de Janeiro (Brazil), where the Olympics and Paralympic Games took place, had one of the highest incidences of ZIKV in the country [40], arousing worldwide concern for the safety of athletes and tourists. Doctors and scientists of various nationalities sent an open letter to the WHO highlighting the risks to all those involved in the events [2].

The ZIKV outbreak in Brazil, with 440,000 to 1.3 million reported cases [40], led to social participation in the search for solutions. Major issues related to the virus were the confirmation of increased cases of microcephaly [31], Guillain-Barré syndrome [4], miscarriages and fetal malformations [30].

Against this backdrop, Brazil developed measures to control the virus vector, the *Aedes aegypti* mosquito, which also transmits dengue, chikungunya, yellow fever, and other arboviruses [35]. Such measures included a national campaign of popular mobilization encouraging citizens to send proposals for innovative actions and to share experiences of successful implementation in the fight against the mosquito [23].

The present study had two objectives: first, to analyze the planning and execution of an idea management campaign entitled the "ZikaZero Education Challenge" based on the four-stage crowdstorming lifecycle proposed by Abrahamson, Ryder, and Unterberg [1]; second, to understand whether socioeconomic aspects and the incidence of ZIKV cases can influence social participation in Brazil. According to Leimeister, Huber, Bretschneider and Krcmar [26], better understanding of participation in the campaign model can make the development and implementation of open government projects more effective. Furthermore, new coordination and crowdsourcing platforms will contribute to disaster relief [15].

To fulfill the objectives, an analysis was conducted of the national campaign of popular mobilization promoted by the Ministry of Education of Brazil, involving processes related to the implementation and use of the technological platform PrêmioIdeia in the crowdstorming approach. Subsequently, the question was investigated whether social, demographic, and economic factors and the incidence of ZIKV are related to access, participation, and decision-making through open government.

The article is structured as follows: after this introductory information, the following section presents a theoretical basis. The third section describes the research methodology, followed by the results and discussions. Lastly, Sect. 5 presents the final considerations and suggestions for future studies.

2   Theoretical Basis

This section presents concepts related to open innovation, crowdstorming, technological platforms, and aspects of social participation.

2.1   Open Innovation Through Crowdstorming and Technological Platforms for Social Participation

The Brazilian democratic scenario is recent, and since the country's democratic restructuring, mutual connections were expected between society and public institutions, including the acceptance of collective decisions and the possibility of greater social integration [8]. After the enactment of the Federal Constitution of 1988, various mechanisms and forms of social participation were instituted, such as councils, conferences, hearings, and participation processes in the public planning and budget cycle.

Today, with the social transformations and the new dynamics that have emerged from globalization, the expectation is that democratic mechanisms interacting effectively with society will solidify through interactive means [37]. Thus, a new trend is emerging called "eParticipation", which, when used to seek innovative solutions, can also be characterized as open innovation [25].

According to Chesbrough [7], open innovation assumes that useful knowledge should be widely shared in a practice known as distributed cocreation and performed around a common good, with the participation of many people and often voluntarily. This type of innovation is closely linked to the concept of crowdsourcing, which uses the collective intelligence present on the Internet to innovate and improve products [21].

This concept is formed from two words: "crowd", referring to the people who participate in the initiatives, and "sourcing" derived from "outsourcing", related to procurement practices for finding, evaluating, and involving suppliers of goods and services [13]. From the initial term, the prefix "crowd" has been integrated into several processes involving people for achieving a common goal.

In turn, crowdstorming is a technique for generating ideas combining the principles of brainstorming with the expansion of the limits of crowds, stimulating innovation, and the inclusion of geographically distant individuals, resulting in broader views of a particular situation or problem [1]. The combination of these concepts, extrapolated to the public sector, can enhance the relationship between citizens and managers, providing value creation for society [20].

This technique can be associated with technological platforms, responsible for providing the necessary infrastructure for interaction between users [34]. An example of a crowdstorming platform is PrêmioIdeia, a platform for managing ideas and open innovation in which challenge themes, scores, and awards are defined, so that citizens, clients, or employees can participate in the ideation process. Employees' answers (ideas) can be liked, commented on, and shared by participating colleagues. In this way, ideas are scored in a gaming process involving the use of games and their intrinsic ability to motivate action [44], solve problems, and enhance learning [14]. Finally, employees with the highest numbers of entries and points are ranked to determine a winner who receives a prize.

In Brazil, this platform has been used for other open government proposals related to crowdstorming, such as "Safe City" [29] and the "Sustainability Challenge" [43,44], which helped not only to identify prospective solutions but also to mobilize and educate communities to support the theme and stimulate the involvement and engagement of participants [44].

Thus, governments have become aware of the use of open innovation to promote interactions with citizens because innovation can be achieved through these interactions [44]. While using crowdstorming to engage large numbers of people in discussing a problem can be beneficial, a poorly planned initiative can result in negative consequences. Gatzweiler, Blazevic, and Piller [16] stress the importance of planning in ideation contests, and Parker et al. [34] argue the importance of structuring the project, i.e., its architecture, and developing laws, rules, and market knowledge for platform governance to be more effective.

Therefore, the planning and the knowledge of well-defined stages for the creation of social platforms are of paramount importance. In this context, the four-stage crowdstorming lifecycle proposed by Abrahamson, Ryder, Unterberg [1] and presented in Fig. 1 was used to fulfill the first objective of this study.

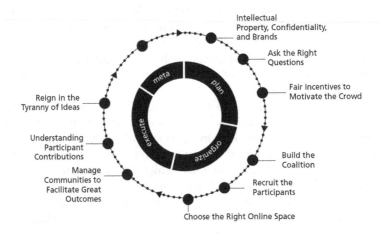

Fig. 1. Four-stage crowdsourcing lifecycle of [1] (Source: Abrahamson, Ryder, Unterberg [1])

2.2   Aspects Related to Social Participation

In general, citizen cooperation, especially when related to the crowdstorming technique, is voluntary; therefore, holistically understanding the issues of the phenomenon associated with participation must be understood. Chang and Chuang [6] and Naranjo-Zolotov et al. [32] addressed this topic, covering several aspects such as personal recognition in certain situations. Based on this literature, we sought to understand how these factors may be related to Brazilian participation in open government initiatives, first examining the ZIKV infection in the country.

For more than a half a century since its discovery in 1947, virtually no records of the Zika virus were found, until 2014, at which time it is estimated to have been introduced into Brazil from the Pacific islands and to have spread rapidly throughout the Americas [35]. With the recent outbreaks, an increase in the incidence of microcephaly, Guillain-Barré syndrome, and fetal malformations and miscarriages in ZIKV-infected mothers was reported. These suspicions were confirmed, as reported by Mlakar et al. [31], Cao-Lormeau et al. [4] and Miner et al. [30], respectively.

Thus, ZIKV became the first infectious disease linked to human congenital defects to be discovered since cytomegalovirus (CMV) in the 1970s [35]. This situation had a global impact, especially when related to the influx of tourists that Brazil was expecting due to the start of the Olympics in August 2016 and the Paralympics in September 2016. The risk of the disease spreading globally worried several scholars, who wrote a letter entitled "Open Letter to Dr. Margaret Chan, Director-General, WHO" [2], proposing changing the date or location of the events due to tourists and athletes' potential exposure to the virus. This letter was released by various media outlets such as the BBC [3], ESPN [12], and The Washington Post [46].

In this context, WHO declared the ZIKV outbreak a public health emergency of international concern (PHEIC) on February 1, 2016 [33]. This was the fourth declared state of emergency since the reformulation of the International Health Regulations in force since 2007. The previous cases referred to influenza A (H1N1) in April 2009, poliovirus in May 2014, and Ebola in August 2014 [47].

Thus, the Brazilian government was pressured to establish measures to combat the vector mosquito, *Aedes aegypti*, which also transmits yellow fever, chikungunya, and dengue, consequently controlling these diseases. Combined with the development and implementation of these measures, the Ministry of Education launched the "ZikaZero Education Challenge" [23], which is of interest for this study mainly because of its objective of promoting a national mobilization campaign to stimulate society to submit proposals for innovative and successful experiences in the fight against the mosquito.

Chang and Chuang [6] found that individuals are positively influenced to cooperate when they can identify with certain situations. These results were corroborated by Naranjo-Zolotov et al. [32] in a study that sought to identify the motivations for open participation.

To better understand the relationship between the regions affected by the ZIKV and participation in the idea challenge, the number of infection cases in the country must be determined. This point is critical, since the clinical estimate is that only 20% of individuals show symptoms of the disease [35] and then seek medical help to confirm the infection based on tests. Thus, the estimate of the Brazilian Ministry of Health was 440,000 to 1.3 million cases by December 2015 [40]; the public body claims to have obtained these figures from the dengue-negative cases and based on international literature, considering only the states with an autochthonous circulation of the ZIKV [39]. Thus, we chose to work with data from the Epidemiological Bulletin issued by the Health Surveillance Secretariat, which presents the confirmed numbers of the incidence of fever due to the Zika virus [41]. These figures are presented by the Brazilian states in Table 1.

Table 1. Incidence of ZIKV infection per 100,000 inhabitants in the Brazilian states

State	Incidence of ZIKV (\100,000 inhabitants)	State	Incidence of ZIKV (\100,000 inhabitants)
Mato Grosso	558.1	Mato Grosso do Sul	23.4
Bahia	265.9	Sergipe	22.2
Rio de Janeiro	230.8	Paraná	18.1
Tocantins	167.3	Pará	16.7
Acre	102.4	Amapá	15.9
Alagoas	73.6	Roraima	15.6
Paraíba	61.7	Federal District	10.5
Amazonas	55.2	Ceará	10
Rondônia	54.3	São Paulo	7.8
Minas Gerais	53.8	Pernambuco	5.3
Rio Grande do Norte	51	Piauí	3
Espírito Santo	48.8	Rio Grande do Sul	2.8
Goiás	39.4	Santa Catarina	1.4
Maranhão	29	-	-

Source: [41]

The second characteristic related to participation in this campaign model was the socioeconomic conditions. Vicente and Novo [48] argue that people with lower purchasing power are digitally excluded, making it impossible to participate in open government initiatives. By analyzing these results in the Brazilian context, we can make an obvious association, since Brazil is a country of continental dimensions with high levels of poverty and unequal income distribution, as demonstrated by indices such as the human development index (HDI) [22]. Brazilian states with the lowest HDIs are also those with the lowest Internet usage rates. In states such as Maranhão, almost 70% of the population does not have access to the Internet [22].

However, other studies contradict this relationship, such as that by Naranjo Zolotov et al. [32], which attempted to understand the motivations for open participation and found no evidence socioeconomic characteristics are related to willingness to participate in open government projects. This dissonance in the literature raises questions about national participation.

To better understand socioeconomic conditions, an international index was developed to represent economic activity, income distribution, and education, resulting in the HDI, an index created to measure the level of human development–based indicators of longevity (life expectancy at birth), education (mean number of years of study in people aged 25 or older, literacy rate, and enrollment rate) and income (GDP per capita) [42]. Its value ranges from 0 (no human development) to 1 (total human development); countries with an HDI of less than 0.499 are considered to have low human development; those with an HDI between 0.500 and 0.799 have average human development; and those with an HDI greater than 0.800 have high human development [22].

The HDI can also be calculated for municipalities and states. For this study, we used state HDI data, as presented in Table 2. Given these data, we can analyze whether the Brazilian socioeconomic characteristics represented by the HDI are related to the level of participation in the idea challenge.

3 Methodology

The present study's methodology is classified as mixed, since qualitative and quantitative data were collected and analyzed to study the same phenomenon: social participation in a campaign of the Ministry of Education of Brazil [9].

The first phase of this study was qualitative, based on documentary research, with the purpose of describing and analyzing the scenario of the application of the technological platform for the management of ideas and "social participation", characterized as open innovation in the public sector. According to Godoy [17], this research model is defined based on the examination of materials of a diverse nature that have not received analytical treatment or for which complementary interpretations remain possible. Thus, the documents analyzed were in the form of data (challenge themes, ideas, and number of likes and comments) collected directly by the technology platform PrêmioIdeia.

From the results obtained by the documentary research, content analysis was carried out using the model proposed by Abrahamson, Ryder, Unterberg [1] to understand if each stage (plan, organize, execute, and meta) and substage was developed from a model already successfully used by other ideation processes in the Brazilian scenario [44,45].

The second phase of this study was quantitative, based on a correlation analysis between socioeconomic factors, virus incidence data obtained by a previous literature review, and social participation in the "ZikaZero Education Challenge" by the Brazilian states. This phase was accomplished using SPSS software. To fulfill this objective, the Pearson correlation test was used to statistically verify the intensity with which parametric data are correlated by comparing the existing association between two datasets and providing a number summarizing the degree of linear relationship between variables [18]. According to David [10] and Harley [19], this test is recommended only if the number of variables is greater than 25, which applies to this study since the variables were analyzed for the 27 Brazilian states.

To analyze the incidence of ZIKV in the country, data presented in the Epidemiological Bulletin provided by the Ministry of Health were used. This document is a free-access publication of a technical-scientific nature in which descriptions of events and diseases with the potential to trigger public health emergencies are published. The bulletin used reported data on the monitoring of cases of dengue fever, chikungunya fever, and Zika fever up to Epidemiological Week 19 of 2016, i.e., until May 14, 2016 [41]. Data of interest for this study were collected and presented in Table 1. For the socioeconomic analyses, the HDI was chosen, a metric used to classify countries by combining data on life expectancy at birth, education, and GDP per capita of the countries. For this study, the most recent data on the HDI made available in 2010 by the Brazilian Institute of Geography and Statistics were used. The data were obtained from the IBGE website [22] and are presented in Table 2.

Table 2. HDIs for the Brazilian states

State	HDI	State	HDI
Federal District	824	Rondônia	0.69
São Paulo	783	Rio Grande do Norte	684
Santa Catarina	774	Ceará	682
Rio de Janeiro	761	Amazonas	674
Paraná	749	Pernambuco	673
Rio Grande do Sul	746	Sergipe	665
Espírito Santo	0.74	Acre	663
Goiás	735	Bahia	0.66
Minas Gerais	731	Paraíba	658
Mato Grosso do Sul	729	Pará	646
Mato Grosso	725	Piauí	646
Amapá	708	Maranhão	639
Roraima	707	Alagoas	631
Tocantins	699	-	-

Source: [22]

Finally, to relate the above data to those who participated in the "ZikaZero Education Challenge", all data generated in the project were extracted directly from the platform's database. After this extraction, the data were imported and organized into a spreadsheet. With this information, the number of ideas and positive experiences submitted, the number of likes and comments, and the educational institutions of the authors were more easily identified. We consider participation as the sum of all positive activities on the platform.

4   Results and Discussion

The idea challenge entitled the "ZikaZero Education Challenge" was carried out by the Ministry of Education of Brazil in partnership with the idea management and open innovation platform PrêmioIdeia. The project was based on the crowdstorming concept, as presented by Abrahamson, Ryder, Unterberg [1], and involved the planning, organization, execution, and meta steps. This section will describe these stages and the participation of schools, institutes, and universities.

4.1 Planning

This stage began with the elaboration of the main objective of the project by experts from the Ministry of Education, which was to promote a national mobilization campaign to combat *Aedes aegypti* and microcephaly, stimulating society to submit innovative proposals for the fight against the mosquito. Based on this objective, the project's theme was "Submit and share proposals for action and reports of positive experiences for combating *Aedes aegypti* and microcephaly".

Next, the managers elaborated the rules that would serve as support for community participation. To make the rules available, an announcement was made presenting information such as project objective, people who could participate, classification and scoring criteria, prizes, deadlines, among others. The notice was published in the Official Federal Gazette, which is one of the National Press' means of communication to make public any and all matters concerning the federal government.

As presented by Souza et al. [44], prizes can be a good way to stimulate public participation. Thus, to stimulate participation, the three participants with the best scores and the ideas were awarded cash in amounts up to US $770.00. For municipal and state schools, federal colleges, and universities, the prizes for the best-placed educational institutions reached up to $7,695.00.

4.2 Organization

To allow large numbers of people to participate, a suitable online space needed to be chosen on which to execute the project. The PrêmioIdeia idea management platform was chosen because it allows adaptations and customizations according to the rules of the public notice.

The community was invited to participate in the idea challenge, and registration on the PrêmioIdeia platform was required. Each participant indicated whether they were representing a municipal or state school, an institute, or a federal university. After registering on the platform and choosing a teaching institution, users could submit ideas and experiences, as well as evaluate (like or not) and enhance (comment) the ideas and experiences of other participants. Each of these activities accumulated points, generating a ranking of participation on the platform. This process entails a virtual social network for generating ideas and open innovation.

The points received by each user also served to rank educational institutions. This process can be classified as coopetition, i.e., innovation in a "healthy competition" among the entities involved. Figure 2 shows the PrêmioIdeia platform with the challenge theme, where the ideas, experiences, and participation of the society were captured.

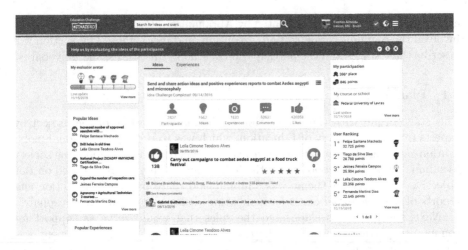

Fig. 2. PrêmioIdeia platform for receiving ideas and experiences. (Source: PrêmioIdeia platform [36])

4.3   Execution

The "ZikaZero Education Challenge" took place from June 29 to September 14, 2016. Over a period of almost three months, the idea challenge received participation from 2,437 people, and 3,195 ideas and experiences were submitted; the challenge had 426,368 likes, 58,631 comments, and the involvement of 23 Brazilian states (88.8%).

The evaluation and moderation of the ideas and experiences posted on the platform were carried out by a judging committee composed of five members appointed by the Ministry of Education. To select the best ideas and experiences, the following criteria were considered: feasibility of implementation, introduction of innovation in relation to previous practices, efficient use of resources (material, financial, human, organizational, and time), and predicted positive outcomes in terms of contributing to the resolution of the challenge or regarding citizens' rights.

4.4   Meta

After the end of the challenge, the experts of the Ministry of Education evaluated and selected 93 actions, which were put together in a collection. The collection's ideas can be implemented by students, teachers, technicians, and public managers or other members of civil society. The actions were grouped into 9 themes: "Use of Technologies"; "Awards, Bonuses, and Incentives"; "Training"; "Awareness, Guidelines, and Combat Efforts"; "Survey, Alerts, and Punishments"; "Traps and Prevention Methods"; "Research"; "Creation and Evolution"; and "Partnerships". In addition to this subdivision, the actions in the collection were assigned an implementation cost and benefit by the experts. The collection is available to the public in the "Mosquito Não" portal of the Ministry of Education.

4.5   Participation of Schools, Institutes, and Universities

As previously shown, when users accessed the PrêmioIdeia platform, they selected a public educational institution (school, institute or university) to represent. Thus, the project was represented by 80 municipal and state schools and 48 universities and institutes from various states in Brazil. Because the educational institutions also competed for awards, many helped to disseminate the project among their students, teachers, and staff.

As the platform presented each participant's institution, the number of participations (sum of the number of ideas, comments, and likes submitted on the platform) by state (sum of the participation of the institutions present in the state) could be extracted (Table 3).

The data in Tables 1 and 2 allowed the Pearson correlation test to be performed using SPSS statistical software. The relationship between social participation with socioeconomic data and the incidence of ZIKV cases was analyzed. For the results to be considered significant, the values obtained by the Pearson correlation test need to have a significance level lower than 5% (0.05).

A highly significant (0.000) relationship exists between the incidence of ZIKV and participation. States with a high number of ZIKV cases tended to participate more in the idea challenge. However, no significant relationship exists between the HDI and social participation.

5   Final Considerations

This article presented the results of an idea challenge entitled the "ZikaZero Education Challenge", promoted by the Ministry of Education of Brazil which had a national scope. The project involved an open innovation, crowdstorming, and social participation platform (PrêmioIdeia); i.e., the study combined the theory and practice of innovation in the public sector.

The project had the objective of capturing ideas and positive experiences to combat *Aedes aegypti* and microcephaly, obtaining promising numbers. The challenge involved 2,437 participants from 22 states plus the Federal District, generated 3,195 ideas and obtained 426,368 likes and 58,631 comments. The PrêmioIdeia platform proved to be suitable for crowdstorming.

After the challenge's completion, the Ministry of Education prepared and made available free to educational institutions and society a collection with the best actions submitted on the platform. These ideas could be implemented by students, teachers, technicians and public managers or other members of civil society. The challenge generated social participation and returns to society, especially for the target audience, educational institutions.

The challenge was elaborated according to proposals in the literature and proposals used by other challenges with the same principle, to involve social

Table 3. Participation in the "ZikaZero Education Challenge"

State	Ideas	Likes	Comments	Participation
Mato Grosso	2	331,221	22,92	356,204
Rio de Janeiro	164	36,931	26	63,318
Minas Gerais	382	30,462	1	32,244
Paraíba	270	15,102	2	17,329
São Paulo	129	4,899	2	7,507
Ceará	97	3,126	3	5,826
Paraná	65	4,008	978	5,051
Rio Grande do Norte	7	447	50	504
Pernambuco	7	44	2	53
Rondônia	4	38	7	49
Bahia	2	21	5	28
Acre	1	21	0	22
Tocantins	0	15	1	16
Piauí	0	11	0	11
Goiás	1	7	0	8
Rio Grande do Sul	0	7	1	8
Sergipe	0	0	5	5
Federal District	0	4	0	4
Espírito Santo	2	2	0	4
Roraima	0	0	4	4
Maranhão	0	1	0	1
Mato Grosso do Sul	0	1	0	1
Santa Catarina	1	0	0	1
Alagoas	0	0	0	0
Amapá	0	0	0	0
Amazonas	0	0	0	0
Pará	0	0	0	0

Source: Prepared by the autors

participation and to develop innovation in the public sector. Thus, the planning, organization, execution, and meta stages in the "ZikaZero Education Challenge" could be identified. The study confirmed the usefulness of the four-stage crowd-storming lifecycle of Abrahamson, Ryder, Unterberg [1].

By using the statistical software SPSS and performing the Pearson correlation test, a significant relationship was found between the incidence of ZIKV and participation in the idea challenge, which reaffirms the study of Chang and Chuang [6]. However, no relationship was found between participation and the HDIs of the Brazilian states, corroborating the results of Naranjo-Zolotov et al. [32].

Finally, the implementation of the ideas submitted in the project is an important object of study for future research. This article does not analyze possible implementations of the proposed actions, which can be considered a limitation. Another limitation is related to the target audience, composed mainly of students. Further studies with a more heterogeneous population and a broader age range are important to broaden the understanding of crowdsourcing and eParticipation.

Once positive proposals and experiences submitted for public consultation stemming from the population have been obtained, managers and others involved in their implementation may show less resistance. However, further research considering the implementation of these ideas is necessary.

Acknowledgements. The authors thank the Conselho Nacional de Desenvolvimento Científico e Tecnológico - CNPq, Fundação de Amparo à pesquisa de Minas Gerais – FAPEMIG e Coordenação de Aperfeiçoamento de Pessoal de Nível Superior - CAPES for the financial support to research. The authors would also like to thanks the National Council for Scientific and Technological Development (CNPq - Brazil) - Process 402789/2015-6 for financial support.

References

1. Abrahamson, S., Ryder, P., Unterberg, B.: Crowdstorm: The Future of Innovation, Ideas, and Problem Solving. Wiley, Hoboken (2013)
2. Attaran, A., Caplan, A., Gaffney, C., Igel, L.: Open Letter to Dr. Margaret Chan, Director-General, WHO (2016)
3. BBC: Zika Crisis: WHO Seeks to Allay Fears Over Rio Olympics, May 2016. https://www.bbc.com/news/world-latin-america-36405689
4. Cao-Lormeau, V.M., et al.: Guillain-barré syndrome outbreak associated with zika virus infection in french polynesia: a case-control study. Lancet **387**(10027), 1531–1539 (2016)
5. Capineri, C., Calvino, C., Romano, A.: Citizens and institutions as information prosumers the case study of italian municipalities on Twitter. Int. J. **10**, 1–26 (2015)
6. Chang, H.H., Chuang, S.S.: Social capital and individual motivations on knowledge sharing: participant involvement as a moderator. Inf. Manag. **48**(1), 9–18 (2011)
7. Chesbrough, H.W.: Open Innovation: The New Imperative for Creating and Profiting from Technology. Harvard Business Press, Brighton (2006)
8. Ciconello, A.: A participação social como processo de consolidação da democracia no brasil. From poverty to power (2008)
9. Creswell, J.W., Clark, V.L.P.: Designing and Conducting Mixed Methods Research. SAGE Publications, Thousand Oaks (2017)
10. David, F.N., et al.: Tables of the ordinates and probability integral of the distribution of the correlation in small samples (1938)
11. Diamantopoulou, V., Androutsopoulou, A., Gritzalis, S., Charalabidis, Y.: An assessment of privacy preservation in crowdsourcing approaches: towards GDPR compliance. In: 2018 12th International Conference on Research Challenges in Information Science (RCIS), pp. 1–9. IEEE (2018)

12. ESPN: Carta aberta à oms sugere adiamento dos jogos por conta do zika vírus, May 2016. http://www.espn.com.br/noticia/602105_carta-aberta-a-oms-sugere-adiamento-dos-jogos-por-conta-do-zika-virus
13. Estellés-Arolas, E., González-Ladrón-De-Guevara, F.: Towards an integrated crowdsourcing definition. J. Inf. Sci. **38**(2), 189–200 (2012)
14. Fardo, M.L.: A gamificação aplicada em ambientes de aprendizagem. RENOTE **11**(1), 1–9 (2013)
15. Gao, H., Barbier, G., Goolsby, R.: Harnessing the crowdsourcing power of social media for disaster relief. IEEE Intell. Syst. **26**(3), 10–14 (2011)
16. Gatzweiler, A., Blazevic, V., Piller, F.T.: Dark side or bright light: destructive and constructive deviant content in consumer ideation contests. J. Prod. Innov. Manag. **34**(6), 772–789 (2017)
17. Godoy, A.S.: Introdução à pesquisa qualitativa e suas possibilidades. Revista de administração de empresas **35**(2), 57–63 (1995)
18. Hair, J.F., Black, W.C., Babin, B.J., Anderson, R.E., Tatham, R.L.: Análise multivariada de dados. Bookman Editora (2009)
19. Harley, B.: A note on the probability integral of the correlation coefficient. Biometrika **41**(1/2), 278–280 (1954)
20. Hilgers, D., Ihl, C.: Citizensourcing: applying the concept of open innovation to the public sector. Int. J. Public Participation **4**(1), 67–88 (2010)
21. Howe, J.: The rise of crowdsourcing. Wired Mag. **14**(6), 1–4 (2006)
22. IBGE: Instituto brasileiro de geografia e estatística, September 2010. https://cidades.ibge.gov.br/brasil/rj/panorama
23. Imprensa Nacional, I.: Diário da união - seção 3. Tech. Rep. N° 90, quinta-feira, 12 de maio de 201664 ISSN 1677–7069, Ministério Público Brasileiro, May 2016. este documento pode ser verificado no endereço eletrônico http://www.in.gov.br/autenticidade.html. pelo código 00032016051200064
24. Koussouris, S., Lampathaki, F., Kokkinakos, P., Askounis, D., Misuraca, G.: Accelerating policy making 2.0: innovation directions and research perspectives as distilled from four standout cases. Gov. Inf. Q. **32**(2), 142–153 (2015)
25. Lee, S.M., Hwang, T., Choi, D.: Open innovation in the public sector of leading countries. Manag. Decis. **50**(1), 147–162 (2012)
26. Leimeister, J.M., Huber, M., Bretschneider, U., Krcmar, H.: Leveraging crowdsourcing: activation-supporting components for it-based ideas competition. J. Manag. Inf. Syst. **26**(1), 197–224 (2009)
27. Lin, Y.: A comparison of selected western and chinese smart governance: the application of ICT in governmental management, participation and collaboration. Telecommun. Policy **42**(10), 800–809 (2018)
28. Loukis, E., Charalabidis, Y., Androutsopoulou, A.: Promoting open innovation in the public sector through social media monitoring. Gov. Inf. Q. **34**(1), 99–109 (2017)
29. Martins, T.C.M., de Souza Bermejo, P.H.: Desafio de ideias para o governo aberto: o caso da polícia militar de minas gerais-brasil. Cadernos Gestão Pública e Cidadania **21**(70), 303–324 (2016)
30. Miner, J.J., et al.: Zika virus infection during pregnancy in mice causes placental damage and fetal demise. Cell **165**(5), 1081–1091 (2016)
31. Mlakar, J., et al.: Zika virus associated with microcephaly. N. Engl. J. Med. **374**(10), 951–958 (2016)
32. Naranjo-Zolotov, M., et al.: Examining social capital and individual motivators to explain the adoption of online citizen participation. Future Gener. Comput. Syst. **92**, 302–311 (2019)

33. Organização Pan-Americana da Saúde, O.: Organização mundial da saúde anuncia emergência de saúde pública de importância internacional, February 2016. https://www.paho.org/bra.../index.php?option=com_content&view=article& id=4991:organizacao-mundial-da-saude-anuncia-emergencia-de-saude-publica-de-importancia-internacional&Itemid=812
34. Parker, G.G., Van Alstyne, M.W., Choudary, S.P.: Plataforma: a revolução da estratégia. Casa Educação-(Casa Educação Soluções Educacionais LTDA) (2017)
35. Petersen, L.R., Jamieson, D.J., Powers, A.M., Honein, M.A.: Zika virus. N. Engl. J. Med. **374**(16), 1552–1563 (2016)
36. Portal Desafio de Ideias do Ministério da Educação, P.I.: Desafio zikazero (2016). http://www.premioideia.com/desafiozikazero/
37. Ribeiro, F.P.: Democracia, expertise e burocracia: relações entre política, técnica e participação. Ciências Sociais Unisinos **49**(3), 297–305 (2013)
38. Royo, S., Yetano, A.: "Crowdsourcing" as a tool for e-participation: two experiences regarding CO_2 emissions at municipal level. Electron. Commerce Res. **15**(3), 323–348 (2015)
39. Ministério da Saúde, B.: Plano nacional de enfrentamento a microcefalia no brasil. Protocolo de vigilÂncia e resposta À ocorrÊncia de microcefalia relacionada À infecÇÃo pelo vÍrus zika, Secretaria de Vigilância em Saúde, December 2015. http://portalms.saude.gov.br/images/pdf/2015/dezembro/09/Microcefalia--Protocolo-de-vigil-ncia-e-resposta--vers-o-1--09dez2015-8h.pdf
40. Ministério da Saúde, B.: Protocolo de vigilância e resposta à ocorrência de microcefalia relacionada à infecção pelo vírus Zika (2015)
41. de vigilância em Saúde, S.: Boletim epidemiológico, May 2016. http://portalms.saude.gov.br/boletins-epidemiologicos
42. Silva, A.B.d.O., Considera, C.M., Valadão, L.d.F.R., Medina, M.H.: Produto interno bruto por unidade da federação (1996)
43. de Souza, W.V.B., et al.: Using crowdstorm to prospect innovations in federal institutions of education in Brazil to reduce its consumption of electric energy. In: 2016 49th Hawaii International Conference on System Sciences (HICSS), pp. 2819–2828. IEEE (2016)
44. de Souza, W.V.B., Cavalcante, C.C.M., Pereira, W.R., de Souza Bermejo, P.H., Martins, T.C.M., Pereira, J.R.: Planning the use of crowdstorming for public management: a case in the ministry of education of Brazil (2014)
45. Souza, W.V.B.D., Bermejo, P.H.D.S., Cavalcante, C.C.M., Domingos, R.N.: Inovação aberta no setor público: como o ministério da educação utilizou o crowdstorming para impulsionar a prospecção de soluções inovadoras (2017)
46. The Washington Post: 150 experts say Olympics must be moved or postponed because of zika, May 2016. https://www.washingtonpost.com/news/to-your-health/wp/2016/05/27/125-experts-say-olympics-must-be-moved-or-postponed-because-of-zika/?utm_term=.fd54cfe55dbf
47. Ventura, D.D.F.L.: Do ebola ao zika: as emergências internacionais e a securitização da saúde global. Cadernos de Saúde Pública **32**, e00033316 (2016)
48. Vicente, M.R., Novo, A.: An empirical analysis of e-participation. the role of social networks and e-government over citizens' online engagement. Gov. Inf. Q. **31**(3), 379–387 (2014)
49. Vidiasova, L., Kachurina, P., Ivanov, S., Smith, G.: E-participation tools in science and business sphere implementation: the case of xpir-platform for participation in education policy. Procedia Comput. Sci. **101**, 398–406 (2016)

50. Wehn, U., Evers, J.: The social innovation potential of ICT-enabled citizen obser-
    vatories to increase eparticipation in local flood risk management. Technol. Soc.
    42, 187–198 (2015)
51. Wijnhoven, F., Ehrenhard, M., Kuhn, J.: Open government objectives and partic-
    ipation motivations. Gov. Inf. Q. **32**(1), 30–42 (2015)

Indicators of Municipal Public Management: Study of Multiple Performance Measurement Systems

Marcus Wilian Pedrotti de Oliveira[1] ⓘ, Renato Neder[1] ⓘ,
Paulo Augusto Ramalho de Souza[1] ⓘ, Cristiano Maciel[1,2(✉)] ⓘ,
Naíse Godoy de Campos Silva Freire[3] ⓘ,
José Marcelo de Almeida Peres[3] ⓘ, Cassyra L. Correa Vuolo[3] ⓘ,
Alexandre Martins dos Anjos[1] ⓘ, and Débora Pedrotti Mansilla[1] ⓘ

[1] Universidade Federal de Mato Grosso, Cuiabá, MT, Brazil
mwoliveira18@gmail.com, renatoneder@gmail.com,
paramalho@gmail.com, crismac@gmail.com,
dinteralexandre@gmail.com, deborapedrotti@gmail.com
[2] Fundação de Apoio da Universidade Federal de Mato Grosso - Uniselva,
Cuiabá, MT, Brazil
[3] Tribunal de Contas do Estado do Mato Grosso, Cuiabá, MT, Brazil
{naise,josemarcelo,cassyra}@tce.mt.gov.br

Abstract. Results-based management as an administrative paradigm can be thought of as a way for private and public organizations to manage their resources with a focus on organizational results. Thus, a multi-stage study is proposed with the aim of examining a public project of results-based management, which is part of a program called Integrated Institutional Development Program (IDP) of the Court of Auditors of the State of Mato Grosso, by means of the analysis of 24 strategic plans of municipalities in the state of Mato Grosso. For methodology, a theoretical framework with 10 dimensions and 63 sub-dimensions was developed, allowing the investigation of 1094 indicators and subsequent analysis of a group of 498 univocal indicators of Public Management. These were obtained through the Strategic Planning System (GPE), which stores and operates multiple Performance Measurement Systems (SMD). As a technical and academic contribution, this work proposes a set of 68 municipal public indicators that could be used in the aforementioned project and in similar cases.

Keywords: Results-based management · Performance measurement system · Strategic management · Municipal indicators

1 Introduction

Public management has been evolving towards the results-based management model since the end of the last century. This management type proposes a paradigm shift, moving the focus of public administration from effort to result. In this sense, Verbeeten

© Springer Nature Switzerland AG 2019
A. Kő et al. (Eds.): EGOVIS 2019, LNCS 11709, pp. 119–132, 2019.
https://doi.org/10.1007/978-3-030-27523-5_9

and Speklé [1] propose that the New Public Administration has been orienting a reform of the public sector for at least 25 years.

Its position in effective management design is based on three key ideas: (1) performance improvement requires a results-oriented culture that emphasizes outcomes rather than inputs or processes; (2) Organizations need to introduce performance management based on goals, monitoring and incentives; and (3) public sector organizations must decentralize decision-making rights and reduce their reliance on rules and procedures [1].

Performance-based management has become widespread in public organizations; many governments have implemented performance management and measurement systems to improve organizational effectiveness.

Souza et al. [2] also point out that performance measurement is key to the development of the New Public Administration. Dialoging with the aforementioned authors, some questions arise: What is result for a public organization? This is a complex question and, as such, does not have a single answer. In this research, we will treat results from the perspective of the Balanced Scorecard (BSC).

Kiriri [3] presents the seminal work of Kaplan and Norton [4] as the origin of BSC and suggests that the methodology arises from a supplementation of the traditional perspective of planning at the time, which saw the financial dimension as hegemonic. To overcome this, Kaplan and Norton [4] propose three more perspectives, namely: Clients, Learning and Growth, and Internal Processes.

In the state of Mato Grosso (Brazil), a relevant effort to improve public management has been developed since 2012 by the Court of Audits of the State of Mato Grosso (TCE-MT) [5, 6]. The Integrated Development Program (PDI), whose objective and focus are "to contribute to the improvement of the efficiency of public services, fostering the adoption of a results-oriented public administration model for society" and the "integrated and permanent development of the TCE-MT, and all public institutions monitored, by means of transference of knowledge, technologies and good management practices". The program is constituted by six projects and had the adhesion of 24 of the 141 municipalities of the state. One of the projects that compose the IDP is the project 01, which supports the Strategic Planning[1] of the municipalities.

Hence, this research will focus on the analysis of the strategic plans developed by the cities acceded to the IDP (TCE-MT), through a qualitative and quantitative study of the 498 indicators circumscribed to the Indicator Monitoring System.

As a research problem, it is pointed out that the lack of standardization of indicators can lead to problems for project management. These indicators cover different themes, nomenclatures and different measurement methods, which makes it difficult – sometimes even impossible – to use other organizations and the comparison of socioeconomic situations and results obtained between different municipalities.

To achieve that, we sought to develop a methodological framework for the analysis of indicators used in the evaluation, monitoring and control of the strategic planning of the municipalities acceded to the IDP. A bibliographical research on public management was carried out. Next, a technical-conceptual framework was developed, allowing

---

[1] Available on: https://www.tce.mt.gov.br/conteudo/index/sid/597. Accessed on: 17th March 2019.

the exploration of the 1094 indicators present in the Monitoring System to reach a standardization of 498 indicators that were later used in the analyzes. Finally, a set of standardized indicators for municipal management was proposed.

2 Theoretical Reference

2.1 Balanced Scorecard in Public Administration

The Balanced Scorecard (BSC) is a management system that provides organizations with an effective connection between their long-term goals and their short-term activities [25]. To do so, this system translates the vision of organizations into four distinct perspectives: Financial; Internal Processes; Learning and Growth; and Customers. From this viewpoint, it proposes the definition of specific objectives, indicators, goals and initiatives, within each perspective, to reach the established vision.

The use of BSC as a methodology for controlling performance in the public management environment is a focus of varied studies, since it was designed to respond to demands of private organizations. However, for Radnor and McGuire [7], the BSC has effective applicability in public management.

In this sense, Maran, Bracci and Inglis [8] observe the relevance of the use of the BSC from the configuration of multidimensional measures of the management that promote the balance of the indicators seeking greater efficiency of the public management.

2.2 Evaluation of Programs and Public Policies

There is a growing research literature on methodologies, measures and indicators for evaluating public policies and programs that deal with developed and developing countries, such as Brazil Kuypers and Marx [9].

There is no consensus as to the correct method for evaluating public policies and programs. Many agents have published studies, guides and manuals on the subject, ranging from regional and international public bodies to groups of public managers and private institutions [10].

The evaluation of public policy programs can be defined as "a systematic analysis of important aspects of a program and its value" in order to provide reliable and usable results Ala-Harja and Hergason [10]. According to the author, evaluations of public programs should raise the quality of information available to public officials and managers, bringing to light the results of the programs being implemented, which would allow more informed decision-making and better program design and implementation, as well as the accountability of its results to society.

Another key role played by the process of evaluation of policies and programs in the public sector is to increase the sense of responsibility and accountability of public officials for the decisions taken, as well as their impacts.

In this regard, Dufour [11] argues that the evaluation process exerts a similar impact on the public sector as competition does in the private sector. The author also emphasizes that efficiency enhancement and modernization of public management is associated with the establishment of measures for evaluation and monitoring of the results and impact of social policies and programs.

According to Francischini and Francischini [12], the evaluation approach must resort to some principles: Productivity; Efficiency; Effectiveness; Use; and Cost.

2.3 Performance Indicators

From the perspective of Francischini and Francischini [12], performance indicators can be understood as measurement frameworks which support the understanding of organizational reality. Thus, these indicators are valuable to understand the ways in which the organization is performing, so that whenever the course is not correct, it can be adjusted.

Understanding the importance of performance indicators from the BSC perspective is crucial for the success of results-based management. According to Francischini and Francischini [12], it is through such indicators that managers and other employees will have an indication of the position in which the organization is in relation to its strategy. Therefore, the construction of valid, measurable and straightforward strategic indicators may be the key to success or failure of planning.

Jannuzzi et al. [13] argue that, in the context of the public sector, indicators should be defined, analyzed, understood and used from the perspective of the formulation and evaluation cycle of public policies. Since each stage of this cycle has its own characteristics, the indicators used in each of them are also different from each other. The authors also classify indicators between analytical and synthetic indicators. The first group is used to analyze specific situations of socioeconomic realities – e.g. percentage of houses with access to treated water and unemployment rate. The second group is used to synthesize aspects of socioeconomic reality that involve multiple dimensions in a single measure.

In the search for a conceptual structure of dimensions that would allow to group the indicators of the studied municipalities, the research identified the following theoretical dimensions. The construction of the theoretical dimensions took into account cases of the Brazilian management environment given the proximity of the management structure of municipal public institutions.

To understand the object of the study, it is necessary to contextualize theoretically the Performance Measurement Systems, which from the perspective of Francischini and Francischini [12], are organized sets of indicators that maintain a relation of cause and effect between them.

Table 1. Dimensions of strategic planning in Brazilian public management.

N°	Dimension	Authors	Perspective
1	Finance	Pereira and Rezende [14]	Municipal public management can improve its financial results through the control and integration of strategic actions using Strategic Indicator Systems
2	Health	Carvalho; Vasconcelos; Arruda and Macena [15]	The development of public health policies in municipalities is related to the monitoring of indicators
3	Education	Santos; Santos and Lira [16]	The effectiveness of municipal public management of educational policies and the strategic decision-making process requires the adoption of mechanisms for the integration and management of strategic indicators
4	Work and economic development	Leite-Filho and Fialho [17]	Economic development in the perspective of municipal public management can be influenced by the measurement and management of strategic indicators in the BSC methodology
5	Environment and land affairs	Giacomini; Catapan; Santos and Santos [18]	The management of public policies at the municipal level focused on the environment can perform positively through the use of strategic indicators based on the BSC methodology
6	Social assistance	Araujo; Araujo; Souza, Santos and Santana [19]	Participation in social programs at the municipal level is related to the monitoring of strategic indicators of social public policies
7	Culture. Sport, leisure and tourism	Petri, Rosa, Bernardo and Bianco [20]	The use of strategic indicators through the BSC methodology provides excellence in the cultural and tourism services offered by municipal public management
8	Processes	Leite and Resende [21]	The use of process indicators in government management at the municipal level, corroborates the more effective management of public resources
9	People	Gomes; Leal and Assis [22]	The performance of municipal administrations, based on efficiency and effectiveness criteria, is influenced by strategic indicators of the institution's people
10	Accountability	Marengo and Diehl [23]	The use of strategic indicators can refer the manager to a long-term vision and enhance the accountability culture of the municipal public institution

3 Methodology

Based on the phenomenon of indicators in the public management environment in Brazil, the research is classified as a multi-case study, which followed an empirical framework for exploratory purposes.

The criterion for selecting the cases for the analysis of the research was based on all the cities participating in the IDP program, which in 2018 already had their structured strategic planning. Hence, 24 cities in the State of Mato Grosso, taking part in the program were selected.

In order to establish the methodological path for conducting the empirical analysis, the following steps are described: Scope delimitation; Theoretical multidimensional model construction; Data collection; Selection of indicators; Data Mining (categorization by size, by sub dimension, and by occurrence); Presentation of results and analysis of the dimensions; and Conclusion.

The data used in the research are from a secondary source and were obtained with the consent of the public institution responsible for the support in the management of the strategic plans of the IDP cities through a SQL query in the Database of the Strategic Management Software and Monitoring of Indicators. This software was developed by the Court of Audits of the State of Mato Grosso and is the main technological tool to support the planning of the municipalities taking part in the program.

Data-mining, based on Hand, Manila and Smyth [24], is related to exploratory analysis and the use of large datasets from exhaustive analyzes, in order to extract strategic information.

It should be noted that for the purpose of this research, only the indicators that account for 20% of the total of 24 municipalities were consolidated. The establishment of a cut-off point for the analysis of the indicators was carried out with the intention of defining a criterion of relevance for the analysis of the data.

The consultation initially brought 1094 indicators, which made it impossible to conduct the study, since many indicators were duplicated. To reduce complexity, 10 theoretical dimensions were developed (Table 1) and 63 sub-dimensions were developed by the authors based on data analysis and presented in Table 2:

Table 2. Dimension – Sub-dimension

Dimension – Sub-dimension	Dimension – Sub-dimension	Dimension – Sub-dimension
1-Expenses with personnel	3-Literacy	6-Poverty
1- Revenue	3-School Fail	6-Assistance
1-Fiscal management	3-School discrepancy	6-Housing
1-Liquidity	3-Evasion	6-Risk and Violated Rights
1-Investment	3-Attendance	6-Vulnerability
1-Municipal dept	3-Transport	6-Social participation
1-Social security	3-Full-time school	7-Culture
1-Budget	3-Research	7-Sport and leisure

(continued)

Table 2. (*continued*)

Dimension – Sub-dimension	Dimension – Sub-dimension	Dimension – Sub-dimension
1-Expenses	3-Meal	7-Tourism
2-Basic attention	4-Agriculture and rural production	8-Processes and systems
2-Diagnostics	4-Family farming	9-Clearance
2-Examinations	4-Employment and income	9-Environment
2-Healthcare	4-Business/Industry	9-Assiduity
2-Mortality	4-Professional qualification	9-Training
2-Preventing	4-Service	9-Ambience
2-Treatment	5-Routes and mobility	9-Performance
2-Vectors	5-Water, sewage and garbage	9-Stocking
3-Performance	5-Accessibility	9-Amount
3-Abandonment	5-Planning and land regularization	10-Satisfaction of society
3-Coverage	5-Public lightning	10- Strategic planning and management
3-School pass	5-Environment	10-Social control

Note: The number before the word refers to which dimension it belongs to (see Table 1).

The methodology allowed, through multiple phases of data mining, to reduce the number of indicators from 1094 to 498. Table 3 shows the conversion of the general indicators of the system into validated indicators, through logical and semantic validation.

Table 3. % of conversion

Dimension	Initial total	Total logical and semantic validation	% of conversion
Finance	142	55	0,387324
Health	143	48	0,335664
Education	177	82	0,463277
Work and economic development	87	58	0,666667
Environment and land affairs	194	80	0,412371
Social assistance	75	40	0,533333
Culture, sport, leisure e tourism	75	44	0,586667
Processes	67	45	0,671642
People	73	26	0,356164
Accountability	61	20	0,327869
Total 24 municipalities	1094	498	0,45521

4   Presentation and Analysis

The indicators found in the 24 municipalities of the IDP project are varied and complex, making them difficult to be analyzed. In order to reduce this complexity, the indicators were subdivided into 10 dimensions (Table 1): health; education; culture, sports, leisure and tourism; social assistance; work and economic development; physical structure, land and environment; finances; people; processes; accountability.

In order to group the unique indicators, 63 sub-dimensions were created (Table 2). This way, through classification and aggregation, the indicators were reduced from 1094 to 498 (See Table 3).

Finally, indicators that occurred in at least 20% of the 24 municipalities were summarized in Table 4. Columns D and O refer respectively to the dimension (See Table 1) and Number of occurrences in municipalities.

4.1   Financial Indicators

The financial indicators were categorized into 11 sub-dimensions: Personnel expenses; Revenue; Fiscal Management; Liquidity; Investment; Municipal Debt; Social Security; Budget; Expenses; and Assets. This structure allowed dividing the financial indicators of the 24 municipalities into a set of 56 unique indicators, which were obtained in the data-mining phase, from the 142 initial indicators. It can be observed from the analysis in Table 4 that the most used financial indicators are related to the revenue dimension (06 occurrences). It is also evident that the indicators related to the assets are not among the most usual. The most used indicator among the municipalities participating in the project is the revenue dimension and is described as the receipt of the active debt, followed by liquidity and personnel expenses.

4.2   Health Indicators

Out of 143 initial indicators 48 remained and were subdivided into 08 sub-dimensions: Mortality, 24 indicators; Diagnostics, 6 indicators; Treatment, 2 Indicators; Healthcare, 4 indicators; Basic Attention, 5 indicators; Prevention, 4 indicators; Exams, 2 indicators; and Vectors 1 indicator. What is notable in the analysis of the 10 indicators that occurred the most in the municipalities is that 10 are indicators of mortality. The analysis of health indicators shows the absence of prevention indicators among the main indicators.

4.3   Education Indicators

In the education dimension there are 82 Indicators subdivided into 13 sub-dimensions: Performance, 31 indicators; School Pass, 4 indicators; Abandonment, 4 indicators; Literacy, 8 indicators; Coverage, 11 indicators; School Fail, 5 indicators; Discrepancy, 3 indicators; Dropout, 8 indicators; Attendance, 3 indicators; Transportation 3 indicators; Full-time school, 2 indicators; Research and School meals, 1 indicator each. Table 4 shows the indicators that occurred in at least 4 cases. The 'Performance' sub-dimension is the most frequent when we analyze education indicators, but the two

Table 4. Dimension, number of occurrence and indicators

D	O	Indicator	D	O	Indicator
1	5	Expenses with payroll of the municipality	4	6	Operational companies
1	5	Debt cost	4	10	Records in the Municipal Inspection Service (SIM)
1	5	Investment	4	11	Assisted families in family farming
1	5	Own revenue	5	4	Preserved rural routes
1	5	Budget outcome	5	4	Sewage treatment coverage
1	6	Index of municipal tax management (general)	5	4	Areas (locality) with selective collection
1	6	Own revenue – ISSQN – PMG	5	6	Recovered rural routes
1	6	Budget enforcement	5	7	Disposal of solid waste
1	6	Own revenue in relation to net current revenue	5	8	Public spaces with accessibility
1	7	Collection of municipal tax revenue	5	8	Urban land regularization
1	7	Own revenue – IPTU - PMG	5	10	Households connected to the sewage network
1	8	Expenses with Personnel	5	10	Green area per capita
1	8	Liquidity	5	11	Households served (water network)
1	16	Receipt of active debt	5	21	Paved urban routes
2	4	Deaths due to diseases of the respiratory system	6	4	Families in need of Special Social Protection.
2	4	Deaths due to external causes	6	5	Families served in relation to those who need Basic Social Protection.
2	4	Deaths due to traffic accident in the municipal area	6	10	Families living in poverty and extreme poverty
2	6	Premature death (30 – 69 years of age) due to Diabetes mellitus	6	13	Housing Deficit
2	7	Premature death (30 – 69 years of age) due to diseases of the respiratory system	7	5	Attendance in cultural activities
2	8	Cure of leprosy cases diagnosed in the cohort years	7	6	Tourists and visitors
2	8	Incidence of dengue	7	10	Attendance in cultural activities

(Continued)

Table 4. Continued

2	10	Premature death (< 70 years) due to Chronic non-communicable diseases	7	11	Participation in sports and leisure practices in the municipality
2	10	Maternal mortality	8	4	Response to requests for information, complaints and reports
2	11	Child mortality	8	5	Mapped internal processes
3	6	Proficiency in the Portuguese Language (final years of Elementary School)	8	6	Response time to request for information, complaint and/or report
3	6	Proficiency in Mathematics (final years of Elementary School)	9	5	Attendant with at least 8 hours of training per year
3	6	Illiteracy	9	7	Organizational ambience
3	9	Basic Education Development Index-IDEB (final years)	9	10	Training of attendants
3	10	Proficiency in the Portuguese Language (early years of Elementary School)	9	14	Performance of attendants
3	10	Proficiency in Mathematics (early years of Elementary School)	9	14	Satisfaction of attendants
3	13	Basic Education Development Index-IDEB (early years)	10	4	Participants in Programs or Social Control Policy
3	16	Potential Coverage in Early Childhood Education (4 to 5 years)	10	13	Strategic planning goals achieved
3	19	Potential Coverage in Early Childhood Education (0 to 3 years)	10	15	Satisfaction of society
4	5	Tones of fish per year	10	15	Participation in events of social control

Note: IPTU Urban Territorial Tax; ISSQN Service Tax.
Note: IDEB - Basic Education Development Index (national indicator calculated by means of an evaluation in schools).

indicators that occurred the most among the 24 municipalities are indicators of educational network coverage. It should be noted that the indicator that most often appeared is: "Potential Coverage in Early Childhood Education (0 to 3 years)". Although the municipality is not obliged to offer places for this age range, there is a growing concern about this issue.

4.4   Work and Economic Development Indicators

A total of 58 indicators, classified into 6 sub-dimensions, were found: Employment and Income, 7 indicators; Family Agriculture, 11 indicators; Agriculture and Rural Production, 17 indicators; Companies and Industries, 18 indicators; Professional Qualification, 3 indicators; Service, 2 indicators. The indicator "Assisted families in family farming" was present in 13 of the 24 counties surveyed. Although Mato Grosso is a predominantly agricultural state, there were no indicators related to agribusiness.

4.5   Indicators of Physical Structure, Land and Environment

Out of the initial 194 indicators, 80 were analyzed. They were classified into 06 sub-dimensions: Routes and Mobility, 27 indicators; Environment, 20 indicators; Water, sewage and waste, 20 indicators; Planning and land regularization, 7 indicators; Public Lighting, 4 indicators; Accessibility, 1 indicator. The most common indicators for this dimension are: Households connected to the sewage network; Green area per capita; Households attended (water network); Paved urban routes.

4.6   Social Assistance

In this dimension, 40 indicators were classified into 6 sub-dimensions: Poverty, 6 indicators; Assistance, 26 indicators, Housing, 4 indicators; Risk and Violated Rights, 2 indicators; Vulnerability and Social Participation, 1 indicator each. Table 1 shows the indicators that appeared in at least 20% of the cases studied. In the Social Assistance dimension there were 75 indicators, which were reduced to 40 after the data mining phase. The indicator that occurred most often is: "Housing deficit" followed by "Families living in poverty and extreme poverty".

4.7   Culture Sports Leisure and Tourism

In this dimension there are 43 indicators out of the 75 initial ones. Indicators are classified in 3 sub-dimensions: Tourism, 9 indicators; Culture, 15 indicators; Sport and Leisure, 20 indicators. In Culture Sports Leisure and Tourism dimension, a predominance of analytical indicators is observed, with 03 on the number of participants and one on the number of tourists who visit the municipalities. The development of outcome indicators that can measure the effectiveness of municipal policies is proposed.

4.8   Indicators of Processes and Systems

The data-mining phase presented 45 indicators of the initial 67. They were subdivided into 2 dimensions (Processes and Systems). Note that these indicators are largely dissipated by municipalities – only 12 of them occurred in more than one municipality. Regarding the mapped internal processes, an attempt is again made to measure effort, when they should measure the impact of the management of their processes.

4.9   People

There are 24 indicators of people remaining from 73 initial indicators. Table 4 shows the classification of the indicators that have occurred in at least one of the four sub-dimensions (Assiduity, 2 indicators; Training, 12 indicators; Performance, 3 indicators; Capacity, Withdraw, Ambience, Quantity and Satisfaction, 01 indicator each). Table 4 shows the classification of indicators that occurred in at least 20% of the cases studied. In this dimension the training indicators are those that most occur – 12 indicators while indicators of performance of the servers are only 3.

4.10   Accountability

In this dimension, there were initially 61 indicators; 20 remained and were classified into three sub-dimensions: Social Control, 6 indicators; Satisfaction of Society, 6 indicators; Planning and Management, 8 indicators. At the end of the data-mining phase there were twenty univocal indicators, and the most frequent occurrences presented in Table 4.

5   Final Considerations

The analysis of 498 indicators proved to be a complex and multifaceted work, in part because there are many different indicators in several municipalities with unique realities. The research developed a unique way, by means of theoretical development of 10 dimensions, which were subdivided into 63 sub-dimensions that, in turn, allowed to reduce from 1094 indicators to 498 singular municipal public indicators.

Theoretically, the survey broadens the perception about Performance Measurement Systems for the development of performance measurement programs for public administration, especially for municipalities.

The perceptions pointed out in the referential by Maran, Bracci and Inglis [7] observe relevance of the use of BSC from the configuration of multidimensional management measures. In the same line, the research proposes a variable structure of planning in which each reality can develop its own dimensions for its specific cases.

From the perspective of the practice, it is proposed that the lack of standardization of indicators in project 01 of the Integrated Development Program (IDP) – responsible for the planning of the municipalities – causes some inconveniences because it makes the analysis of the indicators in group as Performance Monitoring System difficult. The lack of standards also makes it difficult to compare inter-municipalities and municipalities outside the IDP.

In the next round of strategic planning, the proposal is to establish a framework to standardize at least part of the municipal indicators. Also, with regard to practice, a set of 68 indicators have been developed and are widely used in at least 20% of the municipalities surveyed and presented in the Table 4.

Finally, it is clear that this research did not seek to analyze the quality of the indicators, forms of measurement, relation with the short and long term goals, relation with the projects and plans of action and, above all, the relation of the indicators with the municipal strategic objectives. It is, therefore, suggested that these should be the next steps of the research project.

Acknowledgements. We would like to thank the UFMT, TCE-MT and Uniselva Foundation for all the support to develop and publish this research.

References

1. Verbeeten, F.H.M., Speklé, R.F.: Management control, results oriented culture and public sector performance: empirical evidence on new public management. Organ. Stud. **36**(7), 953–978 (2015)
2. Souza, F.S.R.N., Gomes, V., Fernandes Pinto, A., Favero, C.G.: Programa netuno: inovação para a melhoria da gestão na marinha do Brasil. RACE-Revista de Administração, Contabilidade e Economia **15**(3), 843–870 (2016)
3. Kiriri, P.N.: Management of performance in higher education institutions: the application of the balanced scorecard (BSC). Eur. J. Educ. **1**(3), 168–176 (2019)
4. Kaplan, R., Norton, D.P.: The Balanced Scorecard – Measures that Drive Performance. Harvard Business Review, Nova York (1992)
5. TCE-MT, Tribunal de Contas do Estado de Mato Grosso.: Programa de Desenvolvimento Institucional Integrado (PDI). TCE-MT, Cuiabá (2016). https://www.tce.mt.gov.br/conteudo/index/sid/597. Accessed 17 Mar 2019
6. Girata, N.N.H., Maciel, C.: eGov website evolution study within strategic planning. In: 15th Annual International Conference on Proceedings of the 15th Annual International Conference on Digital Government Research - DG.O 2014, Aguascalientes, pp. 69–78. ACM Press (2014)
7. Radnor, Z., McGuire, M.: Performance management in the public sector: fact or fiction? Int. J. Prod. Perform. Manag. **53**(3), 245–260 (2004)
8. Maran, L., Bracci, E., Inglis, R.: Performance management systems' stability: unfolding the human factor – a case from the Italian public sector. Br. Account. Rev. **50**(3), 324–339 (2018)
9. Kuypers, S., Marx, I.: The truly vulnerable: integrating wealth into the measurement of poverty and social policy effectiveness. Soc. Indic. Res. **142**(1), 131–147 (2018)
10. Ala-Harja, M., Hergason, S.: Em Direção às melhores práticas de Avaliação. Revista do Serviço Público **51**(4), 5–60 (2014)
11. Dufour, B.: Social impact measurement: what can impact investment practices and the policy evaluation paradigm learn from each other? Res. Int. Bus. Finance **47**, 18–30 (2019)
12. Francischini, A.S., Francischini, P.G.: Indicadores de desempenho: dos objetivos à ação métodos para elaborar KPI's e obter resultados. Alta Books, Rio de Janeiro (2018)
13. Jannuzzi, P.M., Loloian, A., Conti, V.L.: Elaboração de diagnósticos para programas sociais: a estratégia multimétodos para o Programa Estadual de Qualificação Profissional. Boletim Estatísticas Públicas **9**(10), 113–118 (2014)
14. Pereira, E.T.A., Rezende, D.A.: Planejamento e gestão estratégica municipal: Estudo de caso do controle interno da prefeitura municipal de Curitiba. Revista Economia Gestão **13**(31), 52–72 (2013)
15. Carvalho, F.C.D.D., Vasconcelos, T.B.D., Arruda, G.M.M.S., Macena, R.H.M.: Modificações nos indicadores sociais da região Nordeste após a implementação da atenção primária. Trabalho Educação e Saúde **17**(2), 1–21 (2019)

16. Santos, G.M.A., Santos, A.M., Lira, V.E.: A contribuição do planejamento estratégico na Administração Pública Municipal: um estudo de caso. Revista Caribeña de Ciencias Sociales **20**(67), 1–11 (2015)
17. Leite Filho, G.A., Fialho, T.M.M.: Relação entre indicadores de gestão pública e de desenvolvimento dos municípios brasileiros. Cadernos Gestão Pública e Cidadania **20**(67), 277–295 (2015)
18. Giacomini, M.M., Catapan, A., Santos, R.C., Santos, D.F.: O Balanced Scorecard aplicado na gestão pública de uma empresa de saneamento do Sul do Brasil: Análise da percepção dos usuários. Revista Iberoamericana de Contabilidad de Gestión **11**(22), 1–15 (2013)
19. Araújo, F.R.D., Araújo, M.A.D.D., Souza, F.J.V.D., Santos, D.F., Santana, M.B.: Uma avaliação do Índice de gestão descentralizada do programa bolsa família. Revista de Administração Pública **49**(2), 367–393 (2015)
20. Petri, S.M., Rosa, M.M., Bernardo, F.D., Bianco, P.: Gestão pública através de mapas estratégicos do Balanced Scorecard: um estudo de caso do Festival Floripa Teatro Isnard Azevedo. Revista Catarinense da Ciência Contábil **13**(40), 67–79 (2014)
21. Leite, L.O., Rezende, D.A.: Modelo de gestão municipal baseado na utilização estratégica de recursos da tecnologia da informação para a gestão governamental: formatação do modelo e avaliação em um município. Revista de Administração Pública **44**(2), 459–493 (2010)
22. Gomes, R.C., Santos Leal, A.C., Assis, V.A.: Indicadores Para Avaliar o Desempenho de Prefeituras Municipais. Tecnologias de Administração e Contabilidade-TAC **3**(1), 1–15 (2013)
23. Marengo, S.T., Diehl, C.A.: A divulgação de indicadores não financeiros em sites municipais gaúchos. Gestão Regionalidade **27**(81), 46–58 (2012)
24. Hand, D., Manila, H., Smyth, P.: Principles of Data Mining. MIT Press, Cambridge (2001)
25. Kaplan, R., Norton, D.: Using the balanced scorecard as a strategic management system. Harvard Bus. Rev. 75–85 (1996)

Two Decades of Online Information and Digital Services: Quality Improvements to Municipality Websites and User Preferences

Hanne Sørum[(✉)]

Department of Technology, Kristiania University College,
Christian Krohgs gate 32, 0186 Oslo, Norway
hanne.sorum@kristiania.no

Abstract. A journey through the landscape of quality assessment and website improvement within the public sector in Norway has shown large changes and new ways of interaction and communication between citizens and the public sector. In the past two decades, there has been a tremendous shift in the sense that paper-based communication has largely been replaced with online content and digital services. Key aspects of this transformation have included initiatives taken by the government, changes in users' needs and requirements, and the creation of organizational values because of digitalization. Inspired by this, the aim of the present paper was to investigate the design of public websites, especially those of municipalities. To this end, in this study, we have reported on initiatives taken by the government in the last 20 years. In addition, we have reported a test conducted in a usability lab and qualitative interviews pertaining to users' voices and preferences. Results showed changes related to the design and visual appearance of websites and that users had clear preferences. Search boxes, neutral colors, a clean and simple design, and the structure and grouping of information were preferred. Quality assessments of public websites generally triggered a positive effect, both in terms of organization awareness and increased quality. The findings had implications for the direction the sector should take in the coming years. Concluding remarks have been given at the end of the paper.

Keywords: eGovernment · Public websites · Website quality · User satisfaction · Quality assessment

1 Introduction

The widespread use of online channels to communicate and distribute information requires that organizations facilitate great interactions. This is especially so within an eGovernment context, as in most cases, governments lack competitors and have a monopoly on information and services delivered to citizens. In the new digital age, almost every citizen in Norway has access to public sector service provision. Compared to ten years ago, this is a significant increase. Every citizen in Norway should have equal access to online information and public electronic services provided by the public sector [1]. As stated by the Norwegian Consumer Council, "It is a bit with the municipality as it is with the body. We do not think so much about it being part of us if

© Springer Nature Switzerland AG 2019
A. Kő et al. (Eds.): EGOVIS 2019, LNCS 11709, pp. 133–146, 2019.
https://doi.org/10.1007/978-3-030-27523-5_10

its works" [2]. Here, one can draw a parallel to technology in general; one does not necessarily think about their phone and wireless internet but soon notices when they do not work. This testifies to the importance of great technologies (for example, websites) that satisfy user needs and requirements, and most importantly, that these work as intended.

Norway has about 5.3 million inhabitants and is a well-developed industrial country with a standard of living and life expectancy. The country consists of 422 municipalities spread throughout its length. There is a considerable difference in the size of municipalities in terms of the location, economy, and number of inhabitants. Many municipalities in Norway have spent a lot of money on their websites, including the Oslo municipality (the capital of Norway). In 2015, they announced that NOK 48 million was spent on a new website, viewed by 35,000 unique visitors in one day at that time [3]. The target audience for this website was not only residents but also the media, politicians, and other stakeholder groups. The country has also received great attention from abroad. In 2014, FutureGov suggested that in terms of its design, Norway.no was one of the eight best national eGovernment portals in the world. They announced, "Norway.no is a sleek and simple gateway to online services, with a list of basic topics on the left, an invitation to sign up for SMS text messages, and a prominent search box that lets the user narrow down services by municipality" [4]. Norwegian people use the Internet a lot for various purposes, including business, leisure, and pleasure. Regarding the use of information and communication technologies in the household, one survey reported that 96% of the population had used the Internet over the past three months. Of these, 93% had used it to send and receive emails, 61% to book travel and/or accommodation, and 92% for banking services [5]. This highly use supports the idea that it is important to facilitate good user experiences within the private and public sector in years to come.

To dig into this area of interest, the following two topics have been addressed in this paper: (1) initiatives taken by the government in Norway to improve website quality and digital services within the public sector and (2) the design and visual appearance of municipality websites as perceived by end users. A mixed-method approach was taken by drawing on second hand data retrieved from various web sources and previous work and the results of a lab test. For this test, four municipality websites that had a diverse range of designs were carefully chosen, and the effect of design on perceptions of usability was measured. Additionally, qualitative interviews and a walkthrough of different types of design were conducted with four participants.

The rest of this paper has been organized as follows. Section 2 has provided a review of relevant work, while the method has been presented in Sect. 3. In Sect. 4, the findings have been provided, and this has been followed by a discussion in Sect. 5. Finally, concluding remarks and suggestions for further research have been given in Sect. 6.

2   Relevant Work

"As internet usage continues to increase, e-government websites are undertaking to offer improved performance in meeting citizens' needs. E-government websites now serve a variety of purposes" [6, p. 2]. In eGovernment, electronic services are a key concept and have replaced traditional paper-based communication between citizens and the public sector [7]. Interactions that take place are, therefore, of particular importance, and design plays a vital role. The usability of public websites has been shown to influence how citizens use websites and their overall success [8]. "The Internet, in general, and official websites, in particular, have fundamentally changed the relationship between citizens and their governments by facilitating access to massive amounts of data that can be collected, distributed, and transformed by private firms, journalists, civic organizations, and the public" [9, p. 868]. User groups are, therefore, not homogeneous. Many different needs must be covered, and facilitation is particularly important. Consequently, user experience designers have become concerned with understanding whether sites or applications give value to users, whether users find them easy to use and navigate, and whether users enjoy using them [10]. Many quality aspects must be considered in website design for continuous improvement. Users must be included through usability evaluations that identify their needs and requirements regarding specific websites and digital services to identify future directions in development.

Usability assessments that include real users have been shown to provide valuable insights and feedback [11] and have been distinguished from expert evaluations and technical and/or automated assessment. Nielsen [12], defined usability as "… a quality attribute that assesses how easy user interfaces are to use. The word 'usability' also refers to methods for improving ease of use during the design process". Similarly, the ISO definition of usability is "the effectiveness, efficiency, and satisfaction with which specified users achieve specified goals in particular environments" [13]. Regarding the design and visual appearance of websites, it has been agreed that usability plays a vital role. Design features vital for the success of public websites include large search bars, grouped content, simplicity, icons instead of pictures, responsive design, and content available in different languages [4]. Filling these criteria is not a quick fix, as it requires planning, clear goals, strategy, resources, and user knowledge.

There are many different types of websites within eGovernment environments. Some websites are presented by small municipalities, some have a target group across the country, and some provide solutions related to special services, which may be nationwide or local. A study by Feeney and Brown [14] showed that there were differences between the websites of US municipalities of different sizes and types, and council-manager governments had more advanced websites than mayor-council governments. A study by Aleixo, Nunes, and Isaias [15] stated that usability and accessibility were important in the design of public websites. The authors studied website presence within local governments in Portugal and found an average performance of municipal websites pointing to digital inclusion. Their study was published in 2012 and discussed usability in public websites in terms of concerns about digital inclusion. Cumbie and Kar [16] assessed inclusiveness through measuring the usability, accessibility, and compatibility of 101 local government websites in Mississippi (USA) as well as the number of errors present and the extent to which the sites met national and local standards. They argued that Mississippi was an underdeveloped state with health and social challenges. Their results showed many issues that prevented the delivery of inclusive services, large variations among websites concerning the number of issues found, and an extensive absence of discoverable websites (87 of the 188 websites). These findings indicated a need for more inclusiveness among various user groups with varying needs. Moreover, the quality of information has also been perceived as a vital contributor to success on the Web. Rasool and Warraich [17] conducted a systematic review across several countries to assess the information quality of eGovernment websites. Their findings revealed that information quality was important, and citizens believed that public websites provided high quality information. Information quality can be divided into various aspects, such as relevance, readability, up-to-date and understandable. Concerning this, to design websites that fit users' needs and requirements, Bødker et al. [18] emphasize the use of personas to discuss how this technique could help designers of municipal services. A persona is an imaginary person in a target group and helps to understand the users. They concluded that personas were useful intermediaries, but they could not necessarily replace the involvement of real users in the design process.

3   Method

To investigate the research objectives stated in the introduction, various empirical components have been included in this study. The reason behind choosing a variety of methods was to examine a complex topic that can be explored by taking diverse approaches. The empirical components included are intended to complement each other, while each one provides valuable insights important to the study.

To review how the government has worked over the years, many searches of online sources have been carried out. Academic journals and databases were also reviewed. In Norway, awareness of government involvement has existed for many years, and several articles have been published on the topic. The purpose of the review was to get an overview of various initiatives and activities carried out. This study has not gone into all details but has drawn an overall picture. The purpose was to understand what the public sector has done and how it has worked to raise the quality of its websites, from the static websites of the year 2000 to those produced today. Moving on to the test conducted in a usability lab.

Participants of the lab test included 24 individuals, and there was an equal distribution between genders (12 men and 12 women). One participant at a time in quiet surroundings. Before data collection, all participants signed a consent form and were briefed on the aim and content of the study. They had an opportunity to ask questions in the initial phase. Participants were in the 20–49 year age group (average male age = 28 years, average female age = 35 years) and were recruited from students and staff members at a university college in Oslo (the capital of Norway). Since municipal websites have a wide and slightly homogeneous target group, the participants in this study were selected based on a diverse audience. There was a desire for a variety and therefore a gender and age variation (ranging from 20–49 years).

In total, the websites of four municipalities with slightly different designs were tested, and the aim was to investigate how users experienced the quality of different websites after 60 s of free browsing. Participants were not given tasks to perform and/or specific information for which to search. Drawing on previous research studies that investigated quality in public sector websites [for example, 19], a questionnaire was developed that emphasized the following aspects: design, attractiveness, usability, the use of text and pictures, and participants' overall impression of the site. A five-point Likert scale was used, ranging from strongly disagree to strongly agree. All four websites were representative of public websites in Norway in different ways. As public websites, especially at the municipality level, vary considerably in design and website quality, it was necessary to reflect this diversity in the present study. Consequently, the four websites were carefully chosen from hundreds of public websites. The aim was to get an overview of different types of design and split them into four main categories, which were represented in this study. Descriptive statistical analyses were performed to determine user satisfaction with various quality attributes in the context of different types of website design. Moreover, this study reported on open-ended comments left by participants after the test concluded. To develop insight into the large variety of website designs, participants were asked for their opinion on differences between the sites immediately after the test. These comments were written down by the researcher and organized afterward. The purpose was to get an overall understanding of what participants meant and their immediate reactions after the test.

Additionally, user feedback on how municipality websites appeared on the Web was also measured via qualitative interviews after a walkthrough of different designs. The goal was to obtain fruitful explanations and insights from users' perspectives regarding their preferences. In total, four participants were individually exposed to various types of design. The print screens of seven websites were hung on a wall, and respondents looked at each of them for a few minutes, after which they were asked to form an opinion regarding their design and visual appearance. Then, they actually visited the websites by using a computer and were asked what they thought about each type of website. Notes were taken by the researcher, who asked follow-up questions. Respondents were asked for their immediate response after usage. According to Lindgaard et al. [20], visual appeal on the Web can be assessed within 50 ms, so users form a relatively quick impression.

4 Findings

4.1 Government Initiatives

Since the beginning of the year 2000, hundreds of public websites have been the subject of evaluation initiated by the government (respectively, the Agency for Public Management and eGovernment) in Norway. Different assessment methods based on a set of criteria have been applied during the assessment process. The purpose of annual evaluation has been to focus on quality aspects that are particularly important as well as to present guidelines for organizations regarding investment in online quality. Many organizations have worked closely with the criteria and used it to guide consecutive improvements. Websites that have received high scores in such assessments have been highlighted as good practice examples, which often results in marketing exposure and a positive image among citizens. In addition to initiatives implemented in Norway, similar evaluations have been carried out in other countries over the years. In Denmark, there have been many similarities in how the government has evaluated websites in recent years. From 2001 to 2012, the Agency for Digitization (formerly the National IT and Telecom Agency) measured the quality of public authorities' websites on an annual basis through an initiative called "Bedst på Nettet" (Best on the Web). Danish evaluations also focused on satisfaction among actual users and the business case for improving website quality in the public sector from an organizational point of view. Organizations considered their presence on the Web and the values/benefits they achieved.

In Norway, quality assessments comprised expert evaluations of public websites during 2001–2013, and changes to assessments were made in 2014 (the focus was given to digital online services and not primarily websites). The purpose has been to measure quality and inspire organizations to work purposefully to improve website quality over time. Quality aspects emphasized through such evaluations were related to website content, usability, and accessibility. Many public organizations used these criteria as a guideline for continuous website improvements over time. It has been important to adjust the criteria while keeping them relatively constant to ensure an element of predictability for organizations. No evaluations were carried out in 2012, because there was a need for more time to implement the changes made in 2011. Organizations needed time to incorporate quality improvements related to technical and visual (design) issues – that was anchored in the use of evaluation criteria.

Comparing the results from evaluations conducted in 2001 and 2003, the results showed a significant improvement and that such assessments triggered competition between organizations [21]. Comparing the results from 2007 and 2011, most public websites had a significantly higher quality in 2011 than in 2007, especially regarding website content. In 2007, approximately 30% of websites received 4–6 stars (6 stars are the top score), while approximately 70% got 1–3 stars. In 2011, 4 years later, 65% of websites received 4–6 stars, and 35% received 1–3 stars. Despite this variation, the websites of larger municipalities were of a higher quality than those of smaller municipalities.

Moreover, less than 1% of the websites evaluated fulfilled the accessibility criteria in 2006 [22], and that it was a long way to go for public organizations. Results from prior studies on municipality websites [23] also found that the size of the municipality played a role in website quality and that the sites of larger ones were of higher quality than those of smaller ones. In 2014, 64 state and municipal services were tested, with a focus on online services provided by the public sector rather than websites. In 2016, the average service (public digital services, including municipalities) evaluated reached 60% of the maximum score. Average test scores in 2014 were 61%, so this represented a stagnation. Although not directly comparable, these results indicated that municipalities were developing in the opposite direction. In 2014, the average municipal service scored 58%, while in 2016 it was 53%. This also represented a decrease of 5%

in 2 years [24]. Ideally, the curve would have gone the other way, although it was a small difference.

Another evaluation of public websites, that has been carried out by the Norwegian Consumer Council, also focused on municipal websites. They have tested municipality websites several times since 2005 with clear results showing that the sites of large municipalities were better than those of small ones [25]. The Norwegian Consumer Council evaluated the following aspects: service, availability, and information quality. The quality of the services themselves were not included in this test. They contacted municipalities with questions frequently asked by the populace, such as cost of leisure activities, the processing time for building cases, and the opening hours of the swimming pool. During this contact, researchers posed as citizens. They contacted municipalities via phone and e-mail and inspected the website. After the tests were completed, detailed results were made publicly available on the Internet. The test criteria, methods, and results are transparent and can easily be reproduced. According to the Norwegian Consumer Council, municipality management teams that were concerned with good service were the hallmark of municipalities that succeeded on the Web. This was reflected in their plans, goals, values, and strategies. In these municipalities, the whole organization aimed to provide good service to their citizens, and good dialogue was promoted. Digital communication and interaction were a vital part of this work. They focused on accessibility and offered "a door in" for citizens. For example, such municipalities had a service court, so citizens could get in touch with the municipality easily. In addition, they had great routines for dealing with inquiries from citizens and deadlines for answering inquires. Frequently, user satisfaction surveys were a central element to success [26].

Over the last years, several web awards, such as "beauty contests" on the Web, have also been arranged. In most cases, companies nominate themselves, and participation is voluntary, compared to assessments initiated by the government, which are mandatory. Although the goal of such competitions is to contribute to better user experience on the Web, considering what is evaluated and how, they are more commercial and less predictable. These are privately owned and not public initiatives. In most cases, organizations pay to participate, and winners receive great attention and marketing exposure. However, they can also have a good effect in the way that it is a consciousness related to the importance of offering good digital solutions that the users are satisfied with. While, beyond that, online success can be defined in different ways and need not be the same for all businesses. For one company earning money is highly important, while for another company (or organization) the most important success criteria can for instance be to enlist new members or market a special brand. An awareness of this is important in the development work. As well continuous quality improvements.

4.2 Users Satisfaction in Various Types of Website Design (Lab Test)

Because of the increasing focus on quality on the Web and digital solutions, many organizations have focused on key quality aspects launched within the public sector. For some organizations, how they appear on the Web today can be a result of this. To examine design and visual appearance perceived by end users, four municipality websites are included in the present study.

In the discussion of the results of this study, each website has been given a name. Website 1 is the clean site, Website 2 is the outdated design site, Website 3 is the content-rich site and Website 4 is the somewhat site. The names for the websites were grounded in the presentation and layout of the website's home page (start page). The actual website domains (including organization names) were anonymized, as the aim was to compare various types of designs (which is representative across Norwegian municipalities) and not organizations. In Table 1, a short description of the four municipality websites in the present study has been provided.

Table 1. A brief description of the four websites included in the study.

Website 1 The clean site	Website 2 The outdated design site	Website 3 The content-rich site	Website 4 The somewhat site
This site had a minimalist design and a minimum of design elements on the home page. In general, the layout had a clean design and was simple	This site had many visual elements, including text and pictures on the home page. It appeared cluttered and information-heavy with minimal structure	This site was very information-heavy, and much text was presented. The text was not well organized, and it was hard to get a good overview of the content	This was a typical website representing a municipality. The design did not stand out in any particular way. In many ways, this was an average site

First, a search for the websites in the Internet Archive WayBackMachine (https://archive.org/web/) revealed that all four websites were launched on the Web between 1997 and 2001. The organizations had almost two decades of online experience and had been using technology for communication and interaction purposes within a public sector setting. Moreover, a comparison revealed that many changes and quality improvements were made over the years for each website, although there were differences in how many and the extent of the changes made over the time period. Results from the Web archive showed that during the last few years, the websites had become increasingly modern and minimalist in design, especially the clean site and the somewhat site. In addition, one website, the outdated design site, had been through remarkably few changes during the last two decades. It had mostly the same design and visual look for many years.

The four websites had various designs and different levels of content provision, and there were large differences in quality improvements and maintenance since the first website was launched approximately 20 years ago. To measure perceptions of website quality and user experience for the different types of design, participants were told to browse each website for 60 s without any specific tasks to perform and/or information to identify. Then, they were asked to evaluate the quality of each website based on seven quality indicators derived from previous research studies. In Table 2, an overview of the results from the questionnaire (the lab test performed) and the average scores for each website have been given. Scores on the measurement scale ranged from 1 to 5, with 1 representing the lowest score and 5 the highest score.

Table 2. Results of quality evaluation (average score).

	Website 1 The clean site	Website 2 The out dated site	Website 3 The content -rich site	Website 4 The some what site
I think the website provided a great overview	4.00	1.92	3.21	4.13
I think the website was user friendly	3.79	1.96	3.17	4.21
I think the website has an attractive design	3.25	1.39	2.83	3.92
I think there is a good balance between the use of text and pictures	3.46	1.71	3.08	3.46
I think the website has a great menu structure	3.50	1.75	3.00	4.00
I think the website presents the content in a great way	3.54	1.83	3.13	4.13
In general, I got a great impression of this website	3.83	1.63	3.13	4.04
Average score	3.62	1.74	3.08	3.98

Results in Table 2 showed variation in the perception of website quality among the 24 participants regarding the quality attributes of different types of website design. The average score, based on all statements in the questionnaire, ranged from 3.98 for the best website, the somewhat site, and 1.74 for the worst website, the outdated design site. These results showed huge differences in the perception of the quality of different types of website design. Comparing the average score with the score related to the overall impression of the website, only small differences for the four sites were apparent. Therefore, the average score seems to be representative of the overall impression of the website, which can be linked to the overall user experience after a given period of use. Concerning the average standard deviation of all seven statements, results were similar. The standard deviation of the clean site was the highest (1.10), followed by the content-rich site (1.02), and the outdated site and the somewhat site (both 0.89). Standard deviation did not vary much among the websites included in the study.

In summary, results showed that the somewhat site, which represented typical public sector websites, scored highest. The website did not stand out in any way and presented some information on the home page but not too much. The design was considered user friendly, and the website had a great menu structure and an attractive design. The clean site ranked second in many aspects and was the simplest, with a minimalist design. This site had a clean and simple layout and a large search box, which was clearly visible to users. The content-rich site ranked third in the evaluation. It was not considered attractive by participants, though there was significant potential in terms of the overall usability and organization of the content. The outdated design site was rated as the worst and scored poorly in all quality aspects.

4.3   Qualitative Input After the Lab Test

Qualitative feedback provided by participants immediately after completing the test showed similar results. First, many participants commented on the wide variety of designs, and based on their own experience using different websites, they found that this variation was representative of the public sector. These differences may be due to different factors, but varying allocation of resources to website quality among organizations was probably important. One participant left the following comment, "I did not think there would be such big differences in quality and that there was generally more focus on satisfying users". Another participant said, "Some of the websites were very user friendly, but others (especially one of them) were hopeless to use. There was too much information, and poor structure and organization of the content. The pictures were just disturbing". Regarding the actual design and the extent to which the design was attractive and appropriate for such a website, the majority preferred a minimalist design without too much information or too many options.

A participant said, "I like that it's a simple and comprehensive menu structure. If you do not immediately find what you want, it is nice that the search box is visible and accessible. But it is also important that the search engine works optimally and that the hits (suggestions) that come up are relevant to what I seek information about. Unfortunately, this was not always the case". Other participants pointed out that this may be a problem with many websites. In sum, participants largely had the same perceptions of the website, including the provision of content, digital services, and design issues. They wanted websites to be minimalist and simple with information available in menus and search engines. In addition, they found it interesting to see the large variety of designs and how important design was in their perception of overall user experience.

4.4   Feedback on Visual Appearance (A Walkthrough Various Design)

Valuable feedback also came through qualitative interviews with potential users of municipal websites. After a review of seven websites with different designs, users had clear preferences. One respondent said, "I saw immediately that this was a public website. The sturdy look, a little bit boring and a total absence of advertising". The absence of advertising was perceived as positive. Another one said, "This website seems more professional than the others. It has something to do with color (the website does not use black, but gray). I like the fact that there are not so great contrasts, that it has a large and visible search field and a great use of images". Good use of colors, images, search fields, and the grouping of information were positive. It was also advantageous when information was placed so that the user did not have to scroll the website. Furthermore, one of the respondents commented, "I like menus where I can go into a theme, as long as the menu is still visible. This website is clear and nice, and it is easy for me to remember where I am. I easily can take one step back. It is irritating when new windows appear when you tap a link".

In general, there was agreement between respondents' comments related to the seven websites. Overall, it was considered important that websites were clear and did not contain too much information. Search fields were preferred, and it was preferred that these were visibly placed (preferably high up). Participants agreed that there should not be too much color, that good pictures were important and that websites should be well-organized. Design was important, and participants preferred when information was grouped in relation to themes. Participants responded negatively to cluttered websites with a lot of content, designs that were inconsistent, the use of many different and powerful subjects, lots of space between information, and a lack of opportunities to make quick choices.

5 Discussion

Research topics addressed in the present paper included (1) initiatives taken by the government in Norway to improve website quality improvements and digital services within the public sector and (2) the design and visual appearance of municipality websites as perceived by end users. Electronic services delivered via the Internet are significant within eGovernment and have replaced paper-based communication [7]. Therefore, there is a need to facilitate high quality online interactions. In this regard, Norway and several other countries have developed their online services for many years, and quality assessments of public websites have been conducted since early 2000. These evaluations were initiated by the government and have emphasized aspects of importance to users, including website content, usability, and accessibility requirements. Results of these evaluations showed that most public websites increased significantly in quality over time and that the evaluation triggered a positive effect in public organizations. The evaluations were based on a set of criteria (a list of concrete measures), so organizations received specific goals and guidelines for continuous quality improvement.

Results of such evaluations showed that the websites of large municipalities had better website quality than those of small municipalities [23, 26]. Ølnes [23] also showed that the allocation of resources in an organization, an awareness of evaluation criteria, and collaboration with other municipalities were criteria for success in this regard. This was in accordance with the results of other evaluations of public sector websites and services in Norway [25]. Prior studies also found large variations among government websites [16] and that in many cases, there was huge potential for improvements. Although the results of government rankings have shown a positive trend over the years, there has been a lack of user involvement during evaluation. Evaluations have largely focused on technical quality criteria and commonly comprised expert evaluations.

Usability evaluations that include real users can provide fruitful insights and feedback [11] but are lacking. This might influence evaluation results, as there are differences between expert evaluations and traditional user testing. As usability and accessibility are important in the design of public websites [15], the users opinion and viewpoint should be taken into consideration. In most cases, developing website accessibility is not a quick fix and requires technical changes involving content, visual design, and digital services. Regarding accessibility, the evidence suggests that this is something many organizations have been striving to facilitate and is a process that takes time. Accessibility is also a key quality aspect for websites and is required by law. However, quality assessments initiated by the government have had a positive effect, as websites have generally increased in quality [21]. However, users could have been usefully included in evaluation processes. After 20 years of online experience, many users have clear requirements and recommendations for how websites and services provided by the public sector should appear on the Web. Using personas may help researchers obtain a clear idea of user preferences [18], which may be important in users' perceptions of websites.

As participants in the present study were exposed to websites with a great variety of design features and usability concerns, the different visual appearances of municipality websites were compared (the lab test). The usability of public websites has an impact on citizens' use of websites and contributes to success [8]. Results showed that users clearly prefer websites with a simple minimalist design and a corresponding navigation structure. Moreover, users wanted to achieve great and appropriate interactions. Users did not want the website to be too simple, but they wanted it to be easy enough to navigate quickly and easily in order to find what they needed without spending too much time and effort on the task. There is a lack of competitors in the provision of public online information and services, so compared to an eBusiness website (that often has many competitors and the users can easily switch to another website if they struggle to find what they are looking for), high quality interaction is significant. Although there were many examples of websites with preferred designs, many organizations will need to make a considerable effort to achieve the goals stated by the government, especially in providing great user experiences of online services and information delivery. The present study showed how important website design is in this regard, both in terms of fulfilling government criteria (pertaining to quality indicators launched over the years) and user preference (how actual users in the target group experience a website).

Respondents identified large differences in website quality among municipalities, and some websites were considerably more user friendly than others. This was rooted in design issues, information overload, disturbing pictures, and poor structure and organization of content. Furthermore, respondents stated their preference for a simple design, including a simple menu structure and visible search field. They wanted search engines to work well and made clear references to Google. Therefore, it is essential for municipality websites to have a visible search field and a search engine that works optimally. In addition, a minimal need for scrolling, the use of neutral colors, and available information were considered key quality aspects. These aspects have been, to some extent, covered in government evaluations and have been recommended by DigitalGov [4]. The purpose of visiting a public website, in most cases, is to find specific information, to perform given actions, and/or apply for services provided by the government. Many municipal websites had a lot of information to present to citizens and the challenge was to organize this in a simple way. Managing this was a fine art in the sense that it requires knowledge of several important aspects of design as well as an understanding of users, technologies, information structures, and the purpose of the website. Criteria for success included organizational attention to providing great services for users through plans, goals, values, and strategies. In addition, websites and services should be solidly anchored throughout the organization, with a focus on accessibility and, for instance, service courts. Citizens should be able to get in touch with municipalities easily at any time. In addition, organizations should strive to obtain regular feedback from users and listen to their voice [26].

This study has been conducted in Norway and there are similarities between the Scandinavian countries in relation to evaluations of public websites. Also, regarding the content and type of services provided online. Although this study is limited to Norway, the findings may be relevant to countries beyond this. Public websites often have a lot of information presented and offer different digital self-service solutions, and they are lacking competitors. Knowledge of what is needed to satisfy the users and how organizations can facilitate quality and satisfaction is therefore a vital element in this. While this might vary across countries, there are a selection of universal guidelines, design principles, approaches and methods – that can be shared across borders and subject to discussion.

6 Conclusion

Based on the study results, the following concluding remarks can be made. Despite the public sector's long history and many years of experience of using the Web as a digital channel for interactions, there are large differences in website design within the public sector and no unified way of communicating with users. The Norwegian government has provided guidelines and best practices to communicate expectations and suggestions for quality improvements within the eGovernment context. Compared to some years ago, today, many municipalities have taken these into consideration. The effect of government quality assessment on organizational awareness and the quality of municipality websites has been positive and has influenced the appearance of websites today. Users prefer simple designs, but these should not be too minimal. Content and services should be visible but distinct from each other. Quick and easy access to information is preferable, especially using visible search fields and search engines that work optimally. Large differences in design need not be a problem, but users want specific design features in a domain with few or no competitors. It is critical that users are satisfied and can use the website in a satisfactory manner.

Further research could focus on how to perform this type of quality assessment in the future and what should be evaluated (for example, organizational values/benefits, design, content, user inclusion, and/or technical aspects). This should focus on the possibilities associated with new technologies, the digitization of services, and expectations among citizens. Another approach could be to include to what extent and how public sector websites differ from other business areas, in regard to online information- and digital services provided towards the citizens.

References

1. Moderniseringsdepartementet. https://www.regjeringen.no/globalassets/upload/fad/vedlegg/ikt-politikk/enorge_2009_komplett.pdf?id=2224951. Accessed 28 Feb 2019
2. Forbrukerrådet. https://www.forbrukerradet.no/vi-mener/en-kommune-kommunen-kommuner-alle-kommunene, Accessed 28 Feb 2019
3. Computerworld. http://www.cw.no/artikkel/offentlig-sektor/brukte-48-millioner-pa-nye-nettsider. Accessed 28 Feb 2019

4. DigitalGov. https://digital.gov/2014/12/31/the-best-e-gov-websites-in-the-world/. Accessed 07 Mar 2019
5. SSB. https://www.ssb.no/teknologi-og-innovasjon/statistikker/ikthus. Accessed 14 Mar 2019
6. Hughes, J., Ahluwalia, P., Midha, V.: A heuristic evaluation instrument for e-government online software. Electron. Gov. Int. J. 10(1), 1–18 (2013)
7. Ølnes, S., Jansen, A.: The muddy waters of e-services - the use and misuse of the concept and how to get out of the maze. In: Fallmyr, T., et al. (eds.) NOKOBIT 2012, Norsk konferanse for organisasjoners bruk av informasjonsteknologi, pp. 39–51 (2012)
8. Huang, Z., Benyouce, M.: Usability and credibility of e-government websites. Gov. Inf. Q. 31, 584–595 (2014)
9. Ferreira da Cruz, N., Tavares, A.F., Marques, R.C., Jorge, S., de Sousa, L.: Measuring local government transparency. Public Manag. Rev. 18(6), 866–893 (2016)
10. Interaction Design Foundation. The Basics of User Experience (UX) Design. Amazon Digital Services LLC (2018)
11. de Róiste, M.: Usability measures with real users address limitations of supply side benchmarking. Gov. Inf. Q. 30(4), 441–449 (2013)
12. Nielsen, J.: http://dockerby.com/web/Unit%206%20Validating/Usability%20101_%20Intro duction%20to%20Usability.pdf. Accessed 10 Mar 2019
13. ISO 9241-11: Ergonomic requirements for office work with visual display terminals (VDTs) - Part 11: Guidance on usability
14. Feeney, M.K., Brown, A.: Are small cities online? Content, ranking, and variation of U.S. municipal websites. Gov. Inf. Q. 34(1), 62–74 (2017)
15. Aleixo, C., Nunes, M., Isaias, P.: Usability and digital inclusion: standards and guidelines. Int. J. Public Adm. 35(3), 221–239 (2012)
16. Cumbie, B.A., Kar, B.: A study of local government website inclusiveness: the gap between e-government concept and practice. Inf. Technol. Dev. 22(1), 15–35 (2016)
17. Rasool, T., Warraich, N.F.: Does quality matter: a systematic review of information quality of e-government websites. In: Proceedings of the 11th International Conference on Theory and Practice of Electronic Governance, ICEGOV 2018, Galway, Ireland (2018)
18. Bødker, S., Christiansen, E., Nyvang, T., Zander, T.P.-O.: Personas, people and participation–challenges from the trenches of local government. In: Proceedings of the 12th Participatory Design Conference: Research Papers, Roskilde, Denmark, vol. 1, pp. 91–100 (2012)
19. Barnes, S.J., Vidgen, R.T.: Data triangulation and web quality metrics: a case study in e-government. Inf. Manag. 43, 767–777 (2006)
20. Lindgaard, G., Fernandes, G., Dudek, C., Brown, J.: Attention web designers: You have 50 milliseconds to make a good first impression! Behav. Inf. Technol. 25(2), 115–126 (2006)
21. Jansen, A., Ølnes, S.: Quality assessment and benchmarking of Norwegian public web sites. In: Proceedings of the 4th European Conference on E-Government, Dublin (2004)
22. Ølnes, S.: Accessibility of norwegian public web sites: state of the nation. In: Proceedings of 7th International Conference EGOV, Italy (2008)
23. Ølnes, S.: Small is beautiful or bigger is better? Size of municipalities and quality of websites. In: Proceedings of 13th European Conference on eGovernment, ECEG (2013)
24. Difi. https://www.difi.no/nyhet/2017/07/resultata-fra-kvalitet-pa-nett-2016. Accessed 01 Mar 2019
25. Forbrukerrådet. https://www.forbrukerradet.no/siste-nytt/asker-kommune-beste-i-landet/. Accessed 01 Mar 2019
26. Forbrukerrådet. https://www.forbrukerradet.no/vi-mener/2015/fpa-offentlig-2015/slik-jobber-komm unene-som-gir-best-service/. Accessed 01 Mar 2019

Crowdsourcing Urban Issues in Smart Cities: A Usability Assessment of the Crowd4City System

Ana Gabrielle Ramos Falcão[1], Pedro Farias Wanderley[1],
Tiago Henrique da Silva Leite[1], Cláudio de Souza Baptista[1(✉)],
José Eustáquio Rangel de Queiroz[1], Maxwell Guimarães de Oliveira[2],
and Júlio Henrique Rocha[1]

[1] Information Systems Laboratory, Federal University of Campina Grande,
Campina Grande, Brazil
{anagabrielle,tiagohenrique,juliorocha}@copin.ufcg.edu.br,
{baptista,rangel}@dsc.ufcg.edu.br, pedro.wanderley@ccc.ufcg.edu.br
[2] Centre of Science and Technology, Federal University of Cariri,
Juazeiro do Norte, Brazil
maxwell.oliveira@ufca.edu.br

Abstract. Geosocial networks gather large amounts of voluntarily generated information that can be explored in different contexts, including urban areas. In this sense, we developed the Crowd4City system, which puts together city authorities and citizens focusing on the improvement of their urban spaces. In order to ensure the effectiveness of our proposal, we carried out a usability assessment following the ISO 9241, which covers ergonomics of human-computer interaction. For such, this paper describes a case study using Crow4City in a 3-stage evaluation, involving human volunteers, pre-defined tasks, survey analysis and conformity analysis. The statistical indicators show the usability levels which are useful in the analysis of the user's challenge and motivation on using such a system.

Keywords: Crowdsourcing · Smart cities · Data reliability ·
Geosocial networks · Urban issues

1 Introduction

With the dissemination of social networks among millions of citizens and the evolution and easy access to GPS-enabled devices, location-based social networks (LBSNs), or geosocial networks, have attracted more attention and new followers every day. Geosocial networks, as described by Vicente et al. [1], "provide context aware services that help associate location with users and content (...) and offer different types of services, including photo sharing, friend tracking and 'checkins''. Within this relatively new kind of social network, a large amount

© Springer Nature Switzerland AG 2019
A. Kő et al. (Eds.): EGOVIS 2019, LNCS 11709, pp. 147–159, 2019.
https://doi.org/10.1007/978-3-030-27523-5_11

of voluntarily generated information can be found, including Volunteered Geo-graphical Information (VGI) [2]. Thus, geographical information can be explored in several ways and used in various scenarios.

The world population and the density of urban areas are increasing very rapidly, creating new city management challenges for government entities. The availability of some of the most basic resources – such as clean water, electricity and sanitation – may be in jeopardy, and part of the population suffers from the use of inefficient planning techniques by the local authorities. The techniques already employed have become obsolete as the form and function of urban spaces have become more dynamic [3]. Another problem that has increased with the growth of the population is the deterioration of the environment. Pollution, deforestation, and the disturbance of the regular climate conditions affect the fauna and flora as well as humans' quality of life. As a result, both citizens and authoritative bodies have become more interested in finding solutions to such problems aiming at providing a better quality of life for citizens and take better care of nature and the environment in general.

With these concerns in mind, we aimed to create a system in which citizens could participate more actively in the management of their city. This system enables an exposition of the problems citizens encounter in their city that do not necessarily receive adequate attention from authorities. Users may also use such a system to make suggestions they believe would improve their quality of life and demand explanations of why, for example, a public work (in which their tax money should be spent) is taking so long to complete. To increase usability and provide other features, most activities on the system are conducted using a dynamic map, providing geographical information as submitted by citizens; the spatial dimension is inherent to the system. We also propose the use of the geo-graphical information more extensively, in favor of the visualization and analysis of the displayed information, enabling more personalized and complex searches as well. In this way, authorities will be able to better understand the city's needs. Consequently, it is possible to achieve better planning techniques and provide improved services. Additionally, the resources are used more efficiently, balancing costs and reducing the environmental impact.

A new trend in systems that rely on user interaction is to provide better usability and a better user experience, since it is a key factor in conquering the users as active and helpful sources of information. Basiri et al. [4] and Holm and Laurila [5] highlight that, nowadays, not only the system's efficiency is impor-tant, but also good usability is necessary for user adherence. In geosocial net-works, usability has even more importance, once motivated users are necessary in order to keep the network useful.

Faced with this challenge, this paper describes a usability assessment of the Crowd4City system in a three-stage evaluation approach which combines the monitoring of human volunteers performing predefined tasks, survey applica-tion in order to analyse user profiles and experiences on the system. Finally, a conformity analysis according to ISO 9241 was conducted, which standardizes ergonomic criteria of human-computer interaction. Therefore, the scope of this paper comprises: the presentation of the Crowd4City system's architecture and main features; the description of the approach used for the usability assessment of geosocial networks; and a discussion regarding the results from a case study using Crowd4City in order to evaluate its overall usability indicators.

The remainder of this paper is structured as follows. Section 2 discusses related work. Section 3 addresses the Crowd4City geosocial network and its main features. Section 4 describes the usability assessment in details. Finally, Sect. 5 concludes the paper and highlights further work to be undertaken.

2   Related Work

Recently, frameworks for participatory sensing and retrieval of relevant information using the crowd intelligence have been more explored and have drawn more attention from the community, mainly due to the natural increase in the number of devices (specially mobile ones) that are enabled to gather specialized data (including spatial information) and allow the composition of personalized information [6]. Relating the community to urban planning and geospatial data, Luo, Wei [22] proposed a framework based on three aspects: social, spatial and semantic, where all are interconnected. Doing so, social relations, guided by spatial data related with semantic context, opened a range of research opportunities in the urban context, and are inherent to the study of cities and urban spaces.

The relevance of the information produced by active users of mobile devices such as smartphones and tablets was confirmed by Zhang et al. [7], who studied participatory systems applied on applications for concurrent event monitoring. Guo et al. [8] highlighted interesting approaches regarding studies, technologies, applications and issues when introduced the concept of participatory sensing. As another example of the application of the users' mobile data, Sang et al. [9] explored their check-in data (considering the user context) and developed an algorithm for personalized POI recommendation.

Nowadays we can find a good number of research work and frameworks related to the use of geosocial networks, such as tools enabling the participation of citizens in their city's management. In this regard, we can cite Wikicrimes [10], a LBSN in which users are able to perform crime reports, pointing places where they were, for instance, pickpocketed or where they witnessed armed robberies. Wikicrimes, however, was developed to function only within the security context and is not extendable to other scenarios or settings. Wandhofer et al. [11] and Xia et al. [12] used known social platforms as datasources, the former resulting in the WeGov platform. WeGov [11] was built to enable the connection between citizens and government representatives by retrieving relevant data from consolidated social networks, thus exploring their potential for policy making. Such information is displayed in a map available in their web page, however the map is solely for visualization and there is no further exploration. Spatial queries could have been used to explore the geographic information and relevant knowledge could be derived.

Baykurt [13] performed studies on FixMyStreet[1], a platform implemented and used in the United Kingdom, and could observe that tools that enable citizen engagement in helping improve public services bring to the attention technical and political issues. This way, he concluded that technology should be guided by the civic values, so that the public can be empowered and communities may be improved. Also aiming civic engagement, Hasegawa et al. [21] proposed MyCityForecast[2], an urban planning tool that aims at "what is to come", as it provides information about the future of cities, to generate social awareness and facilitate communication with urban planners. Interestingly, the results obtained, such as changes in urban management habits, are generated by the tool itself, making it easier to obtain conclusions about its effectiveness.

One challenge in these geosocial network initiatives is related to usability. Most of the current geosocial networks do not evaluate usability aspects by listening their users or either monitoring the users behaviours. In addition, the spatial industry does not have a ratings approach for data quality and usability [14]. Usability problems may demotivate users on interacting with such networks. As the number of active users decreases, the network dies, becoming a useless and outdated place. However, there are some approaches which address usability in geosocial networks.

Basiri et al. [4] performed a study on the challenges, requirements and usability of the current location based services', which are key elements that may directly impact in their applications' penetration into the user market. Focusing on indoor Location Based Service (LBS) applications, the authors conducted surveys and considered five categories for the assessment of current technologies' usability: Indoor navigation and tracking; Marketing; Entertainment; Location-based information retrieval; and Emergency and security applications. Moreover, the authors highlight the importance of a geosocial network being easy to use.

Yang et al. [15] proposed the NationTelescope platform, which collects, summarizes and integrates user data from geosocial networks in an interactive map interface for visualization. In a purpose similar to ours in this paper, the authors performed an evaluation of their system's usability using a usability scale survey applied to 18 participants. The System Usability Scale (SUS) survey could attest the platforms good usability and user experience.

Holm and Laurila [5] discussed the importance of usefulness, usability and user experience in a Location Based application developer company. They noted that the emphasis in such applications moved from usefulness to user experience, being one of the most important characteristics in systems relying on user interaction. The authors reviewed the concepts and main topics on usability and user experience, and used the ActionTrack platform as a case study. They performed tests with the company's employees and children of various ages using the system and also experienced with simple paper prototypes which is a valid usability testing tool. However, they did not use surveys in their evaluation.

---

[1] http://www.fixmystreet.com.
[2] https://mycityforecast.net/.

As it could be noticed, usability assessment can be performed mainly by monitoring the user experience and applying surveys. Our work fits with the Yang et al. [15] work since we also developed a platform and we are concerned about user usability. However, we could take more participants in our evaluation and use more than the survey approach, including user behaviour monitoring, user profile analysis, and usability aspects based on ISO 9241. Thus, we develop a more embracing approach for usability assessment.

Such usability assessment techniques are very important in order to validate the systems, once tools with a great potential for changing citizen's quality of life may go into disuse or not live up to their potential if they are not concerned with how the users will be able to interact with them.

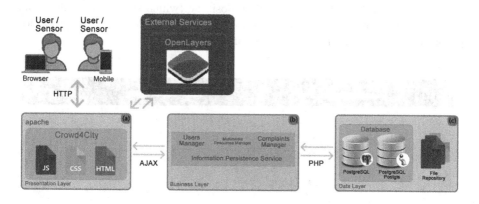

Fig. 1. Architectural project of the Crowd4City system.

3   The Crowd4City System

We developed the Crowd4City system, a geosocial network generated to provide an environment in which citizens could participate more actively in their city's management. The Crowd4City users can share many kinds of urban issues such as locations with high crime rates, places where traffic jams occur frequently, pavement defects, poor lighting, among others.

The information concerning urban issues and complaints are shared publicly by the users and may receive more attention from the authorities and other citizens in the network. Using such data, we intend to validate the effectiveness of using humans as sensors in a smart city context, as stated by Naphade et al. [16].

The Crowd4City system was modelled using the Model-View-Controller architectural pattern (MVC), dividing the application into three interconnected layers, as displayed in Fig. 1.

The user accesses the system via a web browser (whether from a desktop or mobile device), which runs the HTML pages that compose the graphical interface, included into the presentation layer (Fig. 1a). The View layer contains the elements that are displayed for the final users and that can be used by such users (*citizens*) to share information. Apart from HTML pages, the graphical interface also uses scripts written in JavaScript to access the external services of OpenLayers[3] to display the maps and retrieve the geographical information of locations of interest, these spatial data is provided by OpenStreetMaps[4].

The second layer - Controller (Fig. 1b) is responsible for processing the user requests and the system business logic. It is composed of four modules: the user manager; the multimedia resources manager; the complaints manager; and the information persistence service.

Finally, the model layer (Fig. 1c) comprises all the information stored and processed by the system. It consists of a PostgreSQL[5] database (which stores the system's data and interactions); a file repository (which stores the multimedia files); and a geographic information repository with the PostGIS[6] extension for proper management and manipulation of spatial data.

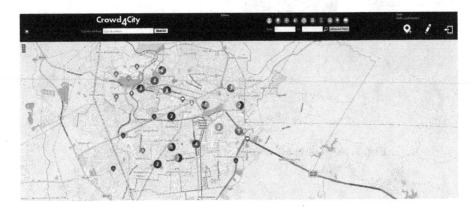

Fig. 2. The Crowd4City's main interface.

As said before, the Crowd4City system (shown in Fig. 2) is an environment in which citizens can voice their dissatisfaction, complaints or suggestions concerning their city. There are two ways a user can create markers (to record complaints) on the system, however both require registration. The users may either sign up filling in a form with all their information and have their name displayed along with the information they submit; or register with an anonymous profile. After logging on Crowd4City, the users may create points, lines or even polygons to represent the city's area associated with the information submitted. This way, they can easily represent precise locations, routes/streets and

---

[3] https://openlayers.org/.
[4] https://www.openstreetmap.org.
[5] https://www.postgresql.org/.
[6] http://postgis.net/.

areas/neighbourhoods which better correspond to the complaint and the system can leverage from the geographic information. Besides the location, the markers must have a title (which briefly summarizes the information) and a description with more detail, and optionally may contain multimedia files such as videos or pictures. In order to enable users' engagement with the submitted information, each marker has buttons for others to "like/dislike" and show their appreciation or discontent with the content. Figure 3 shows an example of the visualization of an urban issue reported in the system, in which a pothole on a street is being reported.

Crowd4City contains nine pre-defined categories (Education, Health, Noise Pollution, Rubbish, Security, Streets and Roads, Transportation) for marker creation, however the user may opt to select the "Other" category to define a new context.

Fig. 3. A pothole complaint shared on the Crowd4City.

We adopted the OpenLayers API in Crowd4City's interface aiming at leveraging from the already available map-driven operations such as pan, zoom and vector/raster data views, and consequently enabling users to explore the city on the social network by using GIS capabilities. In order to bypass the problems emerged with polluted interface once the system is populated with huge volume of information, we created clusters by extending the OpenLayers clustered features and overlay view interface.

A sample marker cluster is shown in Fig. 4. Marker clusters are pie charts which group a number of complaints relatively close to each other in a geographical area. These charts are coloured with the relevant colors from the different complaint categories found in the grouped complaints. The total number of grouped complaints is shown in the middle of the marker cluster. For instance, in the example from Fig. 4, the marker cluster is grouping: two complaints related to transportation issues; and one complaint about street-related issues.

Crowd4City also provides different filters for content exploring. Category and time filters are displayed on top of the main page (top of Fig. 2) and content and spatial filters can be accessed via the "Advanced Filters" button. Using spatial filters we can highlight the buffer and contains spatial functions provided for marker filtering, which can be combined with different Points of Interest (POIs) retrieved from the OpenStreetMap database. For instance, users may search for security complaints within a 200-meter radius from their houses. It is important to note that all filters are cumulative, which enable users to search for more personalized content.

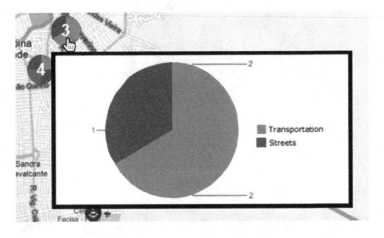

Fig. 4. A sample marker cluster grouping three complaints.

4   Usability Assessment

In order to assess the Crowd4City's usability, we performed an evaluation consisting of three stages. In the first stage, an experiment was carried out with a group of selected volunteers who were asked to use the Crowd4City system by performing a set of predefined tasks – such volunteers were residents of the city

Campina Grande. The second stage consisted of analyzing two surveys answered by the volunteers regarding the system: one applied immediately before performing the tasks in the system (*pre-test*) and other afterwards (*post-test*). Finally, in the third and last stage, we performed a conformity analysis of the Crowd4City system according to the standards defined in ISO 9241, parts 14 [17], 16 [18] and 17 (revised by part 143) [19]. One definition of usability described in ISO 9241 is "the extent to which a system, product or service can be used by specified users to achieve specified goals with effectiveness, efficiency and satisfaction in a specified context of use".

In the experiment (*stage 1*), we were able to recruit 30 volunteer users, consisting of 5 women and 25 men of ages varying from 18 to 35. We developed a script with 6 common tasks of Crowd4City (such as user registration, writing and sharing new complaints, searching and filtering information, among others) and asked the volunteers to perform them on the system. We also recorded the volunteers' activity with a screencasting tool and webcams. Then, we could analyse their actions, facial expressions and reactions to the system's responses without any interference. At this stage, the volunteers were submitted to answer two surveys in order to record useful information regarding their profiles before and after using the system.

The first survey (*pre-test*) was applied before starting the predefined tasks in the Crowd4City in order to enable to assess the volunteers profile and their previous knowledge regarding this type of system. The second survey (*post-test*) was applied after performing the tasks in order to enable to assess the volunteers experience and satisfaction with the Crowd4City. While the pre-test survey was composed of objective questions regarding the user profile and knowledge regarding geosocial networks, the post-test survey was composed of three sections, containing the following items: "The product's use and navigation", "Documentation" and "You and the product". The post-test survey adopts the model proposed by Bailey and Pearson [20] for measuring the overall users sense of satisfaction. The questions were structured according to a Likert scale with five levels of agreement/disagreement, including one option for non-applicability or a neutral instance.

According to the analysis of the volunteers' answers (*stage 2*), we could observe that more than half of them consider Crowd4City a system easy to use and to conclude the tasks, being also easy to read – although 26% of them classified such aspect as moderate. Concerning the instructions and warning messages shown, the results indicate that the users were not comfortable with the system's messages. However, 78% of the users informed that the actions sequence flow for the accomplishment of the required tasks was easy to understand.

Regarding users' behavior concerning error recovery and error messages comprehension, we could note that it was mostly (about 54%) classified as "neither easy nor hard", which means that the errors and their messages were not as clear as expected. Nonetheless, we could notice that none of the occurred errors interfered with the conclusion of the tasks, according to the video analysis from the experiment. Concerning the users' expectations, Crowd4City satisfied 85%

of the users, which represents a high acceptance of the tool and implies on the recommendation rates, which was almost 100%. Lastly, the volunteers classified Crowd4City as objective and easy to use, when comparing the tool with other similar ones. According to the Bailey and Pearson's model [20], the normalized value ranges of user satisfaction concerning a product can be: 0.67 to 1.00 (Extremely Satisfied), 0.33 to 0.66 (Very satisfied), 0.01 to 0.32 (Fairly satisfied), 0.00 (Neither satisfied nor unsatisfied), −0.01 to −0.32 (Fairly dissatisfied), −0.33 to −0.66 (Very dissatisfied), or −0.67 to −1.00 (Extremely dissatisfied). Based on such model, the Crowd4City volunteer users' subjective satisfaction indicator were 0.520, which means the users were classified as "Very Satisfied".

The third and last stage of this evaluation consisted of a conformity analysis of the Crowd4City based on ISO 9241. Once ISO 9241 is huge and involves many ergonomic aspects in the human-computer interaction, we focused on parts 14, 16 and 17 revised, since these parts deal with usability aspects of software. While parts 14 and 16 deal with general usability aspects of any kind of software, we could notice that part 17 revised contains a number of recommendations related to geosocial networks. The ISO 9241 recommends that the inspection results are summarized from an indicator called *Adherence Rate* (*AR*) defined as the rate of the number of recommendations adopted by the product satisfactorily judged by the number of recommendations deemed applicable to the project context.

We analysed the parts 14, 16 and 17 of the ISO 9241 in order to identify the recommendations deemed applicable to Crowd4City in each part. The number of such recommendations is denoted by *Ar* (Applicable recommendations). We then counted, from these identified recommendations, which ones Crowd4City successfully fulfill. The number of these satisfied recommendations is denoted by *Sar* (Successfully adhered recommendations).

Finally, we calculated the percentage for the Adherence Rate *AR* in each one of the three parts of ISO 9241 considered in this study, according to Eq. 1.

$$AR = \frac{Sar}{Ar} \times 100 \qquad (1)$$

Table 1 summarizes the computed adherence rates and its respective applicable and successfully adhered recommendations, analyzed in the conformity analysis of the Crowd4City based on the parts of ISO 9241.

Table 1. Standard conformity assessment of Crowd4City

Standard	Ar	Sar	AR (%)
ISO 9241 Part 14	38	31	81.57
ISO 9241 Part 16	38	31	81.57
ISO 9241 Part 17	59	45	76.27

In Table 1 it is possible to notice that the average values observed for the three conformity standards analyzed is about 80%. This fact indicates that the

Crowd4City presents acceptable usability conditions and that future improvements would not critically affect the system's usability.

The result from the analysis of the data gathered during the experiment concerning user performance and having analyzed the list of problems found with this technique, it was possible to evaluate their impact as: minor (70%), medium (30%), major (0%); and classify them as: consistent (50%), recurrent (50%), and general (0%); which again proves Crowd4City's acceptable usability.

The importance of such usability assessment is to confirm the Crowd4City's usability and, thus, its value and potential for actual use and impact on the society, making it possible for the citizen's to use all os its available features.

5   Conclusion

Our geosocial network system was evaluated in a democracy participation context with the aim of helping authorities better manage cities. This system provides a helpful way for citizens to improve their living conditions, allowing their demands to receive more attention from the authorities and media. As a contribution of our work, the Crowd4City system provides the necessary tools for the users to indicate the features they are unhappy with by using a map, allowing them to save points, lines and polygons, and providing several filters, including the spatial ones. Such combination of features are on top of other similar systems previously developed.

In order to validate our proposal, we performed a usability evaluation in three steps: using a group of volunteers to perform predefined tasks to analyze their behavior; applying pre-test and post-test surveys; and performing a conformity analysis according to standards defined in ISO 9241. From such evaluation, we could notice that the Crowd4City system was considered a system easy to use and to conclude tasks. According to ISO 9241, the average values observed for the conformity standards is about 80%, which indicates acceptable usability conditions.

In future work, we intend to retrieve information for Crowd4City from more widely used social networks, such as Facebook and Twitter, in order to obtain even more data and provide the convenience of not requiring users to move to another environment or system. The social networks these users use in everyday life are likely to represent more friendly atmospheres for them. This may consequently inspire them to contribute more actively. Additionally, the information they input may receive more attention because their peers will not need to leave their comfort zone either.

We also plan to attach external data sources to our LBSN, including non-governmental organizations (NGOs), reliable means of communication (e.g., digital newspapers) and possibly government sectors representatives, to contribute to the content generation and to help shaping more concrete content.

Acknowledgments. The authors would like to thank the CNPq - Brazilian Research Council for funding this research under the grant 428295/2016-9.

References

1. Vicente, C.R., Freni, D., Bettini, C., Jensen, C.S.: Location-related privacy in geo-social networks. IEEE Internet Comput. **15**(3), 20–27 (2011)
2. Goodchild, M.F.: Citizens as voluntary sensors: spatial data infrastructure in the world of Web 2.0. Int. J. Spatial Data Infrastructures Res. **2**, 24–32 (2007)
3. Crooks, A., et al.: Crowdsourcing urban form and function. Int. J. Geogr. Inf. Sci. **29**(5), 720–741 (2015)
4. Basiri, A., et al.: Indoor location based services challenges, requirements and usability of current solutions. Comput. Sci. Rev. **24**(Suppl.), 1–12 (2017)
5. Holm, J., Laurila, K.: Towards action track 3.0: the role of usefulness, usability, and user experience in a startup company developing location-based applications. In: 19th International Conference on Information Visualisation, July 2015, pp. 245–254. IEEE, Barcelona (2015)
6. Guo, B., Yu, Z., Zhou, X., Zhang, D.: From participatory sensing to mobile crowd sensing. In: Proceedings of the IEEE International Conference on Pervasive Computing and Communication Workshops, March 2014, pp. 593–598. IEEE, Budapest (2014)
7. Zhang, B., Song, Z., Liu, C.H., Ma, J., Wang, W.: An event-driven QoI-aware participatory sensing framework with energy and budget constraints. ACM Trans. Intell. Syst. Technol. **6**(3), 42:1–42:19 (2015)
8. Guo, B., Chin, A., Yu, Z., Huang, R., Zhang, D.: An introduction to the special issue on participatory sensing and crowd intelligence. ACM Trans. Intell. Syst. Technol. **6**(3), 36:1–36:4 (2015)
9. Sang, J., Mei, T., Xu, C.: Activity sensor: check-in usage mining for local recommendation. ACM Trans. Intell. Syst. Technol. **6**(3), 41:1–41:24 (2015)
10. Furtado, V., et al.: Collective intelligence in law enforcement - the wikicrimes system. Inf. Sci. **180**(1), 4–17 (2010)
11. Wandhofer, T., van Eeckhaute, C., Taylor, S., Fernandez, M.: WeGov analysis tools to connect policy makers with citizens online. In: Proceedings of the tGovernment Workshop, United Kingdom (2012)
12. Xia, C., et al.: CityBeat: real-time social media visualization of hyper-local city data. In: Proceedings of the ACM International Conference on World Wide Web, pp. 167–170. ACM, New York (2014)
13. Baykurt, B.: Redefining citizenship and civic engagement: political values embodied in FixMyStreet.com. AoIR Selected Papers of Internet Research 1 (2012)
14. Arnold, L.: Improving spatial data supply chains: learnings from the manufacturing industry. In: Proceedings of the Eighth International Conference on Advanced Geographic Information Systems, Applications, and Services (GeoProcessing), pp. 137–145. IARIA, Venice, Italy (2016)
15. Yang, D., Zhang, D., Chen, L., Qu, B.: Nationtelescope: monitoring and visualizing large-scale collective behavior in LBSNs. J. Netw. Comput. Appl. **55**(Supplement), 170–180 (2015)
16. Naphade, M., Banavar, G., Harrison, C., Paraszczak, J., Morris, R.: Smarter cities and their innovation challenges. Computer **44**(6), 32–39 (2011)
17. ISO9241-14: Ergonomic requirements for office work with visual display terminals (VDTs) - Part 14: Menu dialogues. International Organization for Standardization. Geneva, CH, Standard (1997)
18. ISO9241-16: Ergonomic requirements for office work with visual display terminals (VDTs) - Part 16: Direct manipulation dialogues. International Organization for Standardization, Geneva, CH, Standard (1999)

19. ISO9241-143: Ergonomics of human-system interaction - Part 143: Forms (Review of ISO9241-17). International Organization for Standardization, Geneva, CH, Standard (2012)
20. Bailey, J., Pearson, S.: Development of a tool for measurement and analyzing computer user satisfaction. Manag. Sci. **29**(5), 530–575 (1983)
21. Hasegawa, Y., Sekimoto, Y., Seto, T., Fukushima, Y., Maeda, M.: My city forecast: urban planning communication tool for citizen with national open data. Comput. Environ. Urban Syst. (2018, in Press). Corrected Proof. https://doi.org/10.1016/j.compenvurbsys.2018.06.001
22. Luo, W., Wang, Y., Liu, X., Gao, S.: Towards a spatio-socio-semantic analysis framework. Cities Spatial Soc. Netw. **1**, 21–37 (2019)

e-Government Theoretical Background

Value Innovation in the Public Sector: Concept, Determining Factors and Framework

Teresa Cristina Monteiro Martins[1] (ID), André Luiz Zambalde[2] (ID),
André Grützmann[2](✉) (ID), Paulo Henrique de Souza Bermejo[3] (ID),
Everton Leonardo de Almeida[1] (ID),
and Thaísa Barcellos Pinheiro do Nascimento[1] (ID)

[1] Departamento de Administração e Economia, UFLA, Lavras, Brazil
teresacristina@ufla.br, evtufla@gmail.com,
thaisapinheiro35@gmail.com
[2] Departamento de Ciência da Computação, UFLA, Lavras, Brazil
zambaufla@gmail.com, andregrutzmann@gmail.com
[3] Departamento de Administração e Economia, UNB, Brasília, Brazil
paulobermejo@next.unb.br

Abstract. The literature is imprecise about how much new method and technologies used by public organizations could promote effective transformations for citizens. Value innovation is the keystone of the Blue Ocean Strategy for creating new markets by private organizations. And in the public context, what could considerate a value innovation for citizens? This systematic literature review proposed the concept of value innovation in the public sector and framework radar about the value innovation in the public sector. This model has on four dimensions: openness, quality, efficiency and effectiveness; and sixteen factors: openness, usability, accessibility, attractiveness, quality, utility, speed, satisfaction, efficiency, processes, costs, compliance, effectiveness, trust, engagement and social impact. In this context, this framework can support for analyzing and discussing the value generation of "innovation" programs.

Keywords: Public value · Systematic review · Value innovation · Blue Ocean

1 Introduction

The applications of Information and Communication Technologies (ICTs) in the public sector are responsible for generating innovations in public policies and processes. However, governments have invested millions in initiatives involving technologies and innovation without concrete results in terms of the value for the potential beneficiaries of these initiatives, the citizens, and society [1].

Although the literature shows that new technologies have spawned innovations in the public sector, those are incremental improvements - basically, faster processes execution and broader audience reach. There is imprecision about the existence of substantial changes in the public institutions' policies and services. It means that citizens cannot immediately recognize value innovation [2].

© Springer Nature Switzerland AG 2019
A. Kő et al. (Eds.): EGOVIS 2019, LNCS 11709, pp. 163–175, 2019.
https://doi.org/10.1007/978-3-030-27523-5_12

The term value innovation is used in the private sector as a critical element to simultaneously achieve differentiation and low cost, creating a value leap for both clients and organizations [3–5]. This concept pertains to the Blue Ocean Strategy (BOS) and consists of streamlining business aspects through product or service costs reduction while simultaneously identifying new value for customers. This strategy aims to deal with increasing costs creating a new competition-free market [3–5].

In the public sector, value innovation has already been used to describe strategies to redefine social problems for proposing innovative solutions. However, there is little evidence of its applicability.

A concept redefinition or better understanding may be necessary to go beyond the limited vision of efficiency and effectiveness indicators in private organizations. It is about acting considering the society needs, desires, interests, and demands. Those actions require novel techniques and technologies to cope with citizens' values, gathering engagement, and participation besides existing public policies and services. Some questions emerged as drivers for this work: What is value innovation in the public sector? What are the determinants of value innovation in the public sector?

This work aims to conceptualize public sector value innovation and to identify the determinants of this innovative approach. Grounded on value innovation theory [1] plus a systematic literature review the goals are: (i) Define the value innovation concept considering its application in the public sector; (ii) Identify and describe dimensions and determinants of value innovation in the public sector, and (iii) Propose a theoretical evaluation model to value innovation analysis in the public sector.

In the practitioner perspective, this work proposes a preliminary value innovation determinants and a structural model. Those elements can help public agents to develop strategies and assess actions, activities, and processes, aiming for innovation.

The following section presents the theoretical background for this work. The methodology explains the systematic literature review steps and radar proposition. The results section demonstrates the determining factors and value innovation model for the public sector. The final part of this paper was devoted to the conclusions and suggestions of the use of the proposed model.

2 Value Innovation

Value Innovation means the leap of value identified both for buyers and for the company that simultaneously manages differentiated and cost-effective products and services [3–5]. Value innovation is the central concept of the so-called BOS, a methodology proposed by the authors, in which they teach how to rethink an organization's business to generate new demands and create space in a competition-free market.

The authors considered that the value to the buyers of a product or service comes from the utility of the offer less its price, while the value to the organizations comes from the price of the offer minus its cost. Thus, we achieve value innovation when the entire utility, price, and cost system is aligned. For this alignment to occur, the authors propose the reduction of factors that are not main for the buyers and the increase of the elements that this sector never offered, but that could represent a value leap for the buyers [3–5].

According to the authors, the term 'value' differentiates the concept of techno-logical innovation, which is neither a prerequisite for value innovation nor a conse-quence of it [3–5]. Five dimensions characterize value innovation: (i) Assumptions of the sector, (ii) Strategic focus, (iii) Customers, (iv) Assets and capacities, and (v) Product and service offers. The strategic steps for aggregating value through these five dimensions are part of the Blue Ocean Strategy, and one of the decisive steps in the process for offering products and services to create new value demands [3–5].

As a result of the analysis of what is eliminated and reduced and what is raised or created for created the value innovation. Thus, to achieve value, change is needed differentiation and low cost. The first step consists in to identify the factors that determine real and most important benefits for the buyers and raised or created. Moreover, the second step includes in to eliminate or reduce indifferent factors to the buyer, which are not the main reason in their choice to use the service or product.

2.1 Value Innovation in the Public Sector

In the public sector, the BOS, and more precisely, the value innovation theory, has been applied mainly for the development of innovative projects that have an impact on public goods in different areas of government activity.

The first cases of BOS on the Public Sector are about the problem of overcrowding in prisons and high rates of criminal recidivism in California - USA and Malaysia. The governments of these countries overcoming the traditional assumption that all criminals need to keep in prisons. These countries development of recovery centers for small offenders, using barren military lands to house the prisoners, empowering them to raise fish and agricultural production and generate income so they can collaborate with their families and have an alternative to crime [3–5].

In health, BOS was used to propose alternative ways to treat diseases [6]. In the United Kingdom [7] and India, the concept of value innovation has been used to modify the thinking of public administrators, aiming at valuing changes that generate direct benefits to users of services and the reduction of costs by the State. In the education sector, the strategy was used to create an innovative game applicable to public schools, contributing to the quality of public education [8]. Also in the area of education in Malaysia, BOS has been used in universities, either for specific topics such as the libraries modernization [9] or for general issues such as academic gover-nance [10].

In the area of public transport, BOS was used to classify as innovative the strategy to implement a new type of traffic in South Africa [11]. Also, value innovation has been pointed out as the desired result of smart city projects. Thus, the theme of smart cities, also emerging, has been related to BOS [12].

Therefore, value innovation is a desirable result in specific government projects, to generate benefits and reduce costs. However, there is a gap about how much public institution's costs reduce and about what direct profits the governments can create in terms of value for the society.

3   Public Value and Value Innovation

There is a significant difference in the application of innovation and strategy techniques to the public and private sectors since the general context also involves aspects of social and political theory, more complicated conflicts of interest and, mainly, the subjectivity of having the final objective the public good. Despite these significant peculiarities, the public sector tends to import from the private sector concepts and management techniques to innovate its structure and processes.

The innovation of the public sector may be of something new, to introduce a new practice or process, to create a new product (public welfare, public policy or service), adopting new patterns of relationship. Be constituted as the use of something entirely new for a particular place, although it has already been applied elsewhere, and causes a discontinuous or gradual change [13].

Thus, although the definitions are very close to those found in the literature on innovation in the private sector, it is essential to highlight the fact that public sector strategies may differ from those of the private sector. The main difference is because they are driven by the primary objective of creating public value, while the latter aim at the creation of individual value.

In its most common definition, public value is a framework with improved ways to understand what a particular "public" considers to be valuable [14]. Public value can be produced by governmental organizations, private companies, non-profit organizations or other organizations when their management practices guarantee the best possible cohesion between the real results and the expectations of citizens, consumers of these practices [15].

Authors who study the transformational power of the use of technologies in the public sector, for example, argue that the collaboration between citizens and public authority provided by ICTs has built a new paradigm in which it proposes to innovate by focusing on the concrete social and political results of the actions of the TICs. Thus, a new innovative reform would go through the valuation of the concept of public value, which goes beyond the indicators of efficiency and effectiveness of a public management to consider also the measurement of the public good with the improvement of the tools to understand what a particular public.

In this way, measuring the increase in value added in the context of the public sector is more complicated than estimating the rise in value for a buyer, because citizens are not merely clients of public policies. Finally, rather than valuing the strategies that bring them direct benefits, citizens also value universal principles such as equality, justice, and the environment [15]. Therefore, a value innovation in the public sector consists of the creation of strategies and new practices capable of achieving high social impact at low cost.

The public value literature presents some categorizations for organizing these values. Specifically, Jorgensen's work [16] lists a greater variety of public values and ranks them into seven categories:

(a) Public sector's contribution to society, such as common good and altruism;
(b) conversion of civil interests to decisions, such as legitimacy and democracy;

(c) relationship between public administrators and politicians, such as political loyalty and responsibility;

(d) relationship between public administrators and the environment, such as openness-secrecy and neutrality;

(e) intraorganizational aspects of public administration, such as robustness and productivity;

(f) the behavior of public employees, such as professionalism and honesty; and

(g) relationship among government and citizens, such as Legality and equity.

This classification raises some questions because it involves abstract values as well as different actors such as politicians, civil servants, and citizens [2], but being perhaps the most comprehensive list of values sought by the public sector is also one of the most cited classifications for directing the search for characteristics that both citizens and institutions identify as valuable in a society-driven project.

4 Research Method

The present research is applied, exploratory-descriptive, and qualitative research through systematic literature review procedures.

The first objective was to substantiate the concept of value innovation, comprising what citizens and public sector institutions identify as value. Next, we recognize the Critical Success Factors (CSF) for value innovation in the public sector. CSF are commonly used in the management literature to represent areas that must be prioritized so that a given organization achieves the best results or achieves success. A survey was carried out on articles on CSF in public sector innovation projects. Subsequently, these factors were grouped into the categories of the value innovation concept [22], to identify which public values considered a priority for the public institution to achieve excellent results in its innovation projects.

The systematic review of the literature was performed from July to August 2018, using the following keywords: "critical success factors" AND ("public value" OR "governance" OR "public sector"). Scopus databases (which returned 55 articles) and Web of Science (50 articles) consulted. Duplications were eliminated resulting in 98 articles, which were filtered to include only those with the availability of the full text and that deal with the subjects public value and critical success factors in the Public sector, resulting in 55 articles. Of these 55 articles were extracted the critical success factors for value innovation in the public sector.

To associate these factors with the concept of public value, the factors were separated between the areas or categories of impact of the factors [21], i.e.: Which of the following areas will be impacted from the improvement of this factor: (i) contribution of the public sector with society (such as social impact); (ii) transformation of public interests into decisions (legitimacy); (iii) relationship between public and political administrators (integration); (iv) citizens' relationship with the public environment (accessibility); (v) intra-organizational aspects of public administration (efficiency, effectiveness and cost); (vi) the behavior of public employees (receptivity, quality, treatment); and (vii) the relationship between public administration and citizens (interaction, effectiveness of results).

Finally, in order to relate such factors to the concept of value innovation (Blue Ocean Theory), they were grouped according to the following criteria: Which CSF collaborate to aggregate value to: (a) the institutions; and (b) citizens; and which CSF collaborate to reduce costs for (c) the institutions; (d) citizens. The factors present in the two categorizations make up the innovation model of value for the public sector proposed in this research.

In addition to the factors, we have presented cases found in the literature on the use of the Blue Ocean Strategy in public organizations. For this, a new survey was carried out in the period in September 2018 on the scientific bases Scopus (31 articles) and Web of Science (16 articles). The following terms were searched in the title, abstract or keywords of the articles: ("Blue Ocean" AND "public") OR ("Blue Ocean" AND "government") OR ") OR ("value innovation "AND" government "). Excluding duplications and articles that did not address applications of the Blue Ocean Strategy in the public sector, 17 case studies were analyzed.

Finally, after study, analysis, and evaluation, the concept of value innovation for the public sector defined, the critical factors of value innovation identified and the model of the "determinants of value innovation in the public sector" can be proposed. The model was specified in the "radar chart of the determinants" format, aiming at the ease of application and evaluation, basically attending the theoretical approach of the "Radar of innovation" [17]. This mode of representation (radar), as will be seen in the next section (Results and Discussion), is usually composed of critical dimensions, representative of value innovation, associated to determinant factors related to them.

5   Results and Discussion

5.1   Value Innovation in the Public Sector: The Concept

The concept of "value innovation" refers to the Blue Ocean Strategy, whose central objective of value innovation is the creation of a new, competition-free market. Value innovation is achieved through artifacts that lead the employees of organizations to understand the area of business performance and the value that their products or services represent to customers and, from there, devise strategies to redefine market boundaries and reach new customers. Therefore, value innovation refers to prioritizing analyzes involving competition, market, differentiation, strategy, and low cost. These issues are intrinsic to the private sector, which may lead to some questions about the real possibilities of applying BOS in the public context.

However, although there is no competition in the context of most organizations that provide public services, there is a possible need for innovation to follow global trends in public management, to increase efficiency and transparency of processes, and to allow greater engagement of users - citizens or beneficiary organizations.

Thus, in the public sector, we are looking for totally innovative solutions to public problems. It is about providing the innovation beneficiary with a single value, regardless of whether or not the use of new technologies. Innovate in the attributes that the citizen understands as valuable that is, relevant in his decision to join a new service or recognize it as a public management innovation. In short, the objective is not to swim in the blue ocean of non-competition, but instead in new possibilities for public problems solving with the collaboration and participation of all spheres of society.

In this context, the value innovation in the public sector consists of adding value to citizens through the opening of institutions and quality of use of innovations strategically aligned with the efficiency and effectiveness of the processes of creation and maintenance of innovations.

The typical Brazilian case of Banco Palmas [18, 19]. Is pointed out in the literature as a case of social innovation. It is a community bank, created on the outskirts of the city of Fortaleza, CE, aiming at local development through the creation of a common currency that circulates income within the neighborhood limits and offers microcredit to previously excluded groups, strengthening local businesses. In this case, social innovation lies in the fact that the Bank has transformed a social reality, satisfying the basic needs of the local community, creating new relationships and social collaborations [18, 19]. In addition to social innovation, the bank presents characteristics that exemplify the concept of value innovation as specified in this paper. The value innovation occurs because in this case there was a redefinition of a public problem, which gave rise to an innovative solution, differentiated from the existing solutions to the same problem, and put into practice at minimal costs, since the initial contribution to put the idea into practice part of the community itself. The redefinition of the problem consisted in shifting the focus that was focused on the issue of poverty, exclusion and alienation of the community from the current economic system to highlight the leading causes of the problem: the lack of credit and experience to create local businesses and the difficulties of commercialization of products within the limits of the community. From this redefinition of the problem, a strategy differentiated from previous ones was developed starting from the community itself, prioritizing local collaboration to create a new way of making the economy, which culminated in the creation of a local social currency [18, 19].

In this exemplary case, in addition to the differentiation and low cost, the social impact of the initiative is identified in the improvement of the local economy and the image of the community; the efficiency found in the simplification of micro-credit granting processes; the best attendance to the legitimate demands of the community and the opening to the co-creation of the strategy with the community, through meetings of the local Association. Thus, although it is not an innovation that started from the public sector, this case inspires the survey of determining factors that lead to the perception of value innovation.

5.2 Value Innovation in the Public Sector: The Determining Factors

The Critical Success Factors (CSF) are areas, activities, and organizational processes that use the resources available to increase the competitiveness of a given product, service, or organization. The factors founded in the literature were grouped according to their similarities and resulted in the elements specified in Table 1.

Table 1. CSF or determinants of value innovation in the public sector.

Citizens - society

Dimension	Determining factors	Definition	BOS - example
Openness	Usability	Ease of use, user orientation, and attractive design	Digital INSS Initiative - Brazil [20]
	Accessibility	Individual access, differentiation for citizens and particular regions (rural)	Bus rapid transit, South Africa [11]
	Attractiveness	No bureaucracy, convenient, available, and objective	Voxar Puzzle - game fundamental education Brazil [21]
Quality	Utility	Meeting needs - real demands of citizens	Social infrastructure. Smart Cities [12]
	Speed	Access, actions, answers, and quick results	Integration data. Strategic maps social policies [22]
	Satisfaction	Personal satisfaction. Evaluation of feedback, corrections, and evolution	Libraries - perception about service - Malaysia [9]

Organizations - public sector

Efficiency	Process	Strategies for the planning, management, operation, and optimization of processes	Blue Ocean Strategy in Education - Malaysia [10]
	Costs	Reduction of costs of management and operation, in the public context	Model funding for education - Malaysia [23]
	Compliance	Governance, transparency, sustainability. Compliance with laws, standards, and standards	Institutional Theory and IT Governance - Brazil [24]
Effectiveness	Trust	Image of the organization. Positive public perception. Security in relationships	Social vote, positive image of the government - Honduras [25]
	Engagement	Add citizens and society. Collaboration and cooperation, participation in solutions	Urban Living Labs - NGOs - Europe [26]
	Social impact	Effective, positive, and measurable transformation. Public good; social cohesion	Banco Palmas- social innovation - Brazil [18, 19]

There are four dimensions, two related to citizens and society (openness and quality), and two about public sector organizations (efficiency and effectiveness). Three factors represent each one. Therefore, there are a total of twelve factors.

The first two dimensions are the aspects valued by citizens and society. The first dimension is the "Openness" of public institutions to the citizens who are beneficiaries of innovation. It is about facilitating and enhancing the access of different groups to innovation. In this sense, "Openness" encompasses three critical factors: (i) Usability: ensuring that beneficiaries have easy access and use to the proposed innovation; (ii) Accessibility: to guarantee the access of beneficiaries from different regions and with different profiles; and (iii) Attractiveness: so that there are no real or virtual barriers in the context of access to innovative solutions that the beneficiaries are interested and feel comfortable and inspired to use the product or service made available.

The second dimension of the model is "Quality", which encompasses the following determining factors: (i) Utility: complete service to a need, an individual or organizational demand; (ii) Speed: which represents the gains in terms of speed of care and resolution of the problem to the beneficiary, and (iii) Satisfaction: that recipients have a positive evaluation of the innovative product or service made available. It is the evaluation and improvement of the services, of the return related to quality, given by the beneficiary.

The third and fourth dimensions present aspects valued by the institution of the public sector that promotes value innovation. The third dimension to consider is "Efficiency." It is the optimization of internal processes, the search for cost reduction and compliance with laws and regulations in force in a country. Thus, the determinants related to "Efficiency" are as follows: (i) Processes: refers to the proper planning of activities, operations, and actions, aiming at the quality and speed in achieving results. (ii) Costs: relates to the control and optimization of investments, that is, to the economy and management, to the rational and correct use of public resources; (iii) Compliance: refers to compliance with and compliance with current laws and regulations. Include respect for the environment and search for sustainability.

The fourth dimension, in the context of organizations or the public sector, is "Effectiveness." It is the expectation of the promoting institution to solve public problems in an effective and differentiated manner, which occurs when the value innovation strategy used by it reaches its target public, which adheres to that public service or policy, relying on the promoting institution. Thus, the determining factors for the "Effectiveness" of a value innovation strategy are the following: (i) Trust: it is a valuable relationship of the beneficiary with the organization or public sector. It enhances the image of the organization. Positive public perception and security in relationships; (ii) Engagement: beneficiaries, citizens and organizations, begin to interact with the public sector, participate and collaborate in solving problems; and (iii) Social impact: it refers to the positive change brought about by innovation. Finally, effective, positive, and measurable transformation in the context of society.

5.3   The Radar Framework

Finally, dimensions and determinants of value innovation in the public sector were arranged in a circular format diagram to assign equal levels of importance to each factor. The factors were arranged along with the radar and separated into four dimensions. Each dimension corresponds to a quadrant of the diagram, and the dimensions denominated openness and quality refer to what adds value to citizens, while the dimensions effectiveness and efficiency compared to the aspects most valued by public organizations. It should be noted that organizations are also interested in reducing costs, so the dimensions located on the left (public organizations) are also associated with the costs involved to reach these values, such as reducing costs to achieve more significant social impact, engagement, and trust of citizens (Fig. 1).

Fig. 1. Radar framework for public sector value innovation

The model represents the "radar of the determinants of value innovation in the public sector." Unlike the concept of value innovation in the private sector highlights differentiation and costs, radar dimensions highlight the cost management for organizations (efficiency and effectiveness) and value for the citizen (openness and quality).

In summary, the perception of value innovation in the public sector implies that the new idea to be implemented should be more open and convenient to the citizen than the existing services and, at the same time, its implementation should make the public institution more effective and efficient. Therefore, innovation in the public sector can be considered valuable in different aspects.

Thus, from the proposed dimensions and factors, it is possible to understand better who favors innovation and what aspects valued for each group of actors and to provide decision making about strategies, proposals, and projects in the public context.

6   Conclusion

This work aimed to conduct a systematic review of the literature to conceptualize value innovation in the context of public institutions, to identify determining factors and to propose a model of determinants of value innovation in the public sector.

The results were generated based on 55 articles about critical success factors in the public sector and based on 17 case studies found in the literature on value innovation in the public sector.

It was concluded that in the public sector value innovation can be identified when a public problem is deconstructed and understood by another perspective, from which it solved at lower costs for organizations and society, through strategies that differ from current strategies due to greater openness and quality for citizens, with efficiency and effectiveness in the context of organizations.

Thus, from the dimensions of openness, quality, efficiency, and effectiveness were identified in the literature, the determinants of value innovation in the public sector. These factors are usability, accessibility, and attractiveness; utility, speed and satisfaction; processes, costs and compliance; and trust, engagement, and social impact.

Finally, the "radar of the determinants of value innovation in the public sector" model is proposed, which should, in the sequence of the present study, be submitted to a panel of experts for criticism and improvement, based on the proposition as well as a preliminary experimental application in the context of an e-government platform. From these approaches, one should seek the conversion to a structural model and its validation.

In general, with the concept and model of value innovation initially presented, it is hoped to contribute in the theoretical context, to the search for the alignment between the theory of value innovation (Blue Ocean Strategy) and the public sector. On the other hand, in the applied context, to inspire public agents to consider the model as a tool for evaluating the utility of currently used technologies and even in the context of strategies and decision making when proposing innovations.

Acknowledgments. The authors thank the Conselho Nacional de Desenvolvimento Científico e Tecnológico - CNPq, Fundação de Amparo à pesquisa de Minas Gerais – FAPEMIG e Coordenação de Aperfeiçoamento de Pessoal de Nível Superior - CAPES for the financial support to research.

The authors would also like to thanks the National Council for Scientific and Technological Development (CNPq - Brazil) - Process 402789/2015-6 for financial support.

References

1. Yusof, W.Z.M., Tamyez, P.F.M.: Inspired by design and driven by innovation. A conceptual model for radical design driven as a sustainable business model for Malaysian furniture design. In: International Conference on Innovative Technology, Engineering and Sciences 2018. Iop Publishing Ltd., Bristol (2018)
2. Bannister, F., Connolly, R.: ICT, public values and transformative government: a framework and programme for research. Gov. Inf. Q. **31**(1), 119–128 (2014)

3. Kim, W.C., Mauborgne, R.: Value innovation: a leap into the blue ocean (2005)
4. Kim, W.C., Maubourge, R.: Value innovation. Havard Bus. Rev. **70**(1), 71–80 (1997)
5. Kim, W.C., Mauborgne, R.: Blue Ocean Strategy, Expanded Edition: How to Create Uncontested Market Space and Make the Competition Irrelevant. Harvard Business Review Press, Brighton (2014)
6. de Baere, T.: The IR evolution in oncology: tools, treatments, and guidelines. Cardiovasc. Intervent. Radiol. **40**(1), 3–8 (2017)
7. Shim, J.P., French, A.M., McLean, E.R.: Continual growth, inhibitors, and implications of information communication technology in South Korea from a North American perspective. In: 17th Pacific Asia Conference on Information Systems, PACIS 2013 (2013)
8. Silva, V.E., et al.: Voxar puzzle: an innovative hardware/software computer vision game for children development. In: 2015 Xvii Symposium on Virtual and Augmented Reality, pp. 147–153. IEEE, New York (2015)
9. Ahmat, M.A., Jaafar, C.R.C., Azmi, N.A.: The transformation of reference services in Hamzah Sendut Library, Universiti Sains Malaysia. In: Voon, B.H., et al. (eds.) The 6th International Research Symposium in Service Management - Service Imperatives in the New Economy: Service Excellence for Sustainability, Irssm-6 2016, pp. 6–13. Elsevier Science Bv: Amsterdam (2016)
10. Hasan, F.A., et al.: Transformation of universities and the national Blue Ocean Strategy: a case study of Universiti Malaysia Terengganu. J. Sustain. Sci. Manag. **12**(1), 70–78 (2017)
11. Boya, K.S.: Bus rapid transit projects involving the South African government and small operators (as SMMEs): is bus rapid transit a blue or red ocean strategy? Probl. Perspect. Manag. **14**(1), 217–227 (2016)
12. Orlov, A., Chubarkina, I.: Implementation of construction projects for social infrastructure development in smart cities. In: Askadskiy, A. et al. (eds.) XXI International Scientific Conference on Advanced in Civil Engineering Construction - the Formation of Living Environment. Iop Publishing Ltd., Bristol (2018)
13. Mulgan, G., Albury, D.: Innovation in the public sector. Strategy Unit Cabinet Office **1**, 40 (2003)
14. Moore, M.H.: Creating Public Value: Strategic Management in Government. Harvard University Press, Cambridge (1995)
15. Cordella, A., Tempini, N.: E-government and organizational change: reappraising the role of ICT and bureaucracy in public service delivery. Gov. Inf. Q. **32**(3), 279–286 (2015)
16. Jørgensen, T.B., Bozeman, B.: Public values: an inventory. Adm. Soc. **39**(3), 354–381 (2007)
17. Sawhney, M., Wolcott, R.C., Arroniz, I.: The 12 different ways for companies to innovate. MIT Sloan Manag. Rev. **47**(3), 75 (2006)
18. Bataglin, J., Kruglianskas, I., Delatorre, M.: Dimensões da inovação social: o caso do banco palmas. Sustentabilidade e responsabilidade Soc. 7 (2016)
19. Prim, M.A., de Aguiar, R.R.S., Dandolini, G.A.: Banco de Palmas: um caminho para o Empoderamento Comunitários através da Inovação Social. Produção em Foco **7**(1) (2017)
20. Pinheiro, S., Santos, M., Cunha, L.: Digitalização do trabalho no INSS: tensões e estratégias de regulação na implementação do novo modelo de atendimento. Laboreal **14**(2), 62–78 (2018)
21. Silva, V.E., et al.: Voxar puzzle: an innovative hardware/software computer vision game for children development. In: 17th Symposium on Virtual and Augmented Reality, SVR 2015. Institute of Electrical and Electronics Engineers Inc. (2015)
22. BRASIL, E.-E.N.d.A.P.: Iniciativas premiadas no 22 concurso de inovação do setor público (2018). https://inovacao.enap.gov.br/. Accessed 5 June 2019

23. Abdullah, A.: A conceptual model to establish an Islamic Finance Unit at a Malaysian public university. Asian Soc. Sci. **10**(9), 100–107 (2014)
24. Rodrigues, J.G.L.: Diretrizes para implantação da governança de TI no setor público brasileiro à luz da teoria institucional (2010)
25. Joyce, R.A.: Legitimizing the illegitimate: the Honduran show elections and the challenge ahead. NACLA Rep. Am. **43**(2), 10–17 (2010)
26. Concilio, G., Molinari, F.: Urban living labs: learning environments for collective behavioural change. In: Carlucci, D., Spender, J.C., Schiuma, G. (eds.) 9th International Forum on Knowledge Asset Dynamics: Knowledge and Management Models for Sustainable Growth, Ifkad 2014, pp. 746–763. Ikam-Inst Knowledge Asset Management, Matera (2014)

Factors Affecting e-ID Public Acceptance:
A Literature Review

Valentyna Tsap$^{(\boxtimes)}$, Ingrid Pappel , and Dirk Draheim

Information Systems Group, Tallinn University of Technology,
Akadeemia tee 15A, 12169 Tallinn, Estonia
{valentyna.tsap, ingrid.pappel,
dirk.draheim}@taltech.ee

Abstract. This paper presents a literature review that has the main goal to examine what are the factors that are affecting eID public acceptance. We are specifically interested in the perspectives of end-users and the matter of their attitudes towards eID. Our search yielded a rather narrow but concrete range of sources. Among the main themes of interest presented in the literature, we identify factors that are further synthesized in twelve categories. Moreover, we interpret the factors in their original context which allows for understanding which of the factors are mentioned as either drivers, barriers, or both. Based on the analysis of scientific narratives, we point to disparities detected in the existing knowledge of influential factors of eID public acceptance and outline areas that require further research.

Keywords: eID · Public acceptance · Literature review

1   Introduction

Electronic identity is a means to prove that you are the one that you claim to be online and thus granting access to e-services [17]. All over the world, governments have introduced national electronic identity schemes as a part of identity management. Electronic identity plays a vital role in the functioning of digital government infrastructure.

Considering countries' experience of introducing electronic government, it has been realized that for the success of such large-scale systems, the mere implementation of a technologically elegant solution is not sufficient. The importance of end-user acceptance cannot be overlooked. There is currently a struggle taking place when designing e-identity scheme that lies in the attempt of balancing the security of the solution and its usability. Even though, today, there are numerous successful practices, this does not guarantee the applicability and portability of those lessons learned. What works in one country, may not work in another.

As to date, there is no comprehensive study of factors that influence the user acceptance of national eID conducted. Thereby, the current research is exploratory.

A study [10], for instance, explores the aspect of acceptance of electronic identification system as a cross-border interoperability solution by all stakeholders and end-users. Another example can be a study where the focus is also set on the acceptance

A. Kő et al. (Eds.): EGOVIS 2019, LNCS 11709, pp. 176–188, 2019.
https://doi.org/10.1007/978-3-030-27523-5_13

factors of using in this case mobile identification applications [1]. An extent of research [3, 5, 20, 24, 38] focuses on theoretical background of the notion of technological acceptance.

Similar sources are considered within this review in order to present a broader and in-depth perspective on the possible influences of eID.

Hence, the main research question of this review is the following:

RQ: What Are the Factors That Affect eID Public Acceptance?
The intention is to analyze the existing literature in order to gather information about what is known about the particular issue of end users' acceptance of electronic identity that is moderated by the state. The intention is to conduct a search of primary sources and identify the key issues raised by theorists, practitioners, experts, adopters and other stakeholders involved in digital identity domain. We are particularly interested in exploring the studies that focus on the citizens' perspective of eID.

Semantic analysis of the existing literature will be performed to extract knowledge regarding digital identity in the named context. The extracted data will be then distributed to "drivers" and "barriers" categories as per the research question.

With this research, we strive to identify and point to the gap in the existing knowledge in order to spur future research with regards to eID public acceptance. Potentially, the derived results may be applied in building hypotheses and theories, as well as frameworks and evaluations.

2   Method

According to the literature review conduction guidelines [11, 34], the following steps were taken:

1. Identifying the need for literature review.
2. Formulation the research question.
3. Developing a search strategy.
4. Carrying out a comprehensive search of studies.
5. Analyzing and extracting data from the selected studies.
6. Synthesizing the results
7. Writing-up an interpretation of results.

Search Terms. The research question contains the following keywords: "factors, eID, user acceptance."

A list of synonyms for each of the keywords was constructed in order to increase the accuracy of search results. Moreover, the synonyms were selected based on the terms that are common to the researched area (e.g. "user" – "citizen"; "user acceptance" – "public acceptance"). The search terms were adapted to each of the resources searched as not all of them from the list enabled the use of Boolean operators and/or nesting.

Keywords ((*e-ID* OR *"electronic identity"* OR *"digital identity"* OR *"national e-ID"* OR *"national eID"* OR*)* AND (*barrier** OR *obstacle** OR *driver** OR *factor** OR *determinant** OR *influence** OR *impact** OR *affect**)* AND (*"user acceptance"* OR *"public acceptance"* OR *"citizen acceptance"* OR *perception** OR *attitude** OR *"user perception"* OR *"citizen perception" use* OR *usage*)).

Resources Searched. Using the keywords above, the following databases were searched:

- Google Scholar
- Scopus
- ACM Digital Library
- ScienceDirect
- Web of Science
- Springer Link
- IEEE Explore
- Digital Government Reference Library

To increase the number of found materials that fit the search criteria, the keywords were used in a direct search in the key journals and conference proceeding of the area. Additionally, each fitting item's reference list was scanned through for containing possible relevant materials.

Document Selection. The document selection is based on the following inclusion and exclusion criteria:

Authors include studies that:

- directly answer the research question;
- specifically focus on eID and not just e-government;
- mention the issue of acceptance of digital identity by citizens;
- based on empirical data;
- specifically mention societal aspects of technology acceptance of eID;

For this reason, within this study we will not be considering studies that do not provide any insight on the citizen perspective on eID.

Document Retrieval. The search has elicited 146 sources from databases. 88 of those were rejected based on the title and abstract analysis. The remaining sources were then evaluated based on the document selection criteria. The final revised list of selected papers is comprised of 39 items. Among the selected sources such types of documents were included to the review as conference proceedings, journal articles, book chapters, reports, policy documents, theses.

3 Results and Discussion

For the sake of clarification, it must be noted that though the search procedures applied within this study are very much resembling those used in systematic literature reviews (SLRs), we do not claim this review to be one of this kind. This review implements SLR guidelines only partially which is one of the reasons it does not qualify to be fully 'systematic'. As [10, 11] mark, SLR guidelines that originally have been applied in medicine, refer to the coverage of certain clearly identifiable evidence on specific medical treatments, while SLR guidelines outside medicine imply only the rigor of search process. Authors further point out that such limitation nowadays is more than often fails to be acknowledged. Like in SLRs, the upfront search inclusion/exclusion criteria have been introduced with the purpose of delineating and narrowing down the scope of the examined field according to our research aim. Only then, as what is usually done in traditional literature reviews (LRs), we build up criteria for interpreting the findings, i.e. identifying notions and further categorizing them.

The timeframe of selected studies captures the years of 2001–2018. This can be explained by the novelty of the subject of digital identity and its implementation worldwide.

The reviewed studies which outcomes derive from primary data represent country cases from around the globe though European region prevails.

Among 39 selected studies, 13 of them contain case studies with the data samples collected from one country each (Austria, Belgium, Canada, Estonia, Germany, Hong Kong, India, New Zealand, Switzerland, UAE, Ukraine, United Kingdom, USA;) among the rest 26 studies, findings in 17 of them are based on multiple countries data, and the 9 left represent findings of secondary data analysis. The data collected is derived mostly from the European continent which entails a predominantly Western perspective factors that influence eID public acceptance.

The items were selected on the basis of providing explicit insight about citizen perspective on eID. The papers in the final range differ by the extent of provided insight. While some papers had highlighted the eID acceptance by public rather incidentally focusing on other topics, the rest of the studies' aims were directly concerned the object of eID acceptance and the findings were based on primary and secondary data analysis. 9 studies included secondary data, while the rest 30 were presenting results of empirical data analysis.

The review of selected sources has allowed to extract the key notions mentioned by the authors that according to their hypotheses and findings determine the degree of eID public acceptance. The notions were extracted by means of semantic analysis of the selected sources. Categorizing the notions was also reasonable because of the number of synonymous notions that did not differ significantly in their meaning.

Another criterion for creating the categories and assigning their names was the frequency of notion occurring in the sources. For instance, the category of "trust" comprises detected notions concerning the issue of trust which are majorly referred to using the same value in most of the studies. This category also includes studies that mention the same phenomenon but referred to using synonymic notions. Such principle was applied throughout the entire process of categorization. It was decided to implement a condition that if the notion is mentioned less than in 10% of the studies, then it is going to be the category "Other".

The distribution of detected notions, i.e. any phenomenon authors mentioned to infer direct or indirect cause on the eID user acceptance, has allowed to create the following 12 categories: (1) complexity; (2) ease of use; (3) functionality; (4) awareness; (5) trust; (6) privacy concerns; (7) security; (8) control and empowerment; (9) transparency; (10) path dependency; (11) cultural and historical factors; (12) other.

The category "Other" will be further described separately as it contains miscellaneous notions that were not included in the former 11 ones.

Table 1 shows where and how frequently each notion is mentioned in the realm of selected papers.

Table 1. Table captions should be placed above the tables.

Category	Paper references
Complexity	[12, 15, 16, 22, 23, 29, 30, 41, 43]
Ease of use	[1, 3, 5, 6, 16, 20, 22, 24, 29, 31, 34–36, 39–41, 43, 44]
Functionality	[6, 15, 16, 18, 20, 22, 23, 25, 29, 31, 34, 35, 39, 41, 42, 45]
Awareness	[1, 2, 4, 14, 15, 18, 22, 23, 26–28, 31, 32, 34, 35, 39, 41–45]
Trust	[3–9, 12, 14–16, 18, 20, 21, 24, 26, 28, 29, 31–34, 36, 39–45, 48]
Privacy concerns	[1, 3, 5, 7–9, 15, 18, 20–22, 24–26, 30, 32, 34, 36, 39–46, 48]
Security	[1, 5, 7–9, 14, 15, 18, 21, 23, 24, 28, 32, 34, 40–44, 48]
Control and empowerment	[7–9, 12, 16, 18, 26, 27, 41–44, 46, 48]
Transparency	[7–9, 27–31, 33, 42, 43, 45]
Path dependency	[12, 20, 28, 33–35, 40, 45]
Cultural and historical factors	[2, 12, 20, 27, 34, 42, 45]

A number of papers [1, 3–6, 12, 22, 26, 31, 35, 41, 43], studying the acceptance of eID, have incorporated TAM and its extensions [17, 47]. This had an impact on the design of the research by crafting the studies according to the elements of TAM [1, 3–6, 41] or rather providing guidance and serving as a background concept [12, 22, 31, 35, 43]. TAM has also influenced the derivation of notion categories in this review.

Ease of Use. This category echoes the element of TAM that has the same name. This category comprises such notions as "convenience" [1, 12, 15, 16, 24, 35, 42], "user friendliness" [6, 16, 30, 34, 39], "usability" [1, 6, 16, 22, 25, 43], "comfort" [18, 22]. For instance, Kalvet *et al.* uses the term "convenience" when referring to the physical appearance and properties of an eID card [24]. Such terms as "usability". "usefulness", "user friendliness" appear in studies that are having a TAM view within their methods.

Complexity. This category was distinguished despite the thought that it might contradict with the just mentioned notion of ease of use. However, this depends on one's perspective where, for instance, the system that is seen to be complex due to lack of awareness, but on the other hand, can be named so even though another user can understand it regardless [15]. In [46], the term "complexity" is mentioned in the context of information systems and their structure. The issue of complexity in the survey from study [22] is referred as a difficult-to-understand mechanism of the system.

Functionality. This category includes notions that echo the "usefulness" element of TAM. These are the notions "usefulness" (importantly, without implying to TAM), availability of options (such as authentication methods or e-services available). For example, findings of [6] show that availability of services linked to eID is of importance when deciding whether using eID is useful for the citizens.

Awareness. The following category includes such expressions mentioned as "understanding" [15, 22], "seeing reasons/purpose" [30], "knowing how to use" [8], "comprehending". [8] indicates "awareness" in the context of knowing how the systems works and knowing how to use it and connects this notion to the trust. [44] suggests that awareness of, for instance, technical aspects of a currently implemented solution, will not guarantee the acceptance of future updates and changes, which implies the temporariness of this factor.

Control and Empowerment. The given category refers to "control over eID/e-identity/identity" [21], "empowerment of citizens" [2, 15, 16, 26], i.e. their ability to choose whether to use eID, which data to provide, ability to check the status of data, ability to withdraw data, participation. [15] mentions "empowerment" in the context of citizens being able "to access their information without "bureaucracy". In [2], authors use "empowerment" as a reference to access to services, more precisely "so that they can legally control service delivery to their advantage." In [21], "control" appeared as a major theme during analysis of primary data and concerned control of citizens over their personal data as well as the issue of data integrity and disclosure by consent.

Transparency. This category generalizes the understanding of underlying principles of how (accountable) the data is being handled in legal, administrative and procedural sense by authorities [26, 46]. [2] defines "transparency" as a result of a process of "bringing visibility to citizens of the service workflow by means of automated service delivery." The comparative study on citizen perceptions of eID and interoperability [21] provides a formulation of "transparency" given by a citizen as "ALL data that are collected about me should be made available to me, so that I am able to recognize who has collected what data about me." In [31], the context brings up "transparency" along with the approach organizations handle data with.

Path Dependency. This particular category that somewhat represents rather a different perspective than the citizen one, yet it was introduced due to the arguments in studies [12, 33] justifying the fact that paths chosen by countries and the previous setting they possess (including societal) when introducing eID are definitive for the perceptions of stakeholders (including end-users, i.e., citizens).

Path dependency refers to "previous technical, organizational and regulatory settings explain for the differences in the provisioning of national eID systems and thus the heterogeneous landscape of solutions and usage across Europe" [12]. Within our study, we define path dependency as rather an external factor of influence that has not been articulated by end-users within the sample of this review. [33] highlights the need of understanding the scenarios that worked out successfully in one country's case and did not prove itself when applying the same strategies in another country. Authors then state that citizens as one of the stakeholders have a major potential to determine the outcome of each scenario. Hence, they suggest to explore more deeply eID introduction in the socio-material perspective, i.e. citizens' relationships with eID artefacts.

Cultural and Historical Factors. 5 studies [1, 4, 12, 20, 31] have provided insights on the role of culture and history in shaping citizen perceptions and acceptance of eID. An elaborate opinion on how historical events can have a major impact and shape the sense of identity is given in the case study of the Hong Kong eID [20]. In the rest of the studies, history and culture are discussed more in general.

The categories of "privacy concerns", "security" and "trust" are the most frequent within this study. The names of these categories were assigned according to the same notions identified during analysis. All three notions are seen as issues to be leveraged in order to increase their trustworthiness in the eyes of the citizens [12].

Privacy concerns. Notions related to this category are associated with risks, fears, threats to citizens' rights to be violated in relation to their digital identities.

Security. Here, the identified notions are related to data, software, and hardware, their reliability, trustworthiness, safety, and the ability of state to provide this security.

Trust. This category that is the most prevailing one. Even though we do not make any claims about the degree of influence that each identified factor has, trust has been seen and presented by researchers as one the most important pre-conditions of eID success. Trust is interrelated to most of the other categories and could be divided into subcategories or appear as a standalone factor. In [29], "trust" is displayed a two-type concept [48] that included institution-based trust and characteristic based trust. Here, the institution-based trust represents the trust that citizens experience towards public authorities and their activities, whereas characteristic-based trust is the one that end-users put in the system or solution. Another study [32] identifies 'trust' as well as 'distrust' as two independent and separate sides of the same relationship and not as two opposites of one continuum. These two sides, as authors explain, co-exist and evolve as the relationship matures and evolves over time. Here, term 'relationship' is used in the socio-technical and political context. Therefore, ambivalence is the main attribute and finding regarding trust and distrust that variates from country to country clearly influencing the development outcomes.

Other. This category includes notions that have not been assigned to the abovementioned categories. One of the notions is the 'intrinsic motivation to adopt the technology' (i.e. eID) [22]. The same source has identified cost and expenses associated with the use of eID as an influential factor as well as the extent to what the technology has to spread before the user will actually start adopting it him or herself. This tendency particularly echoes the diffusion of innovation theory where such users are known as Late Adopters [38]. Lastly, the survey conducted within the study [20] has also identified as an impact factor the citizens' possibility to receive help from a competent person when using the technology, or in other words, technical support.

Going back, the issue of cost was raised also in [12]. Authors of [5] proposed a model with six key elements that affect the adoption of identity management systems, one of which – 'individual differences' – was distinguished as a notion in our research as well. The element of 'individual differences' is then divided in two sub-elements: demographic variables and situational variables that both have direct and moderating effects. The demographic differences include gender, age and education as characteristic of individuals and the situational ones are referred to as context-sensitive characteristics, i.e., experience, facilitating conditions, subjective norm and cost. A study on the acceptance of biometrics in identity management [24] revealed that "age, gender, education level and occupation do not influence the respondents' views on the acceptability of biometric identity databases in any considerable way." In [33], authors mention such factors as eID user maturity and national differences in perceptions of information systems.

The derived categories can be potentially used as metrics for assessing the acceptance levels of eID. An attempt was made to interpret each identified notion as a driver or barrier of eID acceptance depending in what context it was mentioned. The identified notions were then marked as 'positive', 'negative', 'bilateral', or 'neutral'. In other words, a notion is presented as a driver or a barrier. Moreover, the impact of a notion may range and hereby it can be assigned to both positive and negative group. Lastly, some derived notions were not interpreted neither as positive nor as negative. Additionally, some studies elaborate on the notions in a neutral context by not inferring their positive or negative impact but merely assuming the possibility of impact.

Figure 1 represents the categories and their context in the sources they were extracted from. Depending on the context, a set of indicators was established where "**P**" is "**positive**", "**N**" is "**negative**", "**B**" is "**bilateral**" and "**0**" is "**neutral**". The headings of columns represent the reference numbers of studies that can be found in the References section.

	1	2	3	4	5	6	7	8	9	12	14	15	16	18	20	21	22	23	24	25	26	27	28	29	30	31	32	33	34	35	36	39	40	41	42	43	44	45	46	48
Complexity									P			B	N				0	B						0	B										B		B			
Ease of use	0		P		0	P						P		0		0		0					P		P			P	B	P	P	B	P		P	0				
Functionality				P						P	P	P	P		P	P		0				P		P			P	B		P		P	P			P				
Awareness	0	P		0					P	P		P			P	B			P	P	P			P	P		P	P	P	P	P		P	P	P	B	P			
Trust			N	0	0	P	0	0	0	0	0	P	0	P	0		P		P	P	P	0		B	P	B	P		N	0	P	P	P	P	P	0	N	0	0	
Privacy concerns	0	N		0		N	N	N	N		N		0	N	N		B	N	0	0	P		B		N		N		P	P	B	N	N	N	N	N	0	0		
Security	0			0		N	N	N	N	P	N		0		N		B	P			N			N			N	N		B	N	0	P	0			0			
Control and empowerment						P	P	P	P		P	P			P	P						P	P										P	0	P	0		P	0	
Cultural and historical factors	B										B	0						0						0						0		B								
Path dependency								0				0						0						0				0	0		0				0					
Transparency						B	B	B													0	P	P	0	P		0						P	0	P					

Fig. 1. Derived categories.

4 Limitations

Completeness. The search conducted within this review has elicited a fairly small amount of literature. As the aim of the review was to identify factors that specifically influence public acceptance of eID and not any other component of e-government, it explains the low number of included studies. However, the document selection criteria and search query design allowed for targeting papers which content accurately addresses the issue of eID public acceptance. There were no limitations set regarding the inclusion or exclusion of a particular document type but mostly academic sources appeared in the search results. Further inclusion of policy papers, white papers, and grey literature will be considered when broadening the scope of this research.

Potential Bias. The presented review is conducted within a research for doctoral thesis and hence the likelihood of results influenced by the bias of authors is high. This calls for further validation and assessment of the results by involving other researchers. As the studies in the range of review are mostly displaying findings from data gathered among European countries, generalization is possible only to some extent. As to the process of interpreting and deriving the categories, there is an inevitable effect of subjectivity. To lower this effect, a consensus has to be reached on the basis of a previous review that comes from independent researchers.

Data Synthesis. The findings of papers were analyzed to answer the research question allowing to identify the occurring notions and categorizing them. It is suggested that while grouping them it may have been possible that some of the notions where aggregated into wrong categories as well as there is chance that there could have been created a bigger or smaller number of categories. This serves as an additional motivation to iterate the analysis extending the study.

Future Research. As the eID user acceptance can be viewed from various perspectives, it is more than necessary to extent the study. We consider an attempt to segregate the existing results with those the perspectives on eID public acceptance of other stakeholders. Some papers that were analyzed within this review already provide other stakeholders' perspectives, however, due to the focus of this study, these insights were not considered. The study will benefit if the acceptance factors will be compared and analyzed along with those define the acceptance of similar or larger ISs. A great realm of research and analysis that looks into e-government acceptance as a whole offers much richer outcomes on the subject. As we noted before, it is realized that the derived notions overlap with ones that are also definitive in the case of e-government acceptance, there a still factors that are specific to eID which have to be investigated further.

The prevailing majority of the studies in this review highlighted the issue of trust and privacy concerns which calls for a more detailed analysis of these categories. Even though the goal within this review was to identify factors of impact and through the course of data synthesis and interpretation, each distinguished category was given the same value and weight, the authors of included studies insist on the importance of these notions. Therefore, we also support the idea of this direction to be explored more thoroughly.

The analysis of the studies confirmed that at the moment the body of knowledge contains a rather scarce and fragmented picture of what is of importance for public acceptance of eID especially from citizens' perspective.

5   Conclusion

The findings suggest the eID public acceptance to be a multifaceted phenomenon that is influenced by a wide range of variables with a different degree of impact. The studies with the empirical data analysis provide a sufficient basis only for a primary conceptualization.

Overall, the number of studies elicited by the given criteria leads points to a knowledge gap in the understanding and interpretation of eID public acceptance from citizens' perspective.

While deriving the categories, it has been realized how strongly interconnected these variables are and, in some cases, can imply very similar if not identical or, conversely, ambiguous facts or assumptions. The analysis allowed to construct a list with 12 categories that consist of identified factors influencing eID public acceptance. Composing the list of categories also shed light on a trend among researchers to focus on the issues of trust, privacy and security when it comes to user acceptance of eID. Though a relatively significant body of knowledge on these issues exists, it is encouraged to proceed with going further, especially taking the societal angle. Since derived categories are heavily dependent on each other and hence it is a challenge to establish what is a primary cause for what, needless to point out that this cause-effect relationship varies from country to country.

It is clear that some factors identified, for instance, history, culture and path dependency deserve more attention due to little knowledge about their role in defining citizens' perceptions of eID. This fraction of research would be also interesting to conduct considering the shifts in the notion of identity itself.

Of course, the derived factors and categories are echoing factors that determine the acceptance of e-government services in general. The consistency of our findings with previous research is obvious however the identified gaps evidently call for further research in this particular stream, i.e. eID public acceptance factors.

References

1. Ahrenstedt, S., Huang, J., Wollny, L.: A study on factors influencing the acceptance of mobile payment applications in Sweden. Dissertation (2015). http://urn.kb.se/resolve?urn=urn:nbn:se:hj:diva-26738
2. Al-Hujran, O., Al-dalahmeh, M., Aloudat, A.: The role of national culture on citizen adoption of eGovernment services: an empirical study. Electron. J. E-Government 9(2), 93–106 (2011)
3. Alkhalifah, A., Al Amro S.: Understanding the effect of privacy concerns on user adoption of identity management systems. J. Comput. 12(2), 174–182 (2017). https://doi.org/10.17706/jcp.12.2.174-182
4. Alkhalifah, A., D'Ambra, J.: The role of trust in the initial adoption of identity management systems. In: Linger, H., Fisher, J., Barnden, A., Barry, C., Lang, M., Schneider, C. (eds.) Proceedings of the 2012 International Conference on Information Systems Development, pp. 25–39. Springer, Heidelberg (2013). https://doi.org/10.1007/978-1-4614-7540-8_27
5. Alkhalifah, A.: Factors effecting user adoption of identity management systems: an empirical study (2012)
6. Andermatt, K.C., Göldi, R.A.: Introducing an electronic identity: the co-design approach in the canton of schaffhausen. Schaffhausen Swiss Yearb. Adm. Sci. 9, 41–50 (2018). https://doi.org/10.5334/ssas.122
7. Backhouse, J., Halperin, R.: A survey on EU citizens trust in ID systems and authorities (2007)

8. Backhouse, J., Halperin, R.: Approaching interoperability for identity management systems. In: Rannenberg, K., Royer, D., Deuker, A. (eds.) The Future of Identity in the Information Society, pp. 245–268. Springer, Heidelberg (2009). https://doi.org/10.1007/978-3-642-01820-6_6

9. Backhouse, J., Halperin, R.: Security and privacy perceptions of e- ID: a grounded research. In: Proceeding of the 16th European Conference on Information Systems, ECIS 2008, Galway, Ireland (2008)

10. Boell, S.K., Cecez-Kecmanovic, D.: On being "systematic" in literature reviews in IS. J. Inf. Technol. 30(2), 161–173 (2015)

11. vom Brocke, J., Simons, A., Riemer, K., Niehaves, B., Plattfaut, R., Cleven, A.: Standing on the shoulders of giants: challenges and recommendations of literature search in information systems research. Commun. Assoc. Inf. Syst. 37(1), 205–224 (2015)

12. Brugger, J., Fraefel, M., Riedl, R.: Raising acceptance of cross-border eID federation by value alignment. Electron. J. e-Government 12(2), 178–188 (2014)

13. Budgen, D., Brereton, P.: Performing systematic literature reviews in software engineering. In: Proceedings of the 28th International Conference on Software Engineering, pp. 1051–1052. ACM, May 2006

14. Cap, C.H., Maibaum, N.: Digital identity and its implications for electronic government. In: Schmid, B., Stanoevska-Slabeva, K., Tschammer, V. (eds.) Towards the E-Society - E-Commerce, E-Business, and E-Government; (I3E'01), Zürich, pp. 803–816 (2001)

15. Chauhan, S., Kaushik, A.: Evaluating citizen acceptance of unique identification number in India: an empirical study. Electron. Gov. Int. J. 12(3) (2016). https://doi.org/10.1504/eg.2016.078416

16. Cuijpers, C., Schroers, J.: eIDAS as Guideline for the Development of a Pan-European eID Framework in FutureID. GI-Edition Lect Notes Informatics (2015)

17. Davis, F.D.: A technology acceptance model for empirically testing new end-user information systems: theory and results. Doctoral dissertation, Massachusetts Institute of Technology (1985)

18. European Commission. Special Eurobarometer 359. Attitudes on Data Protection and Electronic Identity in the European Union (2011)

19. European Commission. Electronic Identities - A brief introduction 6 (2015). http://ec.europa.eu/information_society/activities/ict_psp/documents/eid_introduction.pdf

20. Goodstadt, L.F., Connolly, R., Bannister, F.: The Hong Kong e-Identity card: examining the reasons for its success when other cards continue to struggle. Inf. Syst. Manag. 32(1), 72–80 (2015). https://doi.org/10.1080/10580530.2015.983025

21. Halperin, R., Backhouse, J.: A Qualitative Comparative Analysis of Citizens' Perception of EIDs and Interoperability (2008)

22. Harbach, M., Fahl, S., Rieger, M., Smith, M.: On the acceptance of privacy-preserving authentication technology: the curious case of national identity cards. In: De Cristofaro, E., Wright, M. (eds.) PETS 2013. LNCS, vol. 7981. Springer, Berlin (2013). https://doi.org/10.1007/978-3-642-39077-7_13

23. Jones, L.A., Antón, A.I., Earp, J.B.: Towards understanding user perceptions of authentication technologies. In: Proceedings of 2007 ACM Workshop on Privacy in Electronic Society (WPES 2007), pp. 91–98 (2007). https://doi.org/10.1145/1314333.1314352

24. Kalvet, T., Tiits, M., Laas-Mikko, K.: Public acceptance of advanced identity documents. In: Proceedings of the 11th International Conference on Theory and Practice of Electronic Governance – ICEGOV 2018, pp. 429–432. ACM Press, New York (2018)

25. Khan, H., Hutchison, A.: Data privacy implications for security information and event management systems and other meta-systems. In: Felici, M. (ed.) CSP 2013. CCIS, vol. 182 (2013). https://doi.org/10.1007/978-3-642-41205-9_7

26. Adjei, J.K.: A Case for Implementation of Citizen Centric National Identity Management Systems: Crafting a Trusted National Identity Management Policy, 1 edn. Institut for Elektroniske Systemer, Aalborg Universitet (2013)
27. Lips, M.: Rethinking citizen-government relationships in the age of digital identity: insights from research. Inf. Polity 15(4), 273–289. https://doi.org/10.3233/ip-2010-0216
28. Lips, S., Pappel, I., Tsap, V., Draheim, D.: Key factors in coping with large-scale security vulnerabilities in the EID field. In: Kő, A., Francesconi, E. (eds.) EGOVIS 2018. LNCS, vol. 11032, pp. 60–70 (2018). https://doi.org/10.1007/978-3-319-98349-3_5
29. Lockton, V.M.: e-Government and Identity Management in British Columbia: Implementation of the BCeID (2009)
30. Mariën, I., Van Audenhove, L.: The Belgian e-ID and its complex path to implementation and innovational change. Identity Inf. Soc. 3(1), 27–41 (2010). https://doi.org/10.1007/s12394-010-0042-2
31. Marzooqi, S.A., Nuaimi, E.A., Qirim, N.A.: E-governance (G2C) in the public sector: citizens acceptance to E-government systems - Dubai's case. In: Proceedings of the Second International Conference on Internet of Things, Data and Cloud, ICC 2017. https://doi.org/10.1145/3018896.3025160
32. McGrath, K.: Identity verification and societal challenges: explaining the gap between service provision and development outcomes. MIS Q. 40, 485–500 (2016). https://doi.org/10.25300/misq/2016/40.2.12
33. Melin, U., Axelsson, K.: Managing the development of e-ID in a public e-service context: challenges and path dependencies from a life-cycle perspective. Transf. Gov.: People Process Policy 7(2), 240–255 (2013). https://doi.org/10.1108/TG-08-2013-0026
34. Ng-kruelle, G., Swatman, P.A., Hampe, J.F., Rebne, D.S.: Biometrics and e-Identity (e-Passport) in the European union : end-user perspectives on the adoption of a controversial innovation. J. Theoret. Appl. Electron. Commerce Res. 1(2), 12–35
35. Palgin, M.-L.: Diffusion of the estonian ID-card and its electronic usage: explaining the success. Master's thesis, Tallinn University of Technology (2016)
36. Perakslis, C., Wolk, R.: Social acceptance of RFID as a biometric security method. IEEE Technol. Soc. Mag. 25, 34–42 (2006)
37. Petticrew, M., Roberts, H.: Systematic Reviews in the Social Sciences. Blackwell Publ, Malden (2012)
38. Rogers, E.M.: Diffusion of Innovations. Simon and Schuster, New York (2010)
39. Rossnagel, H., Camenisch, J., Fritsch, L., et al.: FutureID - shaping the future of electronic identity. Datenschutz und Datensicherheit 36, 189–194 (2012)
40. Seltsikas, P., O'Keefe, R.M.: Expectations and outcomes in electronic identity management: the role of trust and public value. Eur. J. Inf. Syst. 19(1), 93–103 (2009). https://doi.org/10.1057/ejis.2009.51
41. Seven, A.: Building sustainability and trust in the usage of electronic identification using technology acceptance model. Doctoral Dissertation, Juame I University (2015)
42. Snijder, M.: Security & Privacy in Large Scale Biometric Systems. Special Eurobarometer, p. 359 (2006)
43. Strauß, S., Aichholzer, G.: National electronic identity management: the challenge of a citizen-centric approach beyond technical design. Int. J. Adv. Intell. Syst. 3(1), 12–23 (2010)
44. Tiits, M., Kalvet, T., Laas-Mikko, K.: Social acceptance of ePassports. In: Proceedings of the 13th International Conference of the Biometrics Special Interest Group, 10–12 September 2014, Darmstadt, Germany. LNI, pp. 15–26 (2014)

45. Tsap, V., Pappel, I., Draheim, D.: Key success factors in introducing national e-Identification systems. In: Dang, T., Wagner, R., Küng, J., Thoai, N., Takizawa, M., Neuhold, E. (eds.) FDSE 2017. LNCS, vol. 10646, pp. 455–471. Springer, Cham (2017). https://doi.org/10.1007/978-3-319-70004-5_33
46. van Rooy, D., Bus, J.: Trust and privacy in the future internet – a research perspective. Identity Inf. Soc. 3(2), 397–404 (2010). https://doi.org/10.1007/s12394-010-0058-7
47. Venkatesh, V., Morris, M.G., Davis, G.B., Davis, F.D.: User acceptance of information technology: toward a unified view. MIS Q. 27, 425–478 (2003)
48. Warkentin, M., Gefen, D., Pavlou, P.A., Rose, G.M.: Encouraging citizen adoption of e-government by building trust. Electron. Markets 12(3), 157–162 (2002). https://doi.org/10.1080/101967802320245929

OntoMetrics Evaluation of Quality of e-Government Ontologies

Jean Vincent Fonou-Dombeu[⊠] and Serestina Viriri

School of Mathematics, Statistics and Computer Science,
University of KwaZulu-Natal, King Edward Avenue, Scottsville,
Pietermaritzburg 3209, South Africa
{fonoudombeuj,viriris}@ukzn.ac.za

Abstract. At present, there is a shortage of studies which focus on the analysis of existing e-government ontologies on the web to promote their reuse, maintenance and evolution. This research attempts to fill this gap by identifying and evaluating existing e-government ontologies on the web. Twenty ontologies of the e-government domain are downloaded on the web and a set of quantitative quality metrics adopted from the OntoMetrics ontology evaluation framework are applied to evaluate their schema, knowledge base and graph features. The evaluation results provide insights on the accuracy, understandability, cohesion and conciseness of the e-government ontologies studied.

Keywords: E-government · Ontologies · OntoMetrics · Ontologies quality metrics · Ontologies evaluation

1 Introduction

The popularity of ontologies today is due to their many benefits. Firstly, ontologies are consensual and shared representations of knowledge in various domains; therefore, they can regulate communications between individuals and software agents in those domains. In fact, ontologies use common terminologies and semantics to model a domain through its concepts entities objects and their relationships. At a conceptual level, this may ease the communication between individuals handling the same information that is governed by clearly defined rules or semantics. At the logical level, the common semantics of information may benefit software agents such as web/semantic web services [1] in synchronizing communications and the exchange of messages for a smooth and seamless service provision. The latter is of particular interest in the field of e-government [1,2]. Secondly, ontologies are formally represented in standard languages such as the Resource Description Framework (RDF) and Web Ontology Language (OWL), allowing them to be automatically processed and reasoned by computers on the web. This functionality of ontologies are particularly useful in the distributed and pervasive information systems of today such as that of e-government, in that, it allows automated processing and reasoning of ontology knowledge bases to

© Springer Nature Switzerland AG 2019
A. Kő et al. (Eds.): EGOVIS 2019, LNCS 11709, pp. 189–203, 2019.
https://doi.org/10.1007/978-3-030-27523-5_14

infer new knowledge and provide answers to complex user's queries. Thirdly, the same ontologies may be shared by many semantic-based applications, enabling the interoperability between these applications. In fact, the promotion of ontology reuse in ontology engineering today [3] requires ontologies to be built by merging or integration other ontologies [4]; this results in some ontologies being used in many applications. Such ontologies constitute the require interfaces for the interoperability of the concerned semantic-based applications. In relation to the third benefit of ontologies explained above, one of the aims of this study is to promote the reuse of existing e-government ontologies available on the web.

Apart from the abovementioned benefits of ontologies that make them attractive in semantic-based applications in various domains including e-government today, the advent of linked/open data and ontology libraries has increased the number of ontologies on the web. This in turn has put the issue of ontology reuse at the center of attention in ontology engineering [3,5]. In fact, ontology reuse is beneficial to users or ontologies engineers in that, it (1) reduces the time and cost for building new ontologies *de novo* and may speedup the development of semantic-based applications, (2) improves the quality of the resulting ontologies as the reused ontologies have already been experimented in other applications and (3) enables the interoperability of applications that use the same ontologies. However, ontology reuse requires the users or ontology engineers to select the suitable ontologies amongst the candidate ontologies describing a domain. The task of ontology selection is guided by the evaluation of the targeted ontologies [6]. The evaluation of ontologies entails using qualitative or quantitative metrics [7,8] to assess the quality of the candidate ontologies with the aim of assisting the users or ontology engineers in the choice of the right ontologies for reuse as well as facilitating the maintenance and evolution of these ontologies.

To the best of our knowledge, there is a shortage of studies which focus on the analysis of the quality of e-government ontologies to promote their reuse, maintenance and evolution. This study attempts to fill this gap by identifying and evaluating existing e-government ontologies on the web. A number of 20 ontologies of the e-government domain are downloaded on the web and a set of quantitative quality metrics adopted from the OntoMetrics ontology evaluation framework [9] are applied to evaluate their schema, graph and knowledge base features. The evaluation results provide insights on the accuracy, understandability, cohesion and conciseness of the e-government ontologies studied.

The rest of the paper is structured as follows. Section 2 discusses related studies and the use of ontologies in e-government, and highlights the challenges that may hinder the reuse of e-government ontologies. The OntoMetrics framework for ontology evaluation and its quality metrics adopted in this study are explained in Sect. 3. Section 4 presents the experiments and results and a conclusion ends the paper in the last section.

2   Related Work

Assessing the quality of different aspects of e-government have been of interest to authors in recent years. A theoretical model for assessing the quality of e-government services (e-services) is proposed in [10]. The authors developed an ontology, namely, e-GovQoS to model the quality parameters and metrics of e-government services; they claim that the e-GovQoS ontology would enable the evaluation of quality of service discovery and composition, thereby, assisting in improving the public administration (PA) processes. In [11], the authors stressed the need for governance and evaluation of quality of PA data that transact through e-government systems and proposed a framework that provides a set of metrics for the measurement of the quality of PA metadata. The quality of e-government services is also addressed in [12]. The authors suggest the periodic evaluation of the quality of e-services to ascertain that they meet the expectations of citizens, businesses and organizations. The authors went on to proposed an ontology, namely, QeGS that is suitable for the evaluation of the quality of e-services in different perspectives. Another study in [13] proposed a framework for evaluating the quality of municipalities' e-government systems; the framework provides various metrics for evaluating the design and content of municipalities' e-services systems. The quality of local government e-services is the focus of attention in [14]. The authors proposed a so called multi-layered framework that may assist local governments in the monitoring and evaluation of the quality of their e-services.

None of the previous studies above has tackled the topic of quality of e-government ontologies. Our interest into the analysis of e-government ontologies started in [15]; at the time, we analysed the complexity of the four top level ontologies in the *oeGov* repository. However, ontologies have been used in different aspects of services provision in the field of e-government. Comprehensive reviews of ontology-based e-government projects are provided in [2,16]. Other recent studies on the use of ontologies in e-government can be found in [17–19]. However, most of the e-government ontologies reported in the literature are not available to the public to date. These ontologies are mainly presented in published research and projects reports, giving limited prospect for their reuse in other e-government projects. In fact, only partial views of the majority of these ontologies are revealed in published research and reports; their full codes and structures are hidden to the public [20]. Despite that, some existing e-government ontologies have been loaded in different repositories on the web and are available for download thanks to their authors. These few available e-government ontologies are targeted in this study.

The limited access to the majority of e-government ontologies may undermine the adoption of semantic-based applications in e-government. In fact, as mentioned earlier, it is prescribed in ontology engineering [3,4] to reuse existing ontologies in new projects rather than trying to build new ones from scratch. Ontology reuse [5] reduces the time and cost for building new ontologies as well as the time for developing semantic-based systems. Furthermore, existing ontologies need to be maintained and evolve with the changes occurring in the environment where they are being used. Given the inherent complex nature of ontology [7,8], this can only be achieved if existing e-government ontologies are shared reused and improved in new projects. The materials and methods used in the study are presented next.

3   Materials and Methods

In this study, ontologies of the e-government domain are downloaded from the internet and their quality metrics are gathered via the OntoMetrics online ontology evaluation system [9]. The framework in [20] is applied to search e-government ontologies on the web. The resulting quality metrics of the ontologies are further analysed and discussed to reach the findings of the study. The next subsections present the OntoMetrics framework and its quality metrics adopted in this study as well as the mapping of these metrics to ontologies quality evaluation dimensions/criteria.

3.1   OntoMetrics Framework for Ontology Evaluation

Ontology evaluation is an active research topic in ontology engineering [9, 21–23]. To this end, many approaches have been proposed to address ontology evaluation [23]. The OntoMetrics framework is adopted to evaluate the quantitative quality metrics of e-government ontologies in this study. OntoMetrics was chosen because it is the *state-of-the-art* tool for automated ontology evaluation to date [9]; it (1) offers a free online environment for the calculation of ontology metrics, (2) supports the OWL 2 standard ontology language, (3) provides extensive online documentation on the quality metrics implemented and (4) automatically generates the output of metrics calculation in XML format that can be conveniently analysed later.

Five group of quality metrics of ontologies are available under the OntoMetrics suite including: base, schema, knowledge base, class and graph metrics [9]. The above categories of OntoMetrics quality metrics are further linked to ontology quality dimensions including accuracy, understandability, cohesion, computational efficiency and conciseness [9]. In this study, 11 OntoMetrics quality metrics have been selected and used to evaluate the quality of e-government ontologies based on their correlation with the abovementioned quality dimensions. Moreover, it was cumbersome and impossible to gather the class metrics for each class in the ontologies in the dataset; therefore, the OntoMetrics class metrics are excluded from the metrics adopted in this study. The following subsections present the selected OntoMetrics quality metrics. The selected metrics fall under the schema, knowledge base and graph categories of OntoMetrics suite of metrics.

3.2   Schema Metrics

The schema metrics measure the design of ontology to indicate its richness, width, depth and inheritance of the schema design. The metrics adopted in this study are the attribute, inheritance and relationship richness. These three metrics are defined in Eqs. 1 to 3.

- **Attribute Richness** (AR) - Most of the knowledge in an ontology are represented in its attributes or slots. The AR of an ontology is the average number of attributes/slots per class in the ontology. It is computed as in Eq. 1.

$$AR = \frac{|att|}{|C|} \tag{1}$$

where $|att|$ and $|C|$ are the total number of attributes and classes in the ontology, respectively.

- **Inheritance Richness** (IR) - This metric measures the distribution of information at different levels of the inheritance three of the ontology. It indicates how knowledge is organized into categories and subcategories in the ontology. The IR is given in Eq. 2.

$$IR = \frac{|H|}{|C|} \tag{2}$$

where $|H|$ and $|C|$ are the total number of subclass relations and classes in the ontology, respectively.

- **Relationship Richness** (RR) - This metric provides an indication of the distribution of relations in an ontology. It is defined in Eq. 3.

$$RR = \frac{|P|}{|H| + |P|} \tag{3}$$

where $|P|$ and $|H|$ represent the number of non-inheritance relations between classes and the number of inheritance relations in the ontology, respectively.

3.3   Knowledge Base Metrics

The knowledge base metrics also evaluate the ontology design by measuring the amount of knowledge included in the ontology through criteria such as average population and class richness.

- **Average Population** (AP) - This metric measures the average distribution of instances compared to the number of classes in an ontology. It is the number of instances of the knowledge base (I) over the number of classes in the ontology schema (Eq. 4).

$$AP = \frac{|I|}{|C|} \tag{4}$$

- **Class Richness** (CR) - This metric tells how instances are related to classes in the ontology schema. It is the number of classes that are used in the knowledge base over the total number of classes in the ontology schema (Eq. 5).

$$CR = \frac{|C'|}{|C|} \tag{5}$$

3.4   Graph Metrics

The graph metrics measure the structural features of the ontology graph such as the absolute root and leaf cardinality, average and total number of paths, average and maximum depth and breadth, etc. The graph metrics adopted in this study are defined in Eqs. 6 to 11.

- **Absolute Root Cardinality** (ARC) - This is the property of a directed graph. It represents the number of root nodes in the graph (g). The ARC is represented in Eq. 6.

$$ARC = n_{ROO \subseteq g} \tag{6}$$

  where $n_{ROO \subseteq g}$ is the number of elements of the set of root notes ROO in g.

- **Absolute Leaf Cardinality** (AC) - This metric represents the number of leaf nodes (LEA) in the directed graph (g) of the ontology and is calculated in Eq. 7.

$$AC = n_{LEA \subseteq g} \tag{7}$$

  where $n_{LEA \subseteq g}$ is the number of elements of the set of leaf nodes LEA in g.

- **Average Depth** (AD) - This metric represents the total number of elements on all the paths j belonging to the set of paths (P) of the graph (g). The AD is represented in Eq. 8.

$$AD = \sum_{j}^{P} N_{j \in P} \tag{8}$$

  where $N_{j \in P}$ is the number of elements on the path j belonging to the set of paths (P) of the graph (g).

- **Maximum Depth** (MD) - It is the height of the graph (g) and represented as in Eq. 9.

$$MD = N_{j \in P} \forall i \exists j (N_{j \in P} \geqslant N_{i \in P}) \tag{9}$$

  where $N_{j \in P}$ and $N_{i \in P}$ are the number of elements of each path j belonging to the set of paths (P) of the graph (g).

- **Average Breadth** (AB) - This metric represents how far the ontology has horizontally modelled hierarchies of knowledge. The AB is calculated in Eq. 10.

$$AB = \frac{1}{n_{L \subseteq g}} \sum_{j}^{L} N_{j \in L} \tag{10}$$

  where L is the set of levels/generations in the graph g, $n_{L \subseteq g}$ the number of elements in L and $N_{j \in L}$ the number of elements of each level j in L.

- **Maximum Breadth** (MB) - This metric is the number of elements of each level/generation j in the set of levels L of the graph g. Equation 11 represents the MD.

$$MB = N_{j \in L} \forall i \exists j (N_{j \in L} \geqslant N_{i \in L}) \tag{11}$$

The ontology quality metrics defined above are linked to quality evaluation criteria in the next subsection.

3.5   Correlating Quality Metrics and Evaluation Criteria

As mentioned earlier, the quality metrics in Eqs. 1 to 11 are further mapped to quality dimensions or criteria to evaluate the quality of e-government ontologies. In fact, the quality metrics defined in Eqs. 1 to 11 correlate with four quality criteria [9] as follows:

- **Accuracy** - This quality evaluation criterion indicates to which extend the ontology under evaluation represents the real world domain it is modelling [21]. The schema metrics in Eqs. 1 to 3 and the graph metrics in Eqs. 8 to 11 correlate with this criterion [9].
- **Understandability** - This quality evaluation criterion measures the comprehension of the constituents of the ontologies such as the concepts, relationships/properties, and their meanings [9]. The quality metric in Eq. 7 correlates with this quality criterion [9].
- **Cohesion** - This ontology quality evaluation criterion indicates the degree of relatedness amongst the constituents of the ontologies. In other words, it measures the degree to which the classes of the ontology are related to one another [22]. Two graph metrics in Eqs. 6 and 7 are mapped to this quality dimension/criterion [9].
- **Conciseness** - This quality evaluation criterion measures the degree of usefulness of the knowledge in the ontology [23]. The knowledge base metrics in Eqs. 4 and 5 correlate with this quality criterion [9].

The fifth quality criterion, namely, computational efficiency is not mapped to any quality metric in Eqs. 1 to 11 [9]; furthermore, it is not mapped to any quality metric at all in [9]. Due to this limitation, the quality criterion of computational efficiency is not discussed in this study.

4   Experiments

This section presents the dataset and the experimental results of the study.

4.1   Dataset

The dataset in this study is constituted of 20 ontologies of the e-government domain. Each ontology in the dataset is assigned an index $O_i, 1 \leq i \leq 20$ to ease its reference in the discussions. Table 1 shows the list of ontologies in the dataset with their names and source files. The extensions of these e-government ontologies' files reveal their formats including XML, OWL and KOAN. The XML files are web documents that include the RDF/OWL files of the corresponding ontologies. It is shown in Table 1 that the majority of e-government ontologies downloaded are in OWL format, which is the *state-of-the-art* language for building ontologies. It can also be noticed that the ontologies O_{14} and O_{20} in Table 1 have the same names and different source file extensions; these are two different

Table 1. E-government ontologies in the dataset

Index	Ontology	Source file
O_1	Public contracts ontology	vocabulary_2.xml
O_2	geographica ontology	vocabulary_69.xml
O_3	OntoGov ontology	vocabulary_89.xml
O_4	GovStat ontology	vocabulary_40.xml
O_5	Central Government ontology	central-government.owl
O_6	Government core ontology	gc.owl
O_7	Government ontology	oe1gov.owl
O_8	US government ontology	us1gov.owl
O_9	geopolitical ontology	geopolitical.owl
O_{10}	Quonto quality ontology	quontoV2.owl
O_{11}	Domain ontology	DomainOntology.kaon
O_{12}	Legal ontology	LegalOntology.koan
O_{13}	Life cycle ontology	LifeCycleOn tology.koan
O_{14}	Life event ontology	lifeEventOntology.koan
O_{15}	Organisational ontology	OrganisationalOntology.kaon
O_{16}	CPSV-AP_IT ontology	CPSV-AP_IT.owl
O_{17}	gPAP ontology	administration.owl
O_{18}	Municipal ontology	ontology.owl
O_{19}	Open 311 ontology	open311.owl
O_{20}	Life event ontology	leo.owl

Table 2. Locations of the e-government ontologies

Ontology	Web link
O_1	http://ci.emse.fr/opensensingcity/ns/result/domain/government/
O_2	http://ci.emse.fr/opensensingcity/ns/result/domain/government/
O_3	http://ci.emse.fr/opensensingcity/ns/result/domain/government/
O_4	http://ci.emse.fr/opensensingcity/ns/result/domain/government/
O_5	http://epimorphics.com/public/vocabulary/lg/local-government.html
O_6	http://oegov.us/
O_7	http://oegov.us/
O_8	http://oegov.us/
O_9	http://oegov.us/
O_{10}	http://imu.ntua.gr/software/quonto-quality-ontology-e-gov-portals
O_{11}	https://*/project/ontogov/Ontologies/DomainOntology.kaon
O_{12}	https://*/project/ontogov/Ontologies/LegalOntology.kaon
O_{13}	https://*/project/ontogov/Ontologies/LifeCycleOntology.kaon
O_{14}	https://*/project/ontogov/Ontologies/LifeEventOntology.kaon
O_{15}	https://*/project/ontogov/Ontologies/OrganisationalOntology.kaon
O_{16}	https://dati.gov.it/onto/CPSV-AP_IT.owl
O_{17}	http://lpis.csd.auth.gr/ontologies/ontolist.html#bonsai
O_{18}	https://github.com/structureddynamics/MUNI
O_{19}	http://ontology.eil.utoronto.ca/
O_{20}	https://sites.google.com/site/lifeeventontology/

Table 3. Graph, knowledge base and schema metrics of e-government ontologies

	ARC	AC	AD	MD	AB	MB	AP	CR	AR	IR	RR
O_1	19	19	1,136364	2	5,5	19	0,681818	0,090909	0,59099	0,136364	0,930233
O_2	7	10	3,033333	5	2,142857	7	0,526316	0,105263	0,315789	0,736842	0,222222
O_3	2	10	3,285714	5	2,33333	4	0,352941	0,058824	0	1	0,346154
O_4	3	10	2,076923	3	3,25	6	0	0	0,076923	1,230769	0,407407
O_5	15	42	2,836066	6	3,388889	15	0,016949	0,016949	0,067797	0,779661	0,577982
O_6	3	2	1,5	2	1,5	3	1,166667	0,333333	0,666667	1,333333	0,5
O_7	26	112	3,419162	6	3,604317	33	0,134831	0,02809	0,033708	1,601124	0,2711
O_8	3	2	1,5	2	1,5	3	1,166667	0,333333	0,666667	1,333333	0,5
O_9	1	8	3,416667	4	2,4	4	26	0,583333	7,416667	7,333333	0,169811
O_{10}	26	92	2,447368	4	4,956522	26	1,386364	0,530303	0,106061	1,515152	0,602386
O_{11}	2	7	2,727273	4	2,2	3	4,727273	0,272727	0,363636	0,818182	0,25
O_{12}	2	6	2,375	3	2,666667	5	1,375	0,125	0,375	0,75	0,4
O_{13}	2	6	2,25	3	2,666667	4	1,875	0,125	0,75	0,75	0,333333
O_{14}	2	107	3,801587	4	6,3	17	0,992063	0,007937	0	0,984127	0
O_{15}	2	10	3,285714	5	2,333333	4	0,352941	0,058824	0	1	0,346154
O_{16}	22	22	1,3125	2	2,909091	22	0,54	0,12	0,36	2,12	0,341615
O_{17}	16	56	3,009709	6	2,575	16	0,652174	0,434783	0,217391	1,978261	0,172727
O_{18}							0	0	0,042231	1,130279	0,003862
O_{19}	8	112	3,639706	5	5,666667	25	0	0	0,133333	1,148148	0,093567
O_{20}	8	26	1,84375	3	4,571429	9	1,90625	0,5	0,4375	0,75	0,813956

ontologies developed by different authors. Table 2 provides the web links where the ontologies in Table 1 are located.

It can be noticed that the web links of the ontologies O_{11} to O_{15} in Table 2 include a start (*) symbol; this was included to reduce the length of these links to fit in the table onto one line. The start (*) symbol in these web links can be replaced by *master.dl.sourceforge.net* to get the full links to these ontologies. Furthermore, from the web links in Table 2, it can be seen that some of the e-government ontologies download are located in France, United States, Greece, Italy and Canada. Moreover, the names of some ontologies such as *CPSV-AP_IT.owl* and *quontoV2.owl* in Table 1 are not self-explanatory. The *CPSV-AP_IT.owl* is the Core Public Service Vocabulary Application Profile ontology of the Italian government, whereas, the *quontoV2.owl*, where the acronym QUONTO stands for Quality Ontology is an ontology that formalizes the knowledge needed for a multi-perspective and adaptive evaluation of e-government portals.

4.2   Results and Discussions

The web links of ontologies in Table 2 were used to download their source codes (column 3 in Table 1). The source code of each ontology was loaded into the OntoMetrics online system to compute its 11 quality metrics in Eqs. 1 to 11. The resulting quality metrics of all the e-government ontologies in the dataset are provided in Table 3. It can be noticed in Table 3 that there are no values for the graph metrics of the ontology O_{18}; the reason is that the graph metrics of this ontology were unavailable in the OntoMetrics outputs. Furthermore, the values of certain metrics are zeros for a number of ontologies across Table 3; however, the majority of metrics where successfully gathered for all the ontologies in the dataset. As shown in Table 3, the metrics are small numbers; only the graph metric AC (third column in Table 3) is higher for some ontologies, reaching hundred for the ontologies O_7, O_{14} and O_{19}. The ontologies quality metrics in Table 3 are further used to assess the quality of e-government ontologies in the dataset according to the mapping defined in Subsect. 3.5 next.

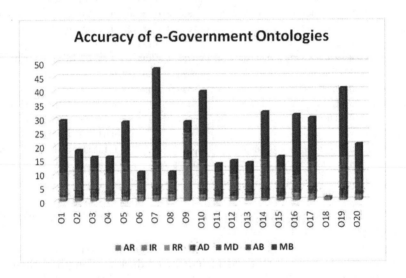

Fig. 1. Accurancy of e-government ontologies

- **Accuracy** - Figure 1 shows the measurement of the accuracy of e-government ontologies. Let's recall that the accuracy quality criterion measures the extend to which an ontology models its target domain. Figure 1 portrays that most of the e-government ontologies in the dataset are not horizontal nor vertical ontologies. In fact, on the one hand, an important part of these ontologies have low IR and relatively high AB; this means there are interesting accounts of detailed knowledge of the e-government domain represented in these ontologies [21]. On the other hand, Fig. 1 reveals that the RR of e-government ontologies in the dataset are small numbers between 0 and 1 and relatively closed to 0; this indicates a substantive amount of subclass relations in these ontologies [21]. The presence of subclass relations in the e-government ontologies in the dataset is also witnessed in their relatively higher values for the MD and MB in Fig. 1. In light of the above, it can

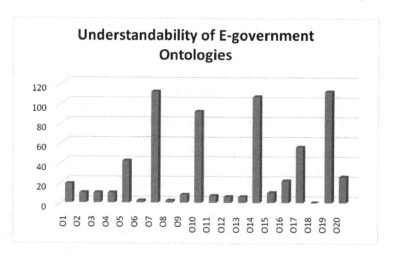

Fig. 2. Understandability of e-government ontologies

be concluded that the e-government ontologies in the dataset include a balanced number of subclass and non-subclass relations; therefore, these ontologies partially represent specialised knowledge of the e-government domain and potentially general knowledge of related domains. This may be an indication that these ontologies have inherited existing taxonomies of knowledge or reused some upper level ontologies.

- **Understandability** - The results of the measurement of how easy it is to understand the e-government ontologies in the dataset is displayed in Fig. 2. It appears in Fig. 2 and Table 3 that the AC of most of the ontologies in the dataset is relatively high compared to the values of the rest of metrics. This indicates that parts of the e-government ontologies in the dataset are taxonomies of subclass relations; this corroborate the finding reached with the analysis of the accuracy criterion above. What could be learned from this as far as the understandability of ontology is concerned is that, an ontology with subclass relations could display unambiguous structure of their classes and relations, thereby, facilitating their comprehension. However, a full comprehension of an ontology would require the use of a qualitative evaluation approach with the involvement of human users to assess the documentations and content of the ontology [9,20]. This aspect of the evaluation is out of the scope of this study and may constitute an avenue for future research.
- **Cohesion** - Fig. 3 portrays the results of the measurement of the cohesion of e-government ontologies. Let's recall that the cohesion quality criterion measures the level of relatedness amongst the classes of the ontology [22]. The graph metrics ARC and AC in Fig. 3 confirm once more that there are substantive subclass relations in the e-government ontologies in the dataset. In fact, it is shown in Fig. 3 that all the e-government ontologies have non-zero values for both metrics (Table 3) and the values of the AC metric for some

ontologies is quiet high. This indicates that components of the e-government ontologies studied are represented with subclass relations.

A similar finding was reached in the analysis of the accuracy and understandability of these ontologies earlier. Therefore, it can be concluded that the classes in the e-government ontologies in the dataset are interconnected and related [22].

- **Conciseness** - The conciseness of e-government ontologies in the dataset is displayed in Fig. 4. This criterion measures the level of utility of the knowledge represented in the ontologies [23]. The measurement of the conciseness of the e-government ontologies in the dataset is done with the knowledge base metrics including the AP and CR (Table 3). These metrics represent the distribution of instances across the classes in the ontologies [21]. Figure 4 and Table 3 portray that the AP and CR metrics have very low values for most of the e-government ontologies in the dataset. This is an indication that the number of instances are very low in the e-government ontologies studied and that these ontologies do not include enough data to exemplify the knowledge represented in their classes [21].

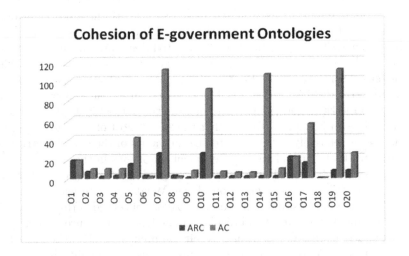

Fig. 3. Cohesion of e-government ontologies

In light of the above analysis of the quality metrics of e-government ontologies against the quality dimensions/criteria, it can be concluded that the e-government ontologies in the dataset have a balanced number of non-subclass and subclass relations. This indicates that these ontologies represent details e-government domain knowledge as well as generic knowledge of related domains inherited from existing taxonomies or obtained through the reuse of other ontologies. The presence of subclass relations in the e-government ontologies in the dataset display their level of cohesion and may ease their understanding. In

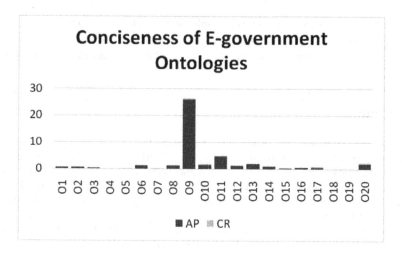

Fig. 4. Conciseness of e-government ontologies

fact, the taxonomy parts of these ontologies represented with subclass relations may provide a clear representation/interconnection of their classes and relations, thereby, contributing to their comprehension. However, as indicated earlier, a better comprehension of these ontologies would require the use of a qualitative method with the involvement of human users to assess their documentations and content. The analysis of the quality metrics of the e-government ontologies in the dataset also revealed that they contain very low number of instances, indicating that these ontologies do not include enough data to use the knowledge represented in them. This shortcoming may be addressed through the reuse and population of these ontologies in other e-government projects.

5   Conclusion

In this study, 11 quality metrics adopted from the OntoMetrics framework for ontology evaluation are used to analyse and evaluate the quality of e-government ontologies against a set of quality evaluation dimensions/criteria. The quality metrics of 20 e-government ontologies are calculated via the OntoMetrics online system. These metrics are further analysed and evaluated. The evaluation results reveal that the e-government ontologies in the dataset are partially accurate as they represent details e-government domain knowledge as well as generic knowledge of related domains. The results also explain the cohesion and understanding of the e-government ontologies on the basis of the presence of non-subclass and subclass relations in these ontologies. Lastly, the results revealed a low number of instances in the e-government ontologies in the dataset; correlating the view that these ontologies do not include enough data to facilitate the use of knowledge represented in them. This drawback may be addressed through the reuse and population of these ontologies with more instances in other projects.

The future direction of research would be to find more e-government ontologies on the web to improve the size of the dataset and to investigate the use of artificial intelligence techniques in the analysis of quality metrics of e-government ontologies.

References

1. Adadi, A., Berrada, M., Chenouni, D., Bounabat, B.: A semantic web service composition for e-government. J. Theor. Appl. Inf. Technol. **71**, 460–467 (2015)
2. Fonou-Dombeu, J.V., Huisman, M.: Engineering semantic web services for government business processes automation. In: Kő, A., Francesconi, E. (eds.) EGOVIS 2015. LNCS, vol. 9265, pp. 40–54. Springer, Cham (2015). https://doi.org/10.1007/978-3-319-22389-6_4
3. Lonsdale, D., Embley, D.W., Ding, Y., Xu, L., Hepp, M.: Reusing ontologies and language components for ontology generation. Data Knowl. Eng. **69**, 318–330 (2010)
4. Bontas, E.P., Mochol, M., Tolksdorf, R.: Case studies on ontology reuse. In: 5th International Conference on Knowledge Management (I-Know 2005), Graz, Austria (2005)
5. Ochs, C., Perl, Y., Geller, J., Arabandi, S., Tudorache, T., Musen, M.A.: An empirical analysis of ontology reuse in BioPortal. J. Biomed. Inform. **71**, 165–177 (2017)
6. Sabou, M., Lopez, V., Motta, E., Uren, V.: Ontology selection: ontology evaluation on the real semantic web. In: WWW 2006, Edinburgh, UK (2006)
7. Yang, Z., Zhang, D., Ye, C.: Evaluation metrics for ontology complexity and evolution analysis. In: Proceedings of the IEEE International Conference on e-Business Engineering, Shanghai, China, pp. 162–170 (2006)
8. Zhang, H., Li, Y.F., Tan, H.B.K.: Measuring design complexity of semantic web ontologies. J. Syst. Softw. **83**, 803–814 (2010)
9. Lantow, B.: OntoMetrics: putting metrics into use for ontology evaluation. In: Proceedings of the 8th International Joint Conference on Knowledge Discovery, Knowledge Engineering and Knowledge Management (IC3K 2016), Joaquim Filipe, Portugal, pp. 186–191 (2016)
10. Corradini, F., Angelis, F., Polzonetti, A., Re, B., Brugnoni, E.: E-GoVQoS: an ontology for quality of e-governmemnt services. In: Wimmer, M.A., Scholl, H.J., Gronlund, A., Andersen, K.V. (eds.) EGOV 2006. LNCS, vol. 4084, pp. 171–178. Springer, Heidelberg (2006)
11. Myrseth, P., Stang, J., Dalberg, V.: A data quality framework applied to e-government metadata - a prerequsite to establish governance of interoperable e-services. In: Proceedings of the International Conference on E-Business and EGovernment (ICEE 2011), Shanghai, China (2011)
12. Magoutas, B., Halaris, C., Mentzas, G.: An ontology for the multi-perspective evaluation of quality in e-government services. In: Wimmer, M.A., Scholl, J., Grönlund, Å. (eds.) EGOV 2007. LNCS, vol. 4656, pp. 318–329. Springer, Heidelberg (2007). https://doi.org/10.1007/978-3-540-74444-3_27
13. Rodríguez, R.A., Giulianelli, D.A., Welicki, L., Vera, P.M.: Measurement framework for evaluating e-governance on municipalities websites. In: ICEGOV 2008, Cairo, Egypt, pp. 381–387 (2008)
14. Candiello, A., Albarelli, A., Cortesi, A.: Quality and impact monitoring for local eGovernment services. Transform. Gov.: People, Process Policy **6**, 112–125 (2012)

15. Fonou-Dombeu, J.V., Kazadi, Y.K.: Complexity based analysis of eGov ontologies. In: Kő, A., Francesconi, E. (eds.) EGOVIS 2017. LNCS, vol. 10441, pp. 115–128. Springer, Cham (2017). https://doi.org/10.1007/978-3-319-64248-2_9
16. Ouchetto, H., Ouchetto, O., Roudies, O.: Ontology-oriented e-gov services retrieval. Int. J. Comput. Sci. Issues **2**, 99–107 (2012)
17. Distinto, I., d'Aquin, M., Motta, E.: LOTED2: an ontology of European public procurement notices. Semant. Web J. **7**, 1–15 (2016)
18. Ferneda, E., et al.: Potential of ontology for interoperability in e-government: discussing international initiatives and the Brazilliang case. Braz. J. Inf. Stud.: Res. Trends **10**, 47–57 (2016)
19. Lamharhar, H., Chiadmi, D., Benhlima, L.: Ontology-based knowledge representation for e-government domain. In: Proceedings of the 17th International Conference on Information Integration and Web-based Applications & Services (iiWAS 2015), Brussels, Belgium (2015)
20. Fonou-Dombeu, J.V., Huisman, M.: Adaptive search and selection of domain ontologies for reuse on the semantic web. J. Emerg. Technol. Web Intell. **5**, 230–239 (2013)
21. Tartir, S., Arpinar, B., Moore, M., Sheth, A., Aleman-Meza, B.: OntoQA: metric-based ontology quality analysis. In: IEEE Workshop on Knowledge Acquisition from Distributed, Autonomous, Semantically Heterogeneous Data and Knowledge Sources, USA, pp 45–53 (2005)
22. Yao, H., Orme, A.M., Etzkorn, L.: Cohesion metrics for ontology design and application. J. Comput. Sci. **1**, 107 (2005)
23. Pak, J., Zhou, L.: A framework for ontology evaluation. In: Sharman, R., Rao, H.R., Raghu, T.S. (eds.) WEB 2009. LNBIP, vol. 52, pp. 10–18. Springer, Heidelberg (2010). https://doi.org/10.1007/978-3-642-17449-0_2

Digitalization and Transparency

Towards Blockchain Technology to Support Digital Government

Reyan M. Zein[1](✉) ⓘ and Hossana Twinomurinzi[2](✉) ⓘ

[1] Sudan University of Science and Technology, Khartoum, Sudan
reyan.aziz@yahoo.com
[2] School of Computing, University of South Africa, Roodepoort, South Africa
twinoh@unisa.ac.za

Abstract. Blockchain technology is considered as one of the fourth industrial revolution technologies that is transforming governments. This study systematically reviews literature on research into blockchain technologies for government with the aim to map opportunities, challenges and gaps. The main findings show that research has ignored the commercial value of blockchain for digital government with the emphasis on sharing, trust and security, as well as the ability to enhance government infrastructure and services. There is an opportunity to investigate further how blockchain could be gradually reinventing the traditional notion of government with its transactional *intermediaries* that are necessary for the classification of G2G, G2C or G2B. The methodological emphasis has been on the design research method, which unsurprisingly relates to the emerging nature of blockchain technology. There is a clear opportunity to begin more reflective research on emergent patterns. Limited research has been conducted in developing countries despite the leapfrogging and governance opportunities that blockchain technology presents.

Keywords: Blockchain · E-government · Digital government · Infrastructure

1 Introduction

Developments in information and communication technologies (ICTs) have allowed governments to use technology for their internal and external transactions, enabling the citizen to obtain information quickly, efficiently and transparently. Blockchains, which were proposed in 2008 by Satoshi Nakamoto for the financial sector [1] are considered to be one of the significant, disruptive fourth industrial revolution technologies [2].

Blockchain technology has a wide range of applications, including cryptocurrency, financial technology, risk control, the Internet of Things, intelligent industries, supply chain and transactions involving digital assets [1, 3]. Blockchain offers an attractive solution to distributed systems challenges relating to performance and security [4]. There are high expectations of the value of blockchain technology due to its key features, namely decentralization, peer-to-peer transactions, persistency, anonymity and auditability [3]. In this paper, we attempt to understand how blockchain technology has been investigated in the context of digital government in order to identify existing challenges, gaps and opportunities.

© Springer Nature Switzerland AG 2019
A. Kő et al. (Eds.): EGOVIS 2019, LNCS 11709, pp. 207–220, 2019.
https://doi.org/10.1007/978-3-030-27523-5_15

The remainder of the paper is structured as follows: The next section contains background information about both digital government and blockchain technology. In the third section, the review methods is outlined. The fourth section contains a classification framework of how the identified papers were selected and analysed. The fifth section contains the findings, and the sixth presents a discussion and research agenda. The final section suggests areas for future research and the conclusions.

2 Background and Motivations

2.1 Digital Government (E-government)

The term digital government, previously known as e-government, refers to the use of ICT to promote innovative, efficient and cost-effective government, and to facilitate access to government information and services. It comprises the utilization of ICTs in public sector administration which can lead to improvement in public services and processes [5]. E-governance is a wider term that covers a state's institutional arrangements, decision-making processes, and the interrelationships between government and the public [6]. Digital government includes organisational, managerial and technological aspects in eight broad categories (Table 1):

Table 1. Digital government categories

Digital government classification	Definition	Description
G2C	Government-to-citizen	Offers generic public services online, specifically electronic service delivery involving exchange and communication
C2G	Citizen-to-government	
G2B	Government-to-business	Assists in driving e-transaction initiatives, such as e-procurement
B2G	Business-to-government	
G2E	Government-to-employee	Launches initiatives to make e-career applications and processing systems paperless in an e-office
G2G	Government-to-government	Enable governments departments or agencies to cooperate and communicate online via the Presidency's mega database
G2 N	Government-to-non-profit	Exchange of information and communication between government, the legislature, non-profit organisations, political parties and social organisations
N2G	Non-profit-to-government	

In this paper, we only focus on the three categories of G2G, G2B and G2C. In addition to the eight categories mentioned, there are other digital government categories, such as digital government maturity and the digital government index (networked readiness index), which are not considered in this paper.

2.2 Blockchain Technology

The essential features of blockchains are their ability to be applied in a decentralized and heterogeneous system, and their ability to ensure the accurate exchange of data between endpoints [7]. Blockchains could be defined as a direct peer-to-peer (P2P) distributed ledger technology for transactional applications that enables safe transactions without centralized supervision when there is a lack of trust among users. They could be considered as the implementation layer in the distribution system to ensure integrity of data [8]. Blockchains are also described as public ledgers where committed transactions appear in a chain of blocks that always grows and increases by appending new blocks [3]. They can work in a decentralized environment and integrate many essential technologies, such as cryptographic hash functions, digital signatures and distributed consensus mechanisms.

The peer-to-peer distributed ledger is useful for cloud computing services because it functions like data source assurance, auditing, digital asset control and distributed consensus management. The consensus technique of blockchains facilitates the structuring of a tamper-proof environment, where transactions are assured using groups of trusted, creditable participants or miners [4]. There are three types of blockchains; public blockchains, private blockchains and consortium blockchains [9]. A public blockchain allows each participant to send transactions and to view the data [7]. Each node in a public blockchain can take part in the consensus process. Transactions in a public blockchain are visible to the public. Data in public blockchains is immutable, since transactions are stored in different nodes in the distributed network – it is nearly impossible to tamper with a public blockchain. Efficiency is however low in public blockchains – it takes plenty of time to propagate transactions and blocks, as there are large numbers of nodes on public blockchain networks. As a result, transaction throughput is limited and latency is high. Everyone can join the consensus process of a public blockchain [3].

A private blockchain offers blockchains access to a known list of entities to create a transaction on the blockchain [7]. Private blockchains are fully centralized as each is controlled by a single group. Every private blockchain is fully controlled by one organization that can determine the final consensus. Transactions in a private blockchain use read permissions to determine visibility. Data in a private blockchain is not fully immutable, because a private blockchain is not tamperproof – if the majority of the dominant organization wants to tamper with the blockchain, it can be done. However, there are fewer validators, therefore private blockchains can be more efficient in terms of time. Private blockchains are permissioned, and each node needs to be certified to join the consensus process [3]. There are two types of private blockchain [10], namely permissionless blockchains and permissioned blockchains. The difference between these types lies in the openness of participation in the consensus mechanism of the blockchain system; they have different requirements for participation in validating transactions. There are therefore two mains private blockchain architectures:

- Permissionless blockchains. Allow all nodes to participate in the consensus mechanism.
- Permissioned blockchains. Use the transaction-consensus mechanism and only a given set of nodes is allowed to participate. Permission is based on criteria determined by the architect of the permissioned blockchain.

Consortium blockchains combine the features of public and private blockchains [7]. They are partially centralized and only a selected set of nodes is responsible for validating the block in consensus determination. Read permission varies in a consortium blockchain, as it can be decided whether the stored information is public or restricted. If the majority of the consortium wants to tamper the blockchain, it can be done. The approach followed by consortium blockchains might be more efficient because they require fewer validators and any one node needs to be confirmed to join the consensus process in a consortium blockchain [3]. Blockchain technology as a newly distributed infrastructure and computational paradigm uses; blockchain data structures to verify and store data; a distributed node consensus algorithm to generate and update data; cryptography to ensure data transmission and access security; and intelligent automation script code contracts to program and operate data [2]. These features offer potential solutions to digital government as they provide the needed security and required consensus.

Blockchain tamper-proof and persistent capabilities are helpful for citizens to access reliable government information, and can as such boost public sector credibility [1]. The value of the blockchain lies in the certainty that it represents a real event or the reality at a particular time, which allows for trust among parties. Conceptually, it performs like a state machine that stores the status of something and changes that status, while keeping an original record of the previous states [11].

Blockchains are characterised by their speed, robustness, openness, portability and extensibility. In addition, blockchain nodes can be made anonymous, which can increase the safety and trust of government transactions. There are many examples of public sector challenges that can be solved with blockchains, such as those posed by financial transactions, criminal activities, legal aspects and economic risks [12, 13]. Modern blockchains are implemented to ensure security, privacy, throughput, size and bandwidth, performance, usability, data integrity and scalability. These contexts give rise to many challenges such as throughput, latency, size and bandwidth, scalability, costs, data malleability, authentication, privacy, double-spending attacks, wasted resources and usability, among others [14]. Another area for development is the hard merging of split chains for administrative or versioning purposes [14, 15].

Batubara et al. [16] identified three categories of blockchain challenges. Technological challenges relate to security, scalability and flexibility. Usability challenges relate to interoperability, computational efficiency, storage size and, importantly, cost-effectiveness. Organizational challenges relate to the need for new governance models and acceptance as required in new contexts with multiple institutions and stakeholders. Other challenges include the implications of blockchain technology, trust and the auditing of blockchain applications. In an environmental context, laws and regulatory support are essential to ensure that users have legal certainty; in other words, they must be sure about the rights and obligations of the parties to the agreement, and informed about legal mans to resolve any disputes.

3   Research Methods

This paper aimed to determine how the application of blockchain technology for digital government has been researched. We followed Okoli and Schabram's [17] guide for conducting a systematic literature review (SLR). The guide includes specific activities, such as the development of a review protocol, defining selection of studies, data extraction and reporting the results. Below subsections are reports on these activities.

3.1   Research Objective

The general objective of the study was to answer the following research question: *How has blockchain technology been researched in the context of the digital government?* The primary question was supported by a secondary question: *What are the opportunities, challenges and risks identified in the research on blockchain technology for digital government?*

3.2   Data Source and Search Strategies

The following electronic search engines were used because of their multidisciplinary nature:

- IEEE Explore (https://ieeexplore.ieee.org/Xplore/home.jsp)
- Springer (www.springerlink.com)
- ACM Digital library (www.portal.acm.org/dl.cfm)
- Google Scholar (http://scholar.google.com/)
- Wiley InterScience (www.interscience.wiley.com/)
- Elsevier Science Direct (https://www.sciencedirect.com)

The search terms and their synonyms are given in the Table 2 below:

Table 2.   Terms and phrases in the search string

Type	Category	Keywords
1	Blockchain technology	Blockchain technology Block-chain technology Block chain technology Blockchain
2	Digital government	Egovernment E-government E government Digital government

The Boolean operator "AND" was used to combine all search elements to select every article that relates to both blockchains and digital government. Moreover, each potential aggregation of one element from Category 1 AND Category 2 was retrieved.

First Stage. Collecting the Related Papers

The following was the refined search string executed for each of the search engines:

(Blockchain technology OR Block-chain technology OR Block chain technology) AND (E government OR Digital government OR E-government OR Egovernment).

Second Stage. The Inclusion and Exclusion Criteria

An exclusion and exclusion criteria were used to select the papers that would be adopted and continue to the next stage of the review:

- Criteria derived from the main research question.
- Restriction by language (English-only papers).
- Restriction by date range (2015–2018).
- The search excluded articles about editorials, discussion comments, news, and summaries of tutorials, panels and poster sessions.

Third Stage. Practical Screening

All the titles, abstracts and keywords of the studies that resulted from stage two were scanned. At this stage, articles with no relevance to the scope of the SLR were excluded. For the papers that were included, the introduction and conclusions of each article was reviewed to determine the relevance. The three steps resulted in the hits as described in Table 3.

Table 3. Results of search string execution for each search engine

Search engine	Returned articles	After exclusion and quality checks
IEEE Explore	4	3
Springer Link	230	69
ACM Digital library	4	4
Google Scholar	264	78
Wiley InterScience	68	16
Elsevier Science Direct	72	31

Fourth Stage. Completing Reading and Quality Checklist

The final criteria were a quality checklist. The questions below were used to determine the quality of the final list of selected papers.

- *Does the paper address the use of any blockchain technology in digital government?*
- *Does the paper discuss any real-life experience of using blockchain technology in digital government?*
- *Is the objective of the paper clearly mentioned?*
- *Does the paper discuss the contextual factors of digital government adequately?*

4   Classification Framework

We adopted a classification framework similar to that used by Amui et al. [18] to map and analyze the selected papers. The classifiers were by scope, focus, research methods, sector, research level, status, taxonomy and region.

Scope refers to the focus of the paper with regard to 1A (sharing, trust and security); 1B (business and the coin market); 1C (the Internet of Things); and 1D (public and social services).

The *focus* of the paper assessed the contribution of blockchain technology to digital government as either contextual or central. The focus was contextual 2A (blockchain as a support theory) if the study did not serve a particular digital government type, but considered digital government in general. The focus was central if it focused on one of the digital government types 2B (G2G); 2C (G2C); and 2D (G2B).

The *research method* indicates the methodological approach of each article as 3A (qualitative research); 3B (quantitative research); 3C (conceptual); 3D (empirical research); 3E (case studies or interviews); 3F (surveys); and 3G (design research). The dimensions of empirical was purposefully included to indicate that primary and not secondary data was used. Case studies, interviews and surveys were included as these represent the dominant methods.

The *sector* was considered in terms of the government technology sector as 4A (infrastructure); 4B (services); and 4C (both infrastructure and services).

The *research level* was categorized according to the level of theoretical engagement as 5A (prescriptive study); 5B (descriptive study); and 5C (conceptual study). Descriptive studies describe, explain and validate studies. Prescriptive studies attempt to determine the strength of cause-effect relationships. Conceptual studies focus on developing new frameworks and emergent theories [20, 21].

The *status* referred to whether the research had already been done or was in the planning phase as 6A (research implemented); and 6B (research proposed).

The *taxonomy* was according to the three types of blockchain; 7A (public block-chains); 7B (private blockchains); and 7C (consortium blockchains). This classification depends on consensus determination, read permission, immutability, efficiency, centralization and consensus processes [3].

The region in which the research was undertaken was broadly adopted from two broad categories: developed economies and developing economies [22]. In this study, transition countries were also categorized as developing countries. The categories were 8A (developed countries) and 8B (developing country).

5   Results and Findings

In this section, the findings are discussed based on the classification framework.

5.1 Scope

Table 4. Distribution based on scope

Scope			
Description	Value	Frequency	Percentage
Sharing and trust; security	A	21	39.6%
Business; coin market	B	9	17%
IOT	C	7	13.2%
Public and social services	D	16	30.2%

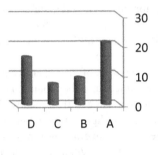

Table (4) above suggests that the greatest focus of the papers is on sharing, trust and security, followed by public and social services. The least focus is on the use of blockchain technologies for the Internet of Things, business and coin markets. We identify that the research has therefore mainly paid attention to the non-commercial value of blockchain technologies. The commercial aspect of blockchains in digital government appears not to generate much research interest. The finding is not surprising when the context of digital government and non-commercial aspects is considered. More research is therefore required into the financial or commercial value of blockchain technologies for digital government, for example in the areas of revenue collection, trade and resource management.

5.2 Focus

Table 5. Distribution based on focus

Focus			
Description	Value	Frequency	Percentage
Blockchain as support theory	A	23	48%
G2G	B	8	16.7%
G2C	C	8	16.7%
G2B	D	9	18.8%

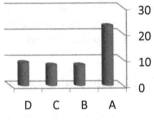

Table (5) reflects the results of the focus indicator and shows that about a half of the studies adopt a theoretical perspective to digital government. The findings suggest a low focus on G2G, G2C and G2B. This could be a result of the blockchain revising the entire notion of how government could work to eliminate the notion of middlemen. The results suggest that each of the major digital government types has nonetheless received some attention. There is therefore a research opportunity to understand how blockchain is re-inventing the notion of digital government and the associated intermediaries that enable the G2G, G2B and G2C.

5.3   Method

Table 6. Distribution based on method

Description	Value	Method Frequency	Percentage
Qualitative	A	10	14%
Quantitative	B	12	16.9%
Theoretical	C	14	19.7%
Empirical	D	7	9.9%
Case studies/interviews	E	9	12.7%
Survey	F	1	1.4%
Design research	G	18	25.4%

Table (6) above suggests that most of the studies use the design research method. The least focus is on surveys. This finding indicates that blockchain technology is still considered to be an emerging technology. As it is a growing technology, design science is more applicable. It suggests that there is an opportunity to combine learning and theory, because the append-only nature of an immutable ledger makes it useful for tracking processes, guaranteeing accountability and supporting transparency. In a public chain that uses open data, these attributes allow blockchain-based systems to be used to improve the transparency of government activities and services.

5.4 Sectors

Table 7. Distribution based on sectors

Sector			
Description	Value	Frequency	Percentage
Infrastructure	A	7	22.6%
Services	B	6	19.4%
Infrastructure and services	C	18	58%

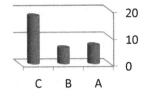

Table (7) above shows that the papers focus on both infrastructure and the services sectors. The work needs to start from scratch as there is very little existing infrastructure that can be used. In other words, the studies have targeted generic infrastructure that could be used to produce various services with a little or no changes, which could reduce the time and effort, and which could lead to an increase in the creation rate of new services. In fact, there is very little infrastructure that could be used in some regions. It is suggested that developed countries should bear the burden of infrastructure development for this technology. However, developing countries may face obstacles to secure the expected infrastructure. They may try to exploit existing infrastructure and tame it to accommodate blockchain technology.

5.5 Research Level

Table 8. Distribution based on research level

Research Level			
Description	Value	Frequency	Percentage
Perspective	A	8	19%
Descriptive	B	17	40.5%
Conceptual	C	17	40.5%

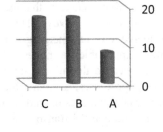

Table (8) above shows that the least research into blockchains has been done at a perspective level. The majority of the research has been done on the descriptive and conceptual levels. Perspective research can be thought of as a frame that serves both to include and to exclude certain things from our view. The finding similarly reflects the practical orientation that the research focuses on with less attention given to reflecting on patterns that could be emerging. There is therefore a gap to investigate the patterns emerging about the role of blockchain in digital government.

5.6   Status

Table 9. Distribution based on status

Status				
Description	Value	Frequency	Percentage	
Implemented	A	13	41.9%	
Proposed	B	18	58.1%	

According to Table (9) above, the status classifier shows that there are more proposed studies than implemented studies. This finding indicates that there are some challenges and obstacles that face blockchain technology implementation. There is opportunity to further reflect on the implementations, identify common practices and seek to apply the practices in the proposals.

5.7   Taxonomy

Table 10. Distribution based on taxonomy

Taxonomy				
Description	Value	Frequency	Percentage	
Public blockchain	A	14	45.2%	
Private blockchain	B	4	12.9%	
Consortium blockchain	C	13	41.9%	

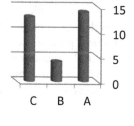

The taxonomy indicator (see Table (10) above) suggests that little research has been done into the private blockchain. More research into the public and consortium blockchains has been found. It is clear that researchers mainly focus on general services and that there are concerns that limit the expansion of the field. While public block-chains seek to give access to information to all, it focuses on protecting this information and the privacy of participants.

On the other hand, private blockchains offer a degree of flexibility concerning access control management and the permissions of each participant in the chain. This type of blockchain offers value to private businesses (e.g. companies and institutions) and enables them to transfer their information systems to another dimension that is provided by blockchain technology. Researchers and developers may therefore find it worthwhile to focus on private blockchains in digital government that may enable the private sector to participate effectively with government.

5.8   Region Type

Table 11. Distribution based on region type

Region Type				
Description	Value	Frequency	Percentage	
Developed country	A	19	61.3%	
Developing country	B	12	38.7%	

According to Table (11), developed countries contribute much more to research than developing countries. The emergent nature of blockchain technology may result in less attention in developing countries whose immediate concerns are probably around social and economic challenges. Nonetheless, the demonstrated failure of digital government in developing countries [23] and the associated challenges in service delivery and corruption, provide vast opportunity for attempts at how blockchain might create new institutional structures which cost less. For example, ownership, property management and voting systems are candidates for blockchain platforms; while smart contracts could manage the transfer of digital assets between parties [24, 25].

6   Discussion and Research Agenda

Blockchain is a fourth industrial revolution technology and its fast expansion in the world is recognised. This study suggests that contribution and adoption of this tech-nology is mainly in developed countries. Some of the reasons might include the stable and available ICT infrastructure and mature governance systems. Blockchain tech-nology is nonetheless a promising technology for developing countries for its potential to introduce governance systems. This is a research gap and opportunity.

The low interest in the commercial aspects of blockchains for digital government appear might highlight the implicit assumption that government is not profit making but service oriented. Blockchains in digital government could nonetheless provide platforms to facilitate for commercial transactions especially in instances where developing the platforms is prohibitive for private entities [26]. This is an area for further research inquiry.

7 Conclusion

This study was a systematic literature review of research about blockchain technology in digital government. The study finds that blockchain technology is an emerging research area that offers unique opportunities for research particularly in the commercial value of blockchains in digital government. Blockchains create secure and immutable information for different sectors in the context of digital government (healthcare, commerce, trade, stock markets, insurance, higher education, supply chains, asset management and banking). These capabilities can prove prohibitive for private entities.

The study shows that there is a lack of Internet of Things (IOT) studies into blockchain technology. Researchers have the opportunity to address the integration of IOT into blockchain technology in several areas, including agriculture, shipping and distribution.

Blockchain technology should be adopted by developing countries to reduce the digital gap and promote governance. Additional challenges and opportunities presented by blockchain technology include technical aspects, such as security, scalability, flexibility, usability, interoperability, computational efficiency, storage size and cost effectiveness. On the other hand, researchers should propose organisational rules to govern the acceptability of blockchains, as well as laws and regulatory support, to ensure that users have legal certainty about the laws that determine the rights and obligations of parties to blockchain agreements.

References

1. Hou, H.: The application of blockchain technology in E-government in China. In: 2017 26th International Conference on Computer Communications and Networks, ICCCN 2017 (2017)
2. Hou, J., Wang, H., Liu, P.: Applying the blockchain technology to promote the development of distributed photovoltaic in China (2018)
3. Zheng, Z., Xie, S., Dai, H.-N., Wang, H.: Blockchain Challenges and Opportunities: A Survey. Int. J. Web Grid Serv., 1–24 (2017)
4. Tosh, D.K., Shetty, S., Liang, X., Kamhoua, C.A., Kwiat, K.A., Njilla, L.: Security Implications of blockchain cloud with analysis of block withholding attack. In: Proceedings - 2017 17th IEEE/ACM International Symposium on Cluster, Cloud and Grid Computing, CCGRID 2017, pp. 458–467 (2017)
5. Assar, S.: Information and communications technology in education. In: International Encyclopedia of the Social & Behavioral Sciences, pp. 66–71 (2015)

6. Otieno, I., Omwenga, E.: Towards the development of a citizen- centric framework for evaluating the impact of eGovernment: a case study of developing countries. In: Conference Proceedings (2014). (978–1)
7. Dukkipati, C., Zhang, Y., Cheng, L.C.: Decentralized, blockchain based access control framework for the heterogeneous internet of things. In: Proceedings of the Third ACM Workshop on Attribute-Based Access Control – ABAC 2018, pp. 61–69 (2018)
8. Bragagnolo, S., Rocha, H., Denker, M., Ducasse, S.: SmartInspect: solidity smart contract inspector. In: 2018 International Workshop on Blockchain Oriented Software Engineering (IWBOSE), pp. 9–18 (2018)
9. Niranjanamurthy, M., Nithya, B.N., Jagannatha, S.: Analysis of Blockchain technology: pros, cons and SWOT (2018)
10. Study, C.C.: The consequences of blockchain architectures for the role of public administrations, pp. 6–7 (2017)
11. Adams, R., Parry, G., Godsiff, P., Ward, P.: The future of money and further applications of the blockchain. Strat. Change **26**, 417–422 (2017)
12. Tama, B.A., Kweka, B.J., Park, Y., Rhee, K.H.: A critical review of blockchain and its current applications. In: ICECOS 2017 - Proceeding of 2017 International Conference on Electrical Engineering and Computer Science: Sustaining the Cultural Heritage Toward the Smart Environment for Better Future, pp. 109–113 (2017)
13. Yli-Huumo, J., Ko, D., Choi, S., Park, S., Smolander, K.: Where is current research on Blockchain technology? - a systematic review (2016)
14. Koteska, B., Mishev, A.: Blockchain Implementation Quality Challenges : A Literature Review Blockchain Implementation Quality Challenges : A Literature Review, pp. 11–13 (2017)
15. Casino, F., Dasaklis, T.K., Patsakis, C.: A systematic literature review of blockchain-based applications: Current status, classification and open issues (2019)
16. Batubara, F.R., Ubacht, J., Janssen, M.: Challenges of blockchain technology adoption for e-government. In: Proceedings of the 19th Annual International Conference on Digital Government Research Governance in the Data Age - DGO 2018, pp. 1–9 (2018)
17. Okoli, C., Schabram, K.: A Guide to Conducting a Systematic Literature Review of Information Systems Research (2011)
18. Amui, L.B.L., Jabbour, C.J.C., de Sousa Jabbour, A.B.L., Kannan, D.: Sustainability as a dynamic organizational capability: a systematic review and a future agenda toward a sustainable transition. J. Cleaner Prod. **142**, 308–322 (2017)
19. Saunders, M., Lewis, P., Thornhill, A.: Research Methods for Business Students. Pearson (2009)
20. Saunders, M., Lewis, P., Thornhill, A.: Research Methods for Business Students (2008)
21. Haussler, S.C.: Handbook for Synthesizing Qualitative Research. Springer, New York (2008)
22. Szirmai, A.: Developing countries and the concept of development, pp. 1–10. Cambridge University Press (2005)
23. Allessie, D.: The Consequences of Blockchain Architectures for the Role of Public Administrations. repository.tudelft.nl
24. Osgood, R.: The Future of Democracy: Blockchain Voting. COMP116: Information Security, pp. 1–21 (2016)
25. Kshetri, N., Voas, J.: Blockchain in developing countries. IT Prof. **20**, 11–14 (2018)
26. Swan, M., de Filippi, P.: Toward a philosophy of blockchain: a symposium: introduction. Metaphilosophy **48**, 603–619 (2017)

Designing an Effective Long-Term Identity Management Strategy for a Mature e-State

Silvia Lips[1(✉)], Krista Aas[2], Ingrid Pappel[1], and Dirk Draheim[1]

[1] Tallinn University of Technology, Akadeemia tee 15a, Tallinn 12616, Estonia
{silvia.lips,ingrid.pappel,dirk.draheim}@taltech.ee
[2] Estonian Police and Border Guard Board, Pärnu mnt 139,
Tallinn 15060, Estonia
krista.aas@politsei.ee

Abstract. Countries that have a well-functioning e-governance ecosystem (infrastructure, processes, interoperability network, user-friendly e-services etc.) reach a particularly high e-governance maturity level. To ensure continuous development and adoption to the changing technological environment the systematic consideration of users' needs is important in the definition of long-term strategical goals. Identity management is a corner stone of each mature e-governance ecosystem. This paper focuses on the process of creating the new Estonian strategy for identity management and identity documents and the analysis of this process from different aspects (responsibilities, engaged stakeholders and interest groups, key competences, scope, implementation). In addition, we give an overview of the underlying strategical and legal regulatory framework. The objective is to map the best practices and bottlenecks of the strategy creation process and propose a model for area specific long-term strategical documents. We aim at understanding best practices and bottlenecks in the process of creating the ID strategy. In service of this, we have conducted qualitative interviews with several high-ranking experts that have been involved as stakeholders in the strategy building process. Based on this, we propose a model for area-specific long-term strategical documents. Furthermore, the research results indicate that it is necessary to invest continuously into public-private partnership.

Keywords: Identity management · Strategy building · Electronic identity · Change management

1 Introduction

Estonia has significant experience in the field of e-governance and e-services from almost twenty years. The established PKI (public key infrastructure)-based e-governance system is intensively used. 98% of the Estonian population have an ID-card that hosts an eID (electronic identity) token; and about 2/3 of them use it regularly. During these twenty years, more than 500 million digital signatures has been given and, at the present time, it is possible to use more than 5000 e-services [1].

Since 2002, the system has remained quite similar with only minor changes. In the end of the year 2018, new contract partner started to issue the fourth generation of eID

A. Kő et al. (Eds.): EGOVIS 2019, LNCS 11709, pp. 221–234, 2019.
https://doi.org/10.1007/978-3-030-27523-5_16

documents. It is clear that the whole system has reached to the maturity level where dealing with concrete developments or needs is not sufficient and there is a clear need for an overall framework and long-term development strategy. Therefore, in September 2017, the Estonian Police and Border Guard Board (PBGB) together with the Estonian Information System Authority (EISA) initiated a process at the level of the public and the private sector level to agree on a long-term identity management view. The process lasted almost one and a half years and resulted into a white paper on identity management and identity documents, henceforth abbreviated as IMIDS white paper or just IMIDS for short.

The current article concentrates mainly on the creation process of the IMIDS white paper and not so much on analyzing the content of the document. The aim is to map the best practices and design an effective model for mature e-states who feel the need for a long-term view.

During the process, common understanding on the terminology level is crucial. If we talk about identity management and identity documents, then it is important to understand the meaning of the term "identity management". There is no single definition of identity management. On a very general level identity management is a security system, which authorizes users to access to certain information or systems [2]. In the current context, identity management means keeping consistent record of a person's identity and managing it by the state during its whole lifecycle. Identity documents are all documents issued by the state and stated in the Identity Documents Act paragraph 2 Section 2 [3]. It means identity card and digital identity card (including e-residency digital identity card), residence permit card, diplomatic identity card, 7 types of travel documents (passports) and mobile-ID [4].

Taking into account previously described framework, it is important to emphasize that in this article we do not focus only on the electronic part of the identity management because the strategical view is much broader covering additionally physical identity management issues, tokens, physical identity carriers, data protection, security issues etc.

In addition, if we talk about identity management and identity documents strategical view then at the same time, we talk at least partly about the strategic management of related information systems and IT innovation. Therefore, it is important to understand if there is an actual need and will for innovation and this type of long-term strategy. The same question raised during the IMIDS creation process – does Estonia actually want to be an innovative and leading country in terms of identity management and eID. According to the answers, Estonia clearly wants to be a successful e-country, but this also means that the country shall be ready for early adoption of new technologies and/or applications [5]. From that point of view, it is crucial to have a long-term perspective and common understating in the identity management area ensuring the implementation and funding of the innovative ideas, solutions and increase user satisfaction [6].

This article contains three main chapters. Firstly, we formulate the research problem and give methodological background with related frameworks. Then, we give an overview about the identity management and identity documents strategy building process and outcomes and analyze different aspects of the process. Finally, we present the most important and interesting findings.

2 Problem Formulation and Frameworks

2.1 Problem Formulation and Theoretical Framework

Central question of the current article is about designing an effective long-term identity management and identity documents strategy for a mature e-state through public and private cooperation. We analyze different aspects like responsibilities, engaged stakeholders and interest groups, key competences, scope and implementation issues. To support the main theme, we give an overview about the identity management and identity documents creation process, outcomes and propose a model of best practices.

Our research methodology is oriented towards action design research (ADR) as we were involved directly to the IMIDS creation process [7]. After the strategy document was ready, we conducted twelve individual structured non-standardized interviews with public and private sector experts who participated in the process (approximate duration one hour each). Five interviewees from the twelve were public and seven private sector representatives. Some of the examples of interviewees: PBGB head of identity and status bureau, EISA head of eID branch, CEO of SK ID Solutions AS, head of citizen markets of IDEMIA, CEO and vice-president of the Estonian Association of Information Technology and Telecommunications (ITL) etc.

Theoretical background of this article bases on the three main concepts: identity theory [8], change management [9] and public private partnership (PPP) [10]. All previously named concepts relate and supplement each other.

2.2 Strategical and Regulatory Framework

In the context of building the national identity management strategy, it is important to understand what kind of legal and strategical documents already exist and how they influence the area. Political and vision documents that has no direct legal impact and legislative acts having direct juridical impact must be distinguished.

On the state level there are in total 47 strategical documents. They are all different in terms of their juridical status, structure, purpose and their relation to the state budget [11]. Directly connected to the identity management area are only two of them: Internal Security Development Plan (STAK) and Estonian Information Society Development Plan (EISDP).

Internal Security Development Plan has eight sub programs and one of the programs is reliable and secure identity management that contains following three main policy instruments: development of secure and smart solutions, effective and systematic administration and management of the identity area, ensuring high quality personal data [12].

EISDP is more detailed policy document focusing inter alia to the eID area. The main aim of the document is to find smart solutions how to use ICT and solve nationwide challenges [13].

Juridical framework is more determined and has direct binding effect to the parties. Therefore, it is important to have an overview of the existing legal regulations related to the identity management and identity documents area. In addition to that, it is important to remark that new technological approaches and innovative solutions might presume changes in the existing legal environment or even establishing new regulatory framework.

Legal framework in the identity management and identity documents area has conditionally three main layers: pre-juridical framework, international law and EU legislation and state law (Fig. 1).

Fig. 1. Identity management legal framework layers.

Pre-juridical framework plays an important role especially in the identity management field consisting different technical standards (ISO, ETSI, PCI etc.) and recommendations (ICAO 9303 etc.) [14]. Even these documents do not have direct juridical impact, they are recognized and accepted worldwide and often used, referenced similarly to legal acts. International and EU law level is a set of different directives and directly applicable regulations that directly or indirectly relate to the identity management area.

On the state level, the main legal acts regulating the identity management regulatory environment in Estonia are Identity Documents Act and Electronic Identification and Trust Services for Electronic Transactions Act [4, 15].

3   Identity Management Strategy Building Process and Outcome

3.1   Strategy Building Process

Estonian identity management field (including eID ecosystem) is complex environment engaging public and private sector expertise and based on a close cooperation of both sectors. It is a well-operating network consisting of different players and roles [16].

During the first half of 2017, EISA initiated to PBGB that they would like to have a long-term view on the eID field. As the topic is wider than digital identity and eID, parties started to build the identity management strategy. 22.09.2017 PBGB and EISA sent an official IMIDS creation proposal to the public sector stakeholders.[1]

Based on the initiative 04.10.2017 public sector stakeholders met in the PBGB. Representatives of three different ministries (Ministry of the Interior, Ministry of Foreign Affairs and Ministry of Economic Affairs and Communications) participated. One of the main concerns brought out in the meeting was the juridical status of the planned strategical document. PBGB and EISA explained that the document becomes an input for already existing political strategical documents. It was clear that public sector did not have a common understanding of different identity management related issues. Therefore, the representatives decided that firstly it is important to achieve common understanding among public sector authorities and then engage private sector stakeholders.

First workshop for public sector stakeholders was 01.12.2017. After brief introduction, the work continued in two main sections: (1) electronic identity and related services (2) physical identity management and related topics. During the first part of the workshop on both sections' participants listed all bottlenecks and shortcomings related to the theme. After that, solution brainstorming followed. The aim was to find innovative solutions to the existing problems and try to think without borders. Finally, both groups presented their results and findings.

Based on the 01.12.2017 workshop results PBGB decided to have one additional internal workshop on 16.01.2018 where all service owners in the PBGB identity and status bureau and one representative of EISA participated. The aim was to think through together once more the broader picture and create links and synergies between different services. Based on the results of these two workshops first draft of the IMIDS was created and sent 02.02.2018 to the PBGB and EISA and shortly after to other public sector stakeholders.

The first draft based on the overlapping part of the mission and vision of the PBGB and EISA, as they are main implementing authorities on the identity management and identity documents field. Second workshop for public sector stakeholders was 03.04.2018. The focus of the meeting was to discuss the received feedback and make amendments to the IMIDS documentation.

01.06.2018 PBGB sent the IMIDS draft to the private sector stakeholders together with a meeting proposal.[2] The meeting was at EISA on 19.06.2018. EISA and PBGB introduced the IMIDS documentation and principles, open discussion followed. Private sector was clearly cautious and expressed their disappointment not being on engaged to the process already earlier. It was clear that there is a need for more meetings.

IMIDS documentation was little bit modified and 06.09.2018 next meeting was held. During the meeting, experts decided to change the document structure. Therefore, the decision was that before planned workshop in October 2018 public and private

---

[1] Ministry of the Interior, Ministry of Economic Affairs and Communication, IT and development center (SMIT), Tallinn Technical University (TeleTech), Estonian Data Protection Inspectorate, former Technical Regulatory Authority now known as Consumer Protection and Technical Regulatory Authority and Centre of Registers and Information Systems.

[2] SK ID Solutions AS, ITL, Estonian Banking Association, Cybernetica AS, Guardtime AS and IDEMIA - representing the interest of information technology companies.

sector experts meet one more time in a smaller circle. The task was to argue and negotiate new IMIDS structure that is acceptable for the private and public sector.

26.10.2018 final public-private workshop took place. Based on already agreed structure and with the help of outside moderator, experts worked in smaller groups. During the workshop, experts mapped relevant services and roles; identified challenges related with the services and offered possible solutions. In the end of December 2018, new draft version of the document was ready.

On February 15, 2019, EISA presented IMIDS to the e-Estonia Council who supported the identity management, eID and identity documents long-term plan [17].

After one and a half years of work, finally the identity management field had a starting point. Experts started to call the IMIDS as "white paper".

3.2 Process Outcome

IMIDS is a valuable set of area specific principles and guidelines and a starting point for the long-term visioning.

During the discussion experts found that term identity management is too broad, and they defined the document scope as follows:

- Identity of a person attributed by the state;
- Identity life cycle – all processes and activities;
- Identity management – management of data, tokens, Online Certificate Status Protocol (OCSP) service etc.;
- Usage - authentication, digital signature, encryption and decryption functionalities, eesti.ee e-mail address, NFC based services, biometrics;
- Ecosystem and cooperation – public vs private sector, research and development activities.

It means that the IMIDS focuses on the state created identities and does not deal with private sector identity solutions like Google or Facebook identities. Document covers the state created identity whole life cycle management and usage from the physical and electronic perspective.

During the process appeared that public and private sector experts understand and use professional terminology differently. For example, term "identity" had already various meanings and experts used it differently. Therefore, experts agreed most important definitions like identity document, identity carrier and carrier management, information service, clients etc. A separate glossary is a part of the document to increase the level of common understanding among public and private sector experts.

The document itself is twenty pages long and consist of five main chapters:

1. Market and Background (Estonia, EU, international level, service providers);
2. Predictable Future Developments;
3. National Identity Management Pillars and Principles;
4. Services Related to the Identity Management;
5. IMIDS Update Mechanisms.

First two chapters give general overview of the existing market situation and possible future trends on the state and international level. Next chapter is a set of general principles and guidelines for the development activities. Fourth chapter is the core of IMIDS and reflects future development vision of identity management related services.

First chapter contains Estonian identity management and identity documents ecosystem brief overview and description of main players and their roles. Estonian identity management framework bases on four main pillars:

- Clients - physical persons, private and public sector entities;
- Identity carriers/tokens – all ID-1 format cards, eID, mobile-ID, smart-ID, travel documents/passports;
- Channels – service points, e-service portal, phone, development environment;
- Services – personal identification, confirmation of the will of the person, validity confirmation services, identity carrier management (including carrier recognition), information services, official e-mail address, development services, service support etc.

In addition to the Estonian identity environment overview, the chapter contains key points that influence and shape the European Union and international market. One interesting finding was that in past three/four years several international service providers in the security documents market have merged. For example, in 2015, Gemalto AG acquired Swiss company Trüb AG and currently Gemalto AG merger process with Thales Group is almost finished. In 2017, French company Morpho S.A.S merged with Oberthur Technologies currently named IDEMIA. This situation illustrates the consolidation of the technologies and competences and the decrease of competition on the international level.

Second chapter analyses possible future developments that affect identity management and identity documents field. Use of biometrics will be one of the key elements in next ten years. Countries experiment with different technologies and biometric identifiers (face, iris, behavioral features etc.). People dependency from the technology and relative importance of the mobile technologies increase. Smart cities become more popular and the block-chain field of application expands. Increasing IoT numbers cause data exchange overload. In the identity management area important developments in the field of machine learning, mathematical modelling of nervous systems and behavior predictability enable accurate identification from the pictures and videos. By 2035, airports have to be able to serve highly increased number of passengers.

Third chapter presents the identity management basic principles. Estonia is open for innovation and ready to pilot new technological solutions. On the other hand, state ensures readiness to cope with technological crisis and creates risk management plan with mitigation measures. To mitigate the risks the state prefers to purchase ID-1 format documents and travel documents from different companies. There is one central identity management database and state analyses possibilities how to offer identification service to the private sector. State wants to review and re-organize the current eID roles and work allocation. These were only some examples of the general principles.

Identity management and related services is a central part of the strategy. Experts pointed out under every service main challenges and directions. Personal identification service challenges are record keeping and access management, international cooperation, aging of the main information system, service availability, and unmanaged risks.

Experts offered solutions for facing these challenges. For example, finding way to process personal data outside of Estonia, implementing automatic biometrical identification system (ABIS), cooperating with international identity providers (GSMA, CITIC etc.).

Carrier management contains different aspects starting from issuance process to risk management. Identity documents application moves to the electronic environment and state engages private businesses in the identity document issuance process. State plans to implement Artificial Intelligence (AI) based solutions in the working processes and searches effective PKI independent and post-quantum solutions.

In the context of digital authentication and signing, state analyzes the possibility to use Estonian eID in international environments (Facebook, eBay, Google) and builds more services on the Near Field Communication (NFC) technology implemented on the new eID card starting from December 2018.

Identity systems developers need more support and attention. Experts suggested different solutions that help to cope with the changing technical environment. Usage of more standardized solutions is just one example.

IMIDS has no separate juridical power, but it will be an input to other political level strategical documents as Internal Security Development Plan (STAK) in the governing area of the Ministry of the Interior and Estonian Information Society Development Plan in the governing area of the Ministry of Economic Affairs and Communications.

According to the strategy document, public and private sector representatives meet once a year in the last quarter initiated by the PBGB and discuss if the document needs to be changed. The full text of the IMIDS is publicly available in Estonian on the PBGB and EISA web pages [3].

4   Important Findings and Discussions

4.1   General Organization

First part of the interviews focused on the IMIDS organizational side. As a warm-up question, we asked about the experience in the identity management field. All interviewees brought out approximate number of years they have worked in the area. Remarkable was the difference in experience between the private and public sector representatives. Public sector median experience in the area was 7.1 years and the same result in private sector was 19.28 years. It is quite remarkable difference and may be one of the reasons why two sectors have different views on the area.

All interviewees evaluated the necessity of the IMIDS on a ten-point scale, where one meant that the creation of the IMIDS was not relevant and ten referred that the strategy document was very necessary. Median score given by all interviewees was 8.92. Public sector median score was 8.8 and private sector score 9. Mainly, the interviewees said that real actions have to follow; otherwise, the strategy document has no practical value. In addition, it is not necessary to repeat already existing principles. Interviewees also marked that the importance was not only coming from the documented part but from the process itself. Experts had not meet to discuss area related issues already long time. Therefore, it was a good opportunity to create mutual understanding among the public and private sector.

Interviewees had a chance to bring out positive and negative elements regarding the IMIDS creation process. The focus of the question was on the overall process structure, meetings held during the process, e-mail communication etc.

Interviewees found positive that the white paper finally created, and the community was around the table. They also pointed out that possibility to meet between private and public sector representatives in a smaller round was very helpful. All interviewees liked 26.10.2018 workshop moderated by professional.

Based on the received feedback it was clear that there is room for process improvement. Most important takeaways and findings are following:

- Engage professional methodical competence already to the strategy preparatory activities.
- Engage public and private sector representatives at the same time.
- Using iterative workshops format is most effective (as many iterations as needed).
- It is important to answer to all comments made during the process.
- Active participation and presence of ministries and policy makers level is very important.
- Interviewees pointed out that engaging the association level (ITL, Banking Association) was not sufficient.
- Telecommunication service providers (mobile operators), public sector IT houses (RMIT, KeMIT, TEHIK etc.) and experts from standardization authority were according to interviewees missing.
- Identity management and identity documents international level and industry view was missing.
- Too many people from the manager level participated.
- Too long periods between the meetings.

Time planning is another relevant issue in every project context. Therefore, we asked from the interviewees their opinion about the time actually spent (one and a half years). It was very interesting how interviewees' opinions about the IMIDS timeframe differed (the range was 3 months to 1.5 years). Most optimal duration seems to be up to six months. However, it is possible to make the document faster. The question is more about the optimal process planning.

4.2 Substantive Analysis

Last part of the interview concentrated on the IMIDS substantive analysis. During the IMIDS building process one of the questions that raised the debate was the juridical status of the document and on what level and by whom it should be approved. There is probably no right or wrong answer but based on the interviewee answers it is possible to fit the document better in the existing framework.

Most of the interviewees (46%) found that juridical status of the document is not necessary or important until the principles stated in the document adopt by the wider political documents like STAK and Information Society Development Plan. Others found that some kind of juridical or legal approval by the government or on the ministry level is important to ensure the enforcement of the document. Others remained neutral or had no opinion about the topic.

Weather the document approved or not, more important is the actual enforcement of principles. The document is expression of expert opinions and the technical environment changes very fast; therefore, it is reasonable to keep the approval procedure rather simple and flexible. The maximum is ministry level, who can organize the introduction of the principles to the government and make the political selection from the IMIDS principles.

Currently PBGB and EISA led the IMIDS creation process. One of the interview questions was about the leadership of the project. Aim was to understand if this kind of dual leadership earned its purpose or are there any good alternatives. Opinions about the leadership were divergent. Interviewees who did not prefer concrete authority brought out that PBGB and EISA could both lead their area of competence separately. Then of course raises the question who will be responsible for putting together the overall picture. More important was the engagement of all related experts and authorities. To summarize this question, the leadership role can be on the ministry or implementation authority level, more important is involvement of the stakeholders and one responsible institution who coordinates the whole process.

In addition to concrete leadership issues, interviewees mentioned that there should be a centralized methodical competence center on a state level, assisting, guiding and advising the creation of similar expert level white papers. The idea is worth of considering if expert level white papers become more common in public sector.

Interviewees brought out following topics that should have been included to the IMIDS or presented more in detail:

- AI and machine learning development (how to use AI in different processes), because it brings lot of benefits and additional risks that need to be analyzed.
- Identity management of the things (AI-s, robots etc.).
- Risk management and related activities.
- Field of biometric solutions.
- Border crossing technical solutions (how to make border crossing faster and more convenient).
- International dimension representation. More specifically Estonian citizens in the international environment with tokens enabling the identification issued by Estonian public and private sector.
- Real actions planning part and input giving to the other implementation plans.

Strategy building and visioning is only one part of the whole picture, because after finalizing the strategy the real planning and work starts. Therefore, we asked from the interviewees how the IMIDS principles become reality. According to the answers, ministries should take a lead and integrate the principles coming from the IMIDS to STAK and ISDP. It was also emphasized that strong community and stakeholder's own attitude is very important, and all engaged parties should take the principles agreed in IMIDS account while planning future activities. One challenge in the implementation process is building up strong public and private partnership again.

Based on the answers it was possible to create a simplified model of the IMIDS implementation cycle. As first step interviewees found that it would be good to meet shortly in a smaller group of public and private sector representatives, prioritize the actions, and select the most important issues that need urgent handling already during the year 2019. After prioritization, the experts have to describe a 10-step action plan and agree responsible authorities.

In the future, the meetings take place regularly once a year preferably in October or November. During these meetings, parties give an overview about implementing status and upcoming activities for the next and for the year after will be discussed (priorities and responsibilities overlooked or set, activities added or removed etc.). The reason for looking year and year after is the state budget planning principles that have direct influence on the implementation actions.

Close question to the previous one was how to keep the IMIDS document itself up to date. According to the document, experts overlook the IMIDS once a year initiated by the PBGB [3]. Interviewees approached to the question differently. Most of them found that need evaluation once a year is enough. Others found that evaluation shall happen more often or based on a necessity without any excessive administrative burden. They found that the focus should be more on flexibility and community-based interaction.

Based on the feedback we should consider CA/Browser Forum work format-based solution as an alternative. It is a strong and active expert community of certification authorities and Internet browser software vendors discussing and influencing international standards and principles [18]. The possibility to use similar format in Estonian identity management field for the public and private expert's cooperation needs further analysis. Therefore, current research is not concentrating to this particular topic in detail.

Two final questions were oriented to the main takeaways from the process and freely expressed comments if interviewees had any. As follows, we present only those takeaways and observations of the interviewees not already covered in the previous chapters:

- Some of the participants did not realize changed context – people who participated in the process were focusing too much to the historical context and did not realize that the situation is changed, and the same models are not applicable.
- Using the same terminology is important (i.e. the term "identity" is overwhelmed).
- Cooperation between the public and private cooperation has become very complex mainly because of the excessive regulatory environment and the feeling of unity is missing.
- Private sector was more active, interested and contributed more.
- Making this kind of white papers should be a common practice in public sector.
- Academic sector could be the bridge between different sectors.

Based on interviewee's answers to these two questions we noticed two main important conclusions. Firstly, interviewees mentioned multiple times that the cooperation between the public and private sector that once was much closer has become more reserved and complex. Mainly because of the too detailed regulatory framework (standards, laws, policies etc.). One of the solutions to overcome this situation offered during the interview was the engagement of academic sector who could be the bridge between the public and private sector. This idea very interesting but of course the concept, format and readiness need separate analysis.

Secondly, interviewees suggested that the format of such white papers as IMIDS should be more widely used in public sector practice. It means that on the expert level in different areas the cooperation will become more active and documented. This wider view and its applicability need also more detailed analysis. As mentioned previously by one interviewee that in such cases there should be on a state level a methodical competence center who helps to guide the process and keeps track of different existing white papers and their changes.

4.3   Recommendations

Based on the analysis of the interviews and outcomes in combination with change management theory and approaches it is possible to design a model for the area specific long-term strategical documents.

The source of the initiative is not that important but usually it comes from the implementation authority who is working on the expert level on the specific area. As a first step, the implementation authority and responsible ministry shall meet and agree the division of labor, general principles and the list of involved stakeholders. After that, it is reasonable to engage methodical help. The role of the methodical help will be coordination and preparation of the meetings and workshops on a joint and smaller working group's level.

It would be good to have the first meeting jointly with public and private parties. The aim of the meeting is to introduce the initiative, agree main principles, work allocation, further steps and time schedule. In addition, the division of work between smaller working groups has to be agreed. Detailed work with concrete proposals shall continue in smaller working groups. The number of meetings in smaller working groups is not limited.

When the working groups are finished their discussions and formed their concrete proposals, the second joint meeting will take place. It is important to consider all proposals, negotiate if necessary and finally prioritize them. To have a systematic and uniform approach to the topic it would be good to use "why-what-how" technique for establishing a hierarchy for the expressed viewpoints [19]. If one meeting is not enough for that purpose, then it is possible to arrange more meetings until achieving mutual understanding and the public and private representatives confirm that the strategy is ready. After that, the document moves on the political level. The responsible ministry introduces the principles to the government, makes selection from the strategy taking into account the priorities, and integrates them in the political strategy document. Implementation actions will follow.

During the implementation, approximately once a year the implementation status and the principles agreed in the strategy will be gone through by the private and public sector representatives and changed if needed.

In addition to already above-mentioned aspects, it is important to keep in mind following principles:

- The whole process should not take more than six months;

- Uniform use of terminology shall be agreed in the beginning of the process;
- Continuous community building and public and private sector cooperation shall be happening as a parallel process;
- State shall provide centrally methodical help and relation management for sector specific strategies.

4.4 Future Direction

In the future, we would like to investigate the applicability of our findings internationally. Every country is different and therefore it is important to find universal aspects and make generalizations while investigating other mature e-countries. As a concrete next step, we will conduct a project with partners from the Netherlands, comparing the Estonian eID solution with cloud-based eID solution in the Netherlands with respect to eIDAS tiers.

5   Conclusion

Identity management and identity documents area is a complex system influencing almost invisibly different areas of life. Estonia as one of the leading e-countries has reached to the maturity level in terms of e-governance and it is crucial to think through the strategic next steps to bring innovation to the existing environment and retain competitive position on the international level.

Therefore, in the beginning of 2017 Estonian Police and Border Guard Board and Estonian Information System Authority initiated the strategy building process in the identity management area. After one and a half years of public and private sector stakeholder's meetings and workshops identity management white paper was finally ready.

Current article focus is on the previously named white paper building process analysis. The aim of the research was to find the answer to the main research question – how to design an effective long-term identity management strategy for a mature e-state. By using approach oriented towards action design research and based on qualitative individual structured non-standardized interviews in combination with theoretical framework, we proposed a model for building strategies on the identity management and identity documents field.

As strategy building is only one part of the change management process it is important that identity management and identity documents strategy does not remain on paper and implementation actions will follow in parallel with the public and private sector community building activities enabling one-step further as a mature e-state.

References

1. e-Estonia Briefing Centre Homepage. https://e-estonia.com/solutions/e-identity/id-card/. Accessed 21 Feb 2019

2. Laurent, M., Bouzefrane, S., Pomerol, J.: Digital Identity Management. ISTE Press, London (2015)
3. Identity Management and Identity Documents. White Paper 1.0. https://www.ria.ee/sites/default/files/content-editors/EID/valge-raamat-2018.pdf. Accessed 13 Mar 2019
4. Identity Documents Act. https://www.riigiteataja.ee/en/eli/526042018001/consolide. Accessed 13 Mar 2019
5. Peppard, J., Ward, J.: The Strategic Management of Information Systems, 4th edn. Wiley, Hoboken (2016)
6. Muldme, A., Pappel, I., Lauk, M., Draheim, D.: A survey on customer satisfaction in national electronic ID user support. In: Terán, L., Meier, A. (ed.) Piscataway 5th International Conference on eDemocracy & eGovernment (ICEDEG), Piscataway, NJ, Quito, pp. 31–37 (2018)
7. Petersson, A., Lundberg, J.: Applying action design research (ADR) to develop concept generation and selection methods. In: Wang, L., Kjellberg, T. (eds.) Procedia 26th CIRP Design Conference, vol. 50, pp. 222–227. Elseiver, Amsterdam (2016)
8. Tsap, V., Pappel, I., Draheim, D.: Key success factors in introducing national e-identification systems. In: Dang, T.K., Wagner, R., Küng, J., Thoai, N., Takizawa, M., Neuhold, E.J. (eds.) FDSE 2017. LNCS, vol. 10646, pp. 455–471. Springer, Cham (2017). https://doi.org/10.1007/978-3-319-70004-5_33
9. Cameron, E., Green, M.: Making Sense of Change Management, 4th edn. Kogan Page Limited, London (2015)
10. Paide, K., Pappel, I., Vainsalu, H., Draheim, D.: On the systematic exploitation of the Estonian data exchange layer X-road for strengthening public private partnerships. In: Kankanhalli, A., Ojo, A., Soares, D. (eds.) 11th International Conference on Theory and Practice of Electronic Governance, ICEGOV 2018, pp. 34–41. ACM Press, Galaway (2018)
11. Development Plans. https://www.valitsus.ee/et/eesmargid-tegevused/arengukavad. Accessed 24 Feb 2019
12. Internal Security Development Plan. https://www.valitsus.ee/sites/default/files/contenteditors/arengukavad/taiendatud_siseturvalisuse_arengukava_2015-2020.pdf. Accessed 13 Mar 2019
13. Estonian Information Society Development Plan. https://www.mkm.ee/sites/default/files/elfinder/article_files/eesti_infouhiskonna_arengukava.pdf. Accessed 25 Feb 2019
14. Järvsoo, M., Norta, A., Tsap, V., Pappel, I., Draheim, D.: Implementation of information security in the EU information systems. In: Al-Sharhan, S.A., et al. (eds.) I3E 2018. LNCS, vol. 11195, pp. 150–163. Springer, Cham (2018). https://doi.org/10.1007/978-3-030-02131-3_15
15. Electronic Identification and Trust Services for Electronic Transactions Act. https://www.riigiteataja.ee/en/eli/511012019010/consolide. Accessed 30 Mar 2019
16. Lips, S., Pappel, I., Tsap, V., Draheim, D.: Key factors in coping with large-scale security vulnerabilities in the eID field. In: Kő, A., Francesconi, E. (eds.) EGOVIS 2018. LNCS, vol. 11032, pp. 60–70. Springer, Cham (2018). https://doi.org/10.1007/978-3-319-98349-3_5
17. E-Eesti nõukogu toetas ID-kaardi ja eidentiteedi 10 aasta arenguplaani. https://www.ria.ee/et/uudised/e-eesti-noukogu-toetas-id-kaardi-ja-eidentiteedi-10-aasta-arenguplaani.html. Accessed 24 Feb 2019
18. CAB Forum Homepage. About the CA/Browser Forum - CAB Forum. https://cabforum.org/about-us/. Accessed 13 Mar 2019
19. APMG-international: Effective Change Manager's Handbook - Essential guidance to the change management body of knowledge, 1st ed. Kogan Page Limited, London (2015)

Toward Value Creation in e-Governance Through Digitalization – An Industry-Based Approach

Domonkos Gaspar and Katalin Ternai[✉]

Corvinus University of Budapest, Fővám tér 8., Budapest 1093, Hungary
dgaspar@gmx.de, katalin.ternai@uni-corvinus.hu

Abstract. Digitalization as trend had matured considerably in the recent years and changed customer expectations in industry as well as end-user environments. The citizens and (state) governance relation is not exempt from this trend. While the importance of digitalization remains in the forefront of the attention, management takes more conscious decisions on digitalization initiatives. In the emergence of changing, break-through and disruptive business models, organizations are challenged in their self-definition and are forced to reflect on their legacy operating model. Information Technology (IT) departments may become the engines of the current sentiment if they master the transformation of their role and position in the Organizational Development efforts. In order to achieve this, Information Technology Leaders need to manage between multiple disrupting fronts: develop understanding and create a coalition for integrated organizational development, while needing to transform their department to meet today's challenges, at times when technology solutions are becoming "everyone's" business in the organizations. The key success factor is the right approach to leveraging on opportunities opened by new digital means as well as managing the demand from, and the implied human side impact on, their customer: the (governance) organization. This practitioner paper offers a response by reflecting on relevant models describing an integrated approach and validates certain assumptions based on the experience of a pilot implementation of the Integrated Change Management model.

Keywords: Digitalization · Change management · Transformation · Operations excellence · Human resource management · Digital dexterity · Integrated change management

1 Introduction and Problem Statement

Standardization and digitalization are high on the agenda of many management and governance boards. This organization, processes and tools related challenge demands a corporate strategic approach and ownership. It can be argued that the successful management of change is crucial to any organization in order to survive and succeed in the present highly competitive and continuously evolving business environment. Public sector governance organizations face comparable challenges towards their customer: the ever more demanding citizen. However, theories and approaches to change

© Springer Nature Switzerland AG 2019
A. Kő et al. (Eds.): EGOVIS 2019, LNCS 11709, pp. 235–246, 2019.
https://doi.org/10.1007/978-3-030-27523-5_17

management currently available to academics and practitioners are often contradictory, mostly lacking empirical evidence and supported by unchallenged hypotheses concerning the nature of contemporary organizational change management.

In the age of the 4th industrial revolution, where technology already outpaced organizational development, IT departments may become the engine room of the corporate transformation if they master the transformation of their own role and position in the Operation Excellence efforts. At times where "disruption" is a preferred state of mind, any past models may be questioned on a basic level, and information technology solutions become "everyone's" business, should IT departments reinvent themselves, or it is possible to capitalize on past robust practices and still deliver their contribution?

This document provides further elaborations on our approach, focusing on sustainability of the changes implemented [1]. We will reflect on existing theories and models, integrating and further developing them based on experience, to come to the description of a model that had proven itself against the challenges Industry 4.0 put on IT and on the entire organization. Our research sets out to empirically validate such a private sector born approach to solve a public sector problem.

2   IT in the Lead of the Transformation

Organizations and processes change dynamically, simultaneously in multiple parts of the organizations, often without coordination, in response to external influence and/or internal needs. These changes almost without exception have a change demand on IT capabilities often impact the same tool/feature(s), eventually causing contradicting requirements. These changes also often join one unified space only in information technology, making the volume and extent of the diverse changes in the organization visible in IT.

In the age of the 4th industrial revolution, organizational units are looking out for digital solutions themselves, increasing demands on the IT organizations both in terms of resources as well as complexities to manage. Organizational anomalies often manifest in insufficient use of foreseen IT tools. More often than justified, the messengers are shot on executive levels, making the inappropriate IT assets and capabilities the reason for those anomalies. While much of the costs, for a change are realized in the IT space, benefits of successful change implementation are realized on other parts of the organization.

In response to these challenges Chief Information Officers, (CIOs) are on the search for effective ways to steer requests from their customer, the business. It is today commonplace, that IT need to align with internal and external domains while remaining/becoming compliant to internal and external regulations and guidelines [2, 3]. IT organization should learn the motivations and operating systems of its business, reach out and provide it with a commonly recognizable approach to manage changes in an integrated way.

In our article we will elaborate on the context of this initiative. We will also extend our approach for such a structure which relies on theories and methodologies, and benchmarked to also serve the needs of no-profit and (state) governance purposes.

3 Principles of the Integrated IT Change Management

3.1 Background and Relevance

Background. In order to be successful in finding a common denominator for change management with business stakeholders, IT needs to critically review its own approach and it must reflect on the key models and approaches driving the way of thinking and acting in management as well as in (service) operations. A consolidated understanding of multiple related domains, drivers of different stakeholders, such as firm theories, corporate culture, change management, industrial and IT operations are necessary to be able to later synchronize the forces acting in an organization.

The search for the reason of existence of firms on open markets has been an area of intensive research for economists since the beginning of the XXth century. From the multiple firm theories Penrose's seminal work, The Theory of the Growth of the Firm, published in 1959, stands out. Competing theories, such as transaction cost theory and agency theory regard the primary organizational problems as incompatibility of individual goals. Penrose's work marked the first attempt by an economist to view firms as real life "flesh-and-blood" organizations [4]. On the path opened by Penrose, Grant's knowledge based theory of the firm gained significance in the age of automation and robotization [5]. Grant argues that beyond knowledge generation, the primary role of an organization is knowledge application and the fundamental task of an organization is to coordinate the effort of many specialists by creating conditions under which individuals can integrate their specialist knowledge. Knowledge is attributable to people, not organizations and maximization of codified (explicit) knowledge is elementary interest of a firm, since transfer of tacit knowledge between people is slow, costly and uncertain [6].

Corporate culture scholars agree with the importance of the individual, they argue though that human aspects and related corporate cultures are multi-dimensional subjects and they are indispensable for the company`s value creation [7, 8]. There is a recent paradigm shift in the ways that organizations balance stability and dynamism: research show that in the past century hierarchy and specialization focused, once highly successful (so called "machine") organizations have been overtaken by quickly mobilizing, agile, nimble and empowered, in short: agile organization which see organization as living organism [9]. Schein, a leading scholar in the domain, defines culture as "a pattern of shared basic assumptions that was learned by a group as it solved its problems of external adoption and internal integration" [10]. He argues that there are three basic levels of corporate culture, such as Artifacts, Espoused Values and Basic Underlying Assumptions, with the latter level being decisive for employees` actions. In general, the layers can be understood as defense mechanisms against any kind of change.

An institution in an ever vibrant environment requires effective focus on continuous improvement, through transformation, so to remain existent and propagate [11]. Industrial companies have in the 1950s and 1960 developed a number of manufacturing methodologies, from which the model developed by Toyota Motors, called Toyota Production System (TPS) is seminal [12]. Together with LEAN, an evolution of TPS, they are today the industry reference [13]. A key common point of these approaches is the establishment of the Continuous Improvement (CI) process as operational initiator of changes. The CI process progresses through "incremental" improvement over time or "break-through" improvement all at once. Among the most widely used tools for CI is a four-step quality model – the Plan-Do-Check-Act (PDCA) is stands out and it remains inspirational for other approaches [14–16].

In order to address the imminent need of strategic alignment between IT and other departments, the Business Process Management (BPM) approach was developed [17]. The BPM lifecycle is widely used in IT related projects and it has a potential to be utilized for process improvement as well [18]. Its stages can well be put in relation with the PDCA cycle, providing a potential for common denominator in projects approach with industrial stakeholders (Fig. 1).

Business Process Management Life Cycle	Shewhart Cycle
Process Documentation	Plan
Process and System Analysis	
Implementation and change management	Do
Process Operation	
Process Controlling and Monitoring	Check
Business Process Strategy	Act

Fig. 1. Alignment between the process steps of the Business Process Management Lifecycle and the Shewhart (PDCA) Cycle (Source: own work based on [14, 17])

The Infrastructure Technology Information Library (ITIL) provides a set of detailed practices for IT service management, Project - and Program management principles used in IT environment, such as PRINCE2 and Managing Successful Programs (MSP) also provide orientation for change management handling [19, 20]. There is argumentation though, in line with our experience, that while they define processes for most relevant information technology related aspects, their governance processes lack the right strategic view for achieving the objectives of the business in the organizations [21, 22].

The introduction of change within the organization can have strong repercussions. The instinctive reaction to change is rejection [23]. While seminal considerations are put into finding ways of managing organizations through change and the influence of firm theories on the domain is beyond doubt, organizational change management models tend to resort to the terminal choice that an individual leaves the organization in case it is unable or unwilling to adhere to the change [24]. In the age of knowledge-based, information-driven economy this option is not affordable especially in organizations where high proportion knowledge elements are (still) tacit either due to high proportion of non-codified knowledge or for the coded knowledge being out of date or not adhered to. We argue that the emergence of individuum focused change management methodologies and consideration of applicability of psychological research is the future direction of evolution is the most adequate response to organizational change management in the age of digitalization [25–28].

IT organizations setting out to build a cross-domain framework for change management will find though that despite imminent correlation between firm theories, organizational culture, industrial models and change management, relatively little cross-fertilization took place between these domains. An end-to-end model and commonly recognized translation between domains are not available to support their approach.

Relevance. To respond adequately to Industry 4.0 challenges, a cross departmental evaluation of opportunities and rethinking of processes and change execution are necessary. Integration of production machinery and other systems requires collaboration between IT and other departments even on areas, which were previously no common domains. The current momentum created by Industry 4.0 could be leveraged by the IT departments to rethink their approach for better alignment and conclusively more value add collaboration with the business stakeholders. When successful, IT departments will be able to maintain their position as key value creator in the organizations. Establishing an improved way for Change Request management may just be the right first step.

3.2 Integration with Business Process Management

Managing business processes means focusing on the important activities and resources of a company, such as: markets, strategy, people, financial aspects, material management, intellectual properties, data and information. The aim is to design and control the organizational structures in a very flexible way so they can rapidly adapt to changing conditions.

The BPM applications help to describe the organizational processes, together with the required information and other resources (amongst others human resources) needed to perform each activity. Business processes are defined as sequence of activities. Each elementary task should have an organizational actor to perform it. A well-described process model contains all the relevant tasks and their description. In our opinion it is required to define unambiguously, who is responsible for the execution of each activity in terms of the RACI matrix (abbreviated from Responsible, Accountable, Consulted, Informed), bridging the organizational model and the process model [29, 30].

One of the objectives of BPM is the transformation of informal knowledge into formal knowledge and facilitates its externalization and sharing [31]. The relevant knowledge is embedded and strongly related to the roles as building element of the organizational structure. The competences relate to the job role, considered as content. Competences mean knowledge, skill and attitude that is necessary to sufficient execution.

In the turbulent environment both the roles and required competencies are changing, therefore the knowledge articulation cannot be independent from the permanently updated business process model.

BPM steps include modeling and analyzing the current process and optimizing and redesigning of new process. Process design is, therefore, a continuous process due to several reasons.

BPM includes process engineering (design and modeling), execution, monitoring, optimizing and re-engineering. Additional feature of these applications of process models the ability for simulation.

It is not easy to analyze business processes, to define them and to install them, because a lot of business information, such as information about events, actors, conditions and artifacts, is needed to understand the process. If businesses and business strategies are changing, the underlying business processes also have to be changed and adopted. Once a model of a business process is available, various analytical methods can be used to check if the process delivers the product or service in the most optimal and cost-effective way. In particular, each task can be analyzed to ensure its added value to the business and to prevent wasting time and resources [32, 33].

As mentioned above, the BPM life cycle approach aligned with the company's CI structure is sufficient for a common denominator with the business stakeholders on change management. In our work we will expand the theoretic basis with IT change relevant aspects to define a conceptual model which will be referred to later. Our key statement is that an IT change can only be successful, if the related organizational, process and data changes are handled simultaneously in an integrated way. In an earlier work we have in detail described how we have integrated the Business Process Management lifecycle (based on Gabor et al. [34]) with IT Change Management components.

3.3 Culture and Knowledge Management, Digital Dexterity

Cultural and knowledge management are key elements in assuring the sustainability of the implemented process. Experience shows, that processes and related benefits do not get fully realized and/or erode if knowledge management and more broadly, embedment of change in the organization are left to the software training only. Knowledge management drives organizational learning which takes place during the entire Business Process Management lifecycle and change embedment drives sustainability of the results. A conscious approach to culture and knowledge management improves efficiency of implementation of a change and the maintenance of the result of the change and drives digital dexterity in the organization [35].

3.4 Employee Impact Map

As discussed in earlier chapters, appropriate change management on organizational and human side are elementary success criteria. For a structured approach, we have developed the Employee Impact Map. Addressing the matter on the individual level needs to recognize two key dimensions of the impact of a change on an employee:

- Nature of the impact – the nature of the impact may be direct or indirect. An employee is directly impacted when the change happens to his person. An employee is indirectly impacted when the change has no direct impact on him or her, but it takes place in his or her surroundings.

• Relevance – relevance of a change may be situational or dynamic. Situational relevance are changes which impose immediate and lasting impact on the employee. Dynamic relevance deals with changes imposed on future objectives and outlooks of an employee.

The following figure demonstrates the Employee Impact Map along the above dimensions and provides examples of each impact type (Fig. 2).

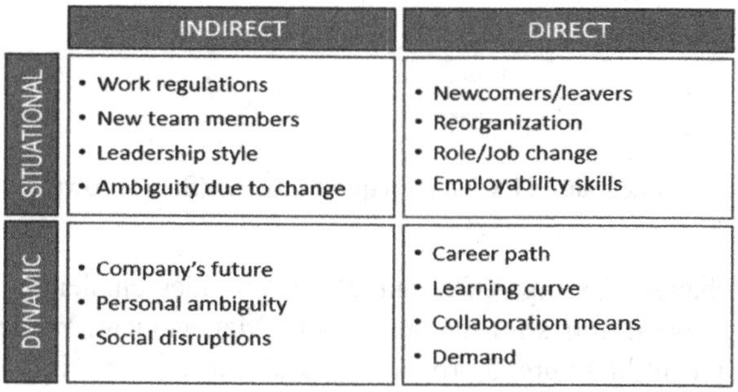

	INDIRECT	DIRECT
SITUATIONAL	• Work regulations • New team members • Leadership style • Ambiguity due to change	• Newcomers/leavers • Reorganization • Role/Job change • Employability skills
DYNAMIC	• Company's future • Personal ambiguity • Social disruptions	• Career path • Learning curve • Collaboration means • Demand

Fig. 2. The Employee Impact Map with typical impact types (Source: own work)

Objective of change management on organizational and human side should aim to empower employees through impact-based, tailorable and measurable actions. It is to be noted too, that an impact of a change may evolve, thus revision of the impact map and adjustment of the measures should be revisited over time.

3.5 Integrated Approach to Change Management

IT Change management is often understood purely in IT context. Build new functionalities, test and deploy. We argue that in case of an IT change all elements, need to be mapped, analyzed and managed in an integrated way: Organization and process, Data and System – in this sequence of priority. The underlying logic is that a process being executed be an organization processes certain information (data) in every step. Systems need to assure that the appropriate data is available at the needed time and in required quality. Process automation through systems must also be viewed in the light of the Organization and process as well as data context [1].

3.6 Industry as a Benchmark for Customer Oriented Governance

Since the onset of the 1980s scholars have argued that a paradigm change becomes necessary in the public sector governance [36]. At the beginning cost-efficiency considerations prompted to the development of the Entrepreneurial Government theory, which included a thesis about Customer-driven Government. Later citizen demands for more convenient (customer oriented) governance processes in the public sector fueled

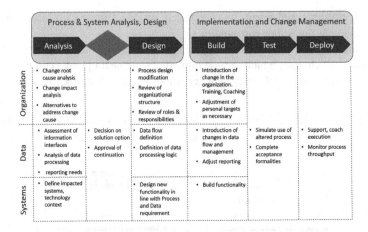

Fig. 3. Integrated IT Change request process (Source: own work)

the need for a change. The age of digitalization provides challenges while provides ground breaking opportunities for the New Public Management. While success stories are available in recent literature, a proven approach for digitalization driven, customer focused governance transformation did not yet emerge [37–39].

Customer focus has been the key driving force if the private economy since its inception. Therefore benchmarking private sector practices for the benefit of the public sector challenges is obvious.

4   The Approach

4.1   The Integrated IT Change Request Process

Basis for our selected approach is the IT Change Request Process, which contains the essential elements of an integrated approach. During the development of the model the frequent scenario was considered, where a new process, task, or data flow is often not possible to test without the readiness of the supporting system. Therefore, from the Phase "Build" onwards the model merges the three elements into one course of action.

Previous implementation cases show that the defined approach is useable with "agile" and with "waterfall" delivery models alike, with little adaptation, although here to further studies are needed. Due to its role based approach organizations of different size and management models can find it applicable. Well known management approaches as well as new disciplines suggest to define roles that can be sized and assigned to people (one person can have multiple roles) rather than jobs, in order to make the model universally applicable in different delivery and management methodologies [16, 40].

4.2   Process Analysis Framework

Business Process Re-design and Transformations in their execution on business processes and information systems can in their essence be regarded as larger scale Change Requests. We argue that, with certain enhancements, the integrated Change Management approach can serve as basis for those large-scale re-design and transformation approaches.

In order to host the complexity that a business process redesign presents, extensions and changes were needed in the "Organization" category which had formerly comprised all, the process, organizational and change management perspectives. In order to retain clear focus on organizational system (of systems) engineering and to manage the specific needs of the "human" aspects most adequately (e.g. targeted application of the Employee Impact Map), the domain "Organization" was split to "People" and "Process & Organization" and enhanced accordingly.

Furthermore, the domain of Business Processes requires an extension in definition and approach. The below figure depicts the process approach and its integration with the aforementioned categories (Fig. 4).

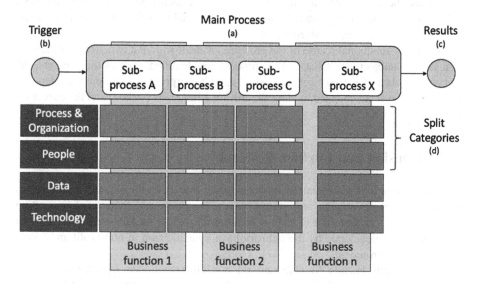

Fig. 4. Process analysis framework (Source: own work)

Setting the scope right in a re-design or transformation initiative is key driver of the embedment and overall efficiency of its result in all of the categories. Narrowly set scope may result in local efficiencies on the cost of overall efficiency throughout the value chain, and too broad scope will over-stretch the resources of the organization while increasing risks in business continuity.

Our framework adapts an end-to-end approach, in which the process is considered to be a set of activities (steps and decisions), eventually through a number of sub-processes, in response to a triggering event that achieves a defined result for each process stakeholder. Main Process (a) is such which has an identifiable single "token" moving through all the sub-processes, events and decision points to deliver a result. If the Result of the sub-sequent (sub-)process is in 1:1 relationship with the Trigger of the following (sub-)process, then the relevant (sub-) processes belong to the same Main Process. 1:n or n:1 relationships however mark the boundaries of Main Processes.

Starting point of a Main Process is the Trigger (b) which may be of three kinds: Action (decision-based), Temporal (time-based) and Conditional (data based). A process may have alternative triggering events, of different types. Always the earliest trigger is considered.

Results (c) are generally of three types: a service, a good or an information. The result (output) of a process is always the final one for the process, and it is not necessarily the same than the objective (performance target) of the process.

The above figure also highlights the split of the category (d) of the original "Organization" into "Process & Organization" and "People" compared to the base approach as shown on Fig. 3.

As an example of the above definitions "Student admittance" with its numerous subprocesses would be a Main Process in the complex process landscape of an University, because it has a single "token" (the Student) processing through from Trigger (e.g. student met entrance criteria – Conditional trigger) to the Result of being "ready to attend classes" (Information).

The cross-functional nature of the processes is dealt with in a two-step approach. In first step the subjective ("what") of the process are identified, such as the Triggers, the Results, the Activities (also: sub-processes) and Cases (process variations). In step two the process flows are mapped, adding the Business functions ("who") and the execution means ("how").

5 Conclusion and Further Research

The current attention to Digitalization is having an impact on the citizens' expectations from the (state) governance institutions. The terminology and focus of digitalization may be originating from the industrial scene, nevertheless we are strongly convinced that approaches developed by the industry have a justification in non-profit and (state) governance environment.

Our research intends to elaborate on our aforementioned hypothesis, that an industry based approaches can be benchmarked for improving public sector governance:

- Empirically test the integrated change and process management in an industrial environment, where the roots of the approach are lying.
- Following verification in the industrial scene, apply the integrated change and process management approach in an indicative non-profit or governance case.
- Investigate if currently available Business Process Management tools are adequate for supporting the integrated change and process management.

Conclusively, highly integrated approach to change and process management supported by current technology, will remain a key vehicle for sustainable organizational value creation. It also bears the opportunity for IT organizations to remain, independently of the current trend, in the center of gravity for value creation in operations.

References

1. Gaspar, D.: Organizational value creation by IT in Industry 4.0. In: Buchmann, R.A., Karagiannis, D., Kirikova, M. (eds.) PoEM 2018. LNBIP, vol. 335, pp. 274–287. Springer, Cham (2018). https://doi.org/10.1007/978-3-030-02302-7_17
2. Henderson, J.C., Venkatraman, N.: Strategic alignment: leveraging information technology for transforming organisations. IBM Syst. J. **32**(1), 4–16 (1993)
3. SMME: ITIL V3 Foundation – Student Manual; Ver 5; Leuven, pp. 234–272 (2009)
4. Pitelis, C.: Edith penrose, organisational economics and business strategy. Manag. Decis. Econ. **26**, 67–82 (2005)
5. Grant, R.M.: Toward a knowledge-based theory of the firm. Strateg. Manag. J. **17**, 109–122 (1996)
6. Kogut, B., Zander, U.: Knowlwdge of the firm, combinative capabilities and the replication of technology. Organ. Stud. **3**, 387–397 (1992)
7. Boda, G., Virag, I.: Utemvaksag; Kozgazdasagi Szemle Volume LVII, pp. 1087–1104 (2010)
8. Wien, A., Franzke, N.: Grundlagen der Unternehmenskultur. In: Wien, A., Franzke, N. (eds.) Unternehmenskultur – Zielorientierte Unternehmensethik als entscheidender Erfolgsfaktor, pp. 29–45. Springer, Wiesbaden (2014). https://doi.org/10.1007/978-3-658-05993-4_2
9. Aghina, W.: The 5 Trademarks of Agile Organisations, pp. 2–5. McKinsey & Company, New York City (2017)
10. Schein, E.: Organisational Culture and Leadership: A Dynamic View, p. 4, 17. Jossey-Bass, San Francisco (1992)
11. Black, J.A.: Fermenting change, capitalising on the inherent change found in dynamic non-linear systems. J. Organ. Change Manag. **13**(6), 520–525 (2000)
12. Ohno, T.: Toyota Production System: Beyond Large-Scale Production (English translation ed.), pp. 75–76. Productivity Press, Portland (1988). ISBN 0-915299-14-3
13. Womack, J.P., Jones, D.T., Roos, D.: The Machine That Changed the World (1990). ISBN 978-0-7432-9979-4
14. Shewhart, W.A.: Statistical Method from the Viewpoint of Quality Control. Dover Publications, New York (1986). ISBN 0-486-65232-7, S. 45
15. Tennant, G.: SIX SIGMA: SPC and TQM in Manufacturing and Services, pp. 3–4. Gower Publishing, Ltd. (2001). ISBN 0-566-08374-4
16. Moen, R., Norman, C.: Evolution of the PDCA Cycle (PDF). Accessed 12 Feb 2017
17. Scheer, A.-W., Abolhassan, F., Jost, W., Kirchmer, M.: Business Process Excellence - ARIS in Practice. Springer, Heidelberg (2002). https://doi.org/10.1007/978-3-540-24705-0
18. Josic, D.: Kritische Analyse der Prozessoptimierung als wesentliches Element des Change Managements. GRIN Verlag, München (2016)
19. Berry, D., et al.: Managing Successful Projects, pp. 251–291. TSO Publishing, London (1996)
20. Sowden, R., et al.: Managing Successful Programmes, pp. 47–75. TSO Publishing, London (2007)
21. Alonso, I.A., Verdún, J.C., Caro, E.T.: Description of the structure of the IT demand management process framework. Int. J. Inf. Manag. Part A **37**(1), 1461–1473 (2017)

22. Rahimi, F., Møller, C., Hvam, L.: Business process management and IT management: the missing integration. Int. J. Inf. Manag. **36**(1), 142–154 (2016)
23. Morton, S.: The Corporation of the 1990's: Information technology and Organisational Transformation. Sloan School of Management. Oxford University Press, New York (1991)
24. Kazmi, S.A.Z., Naarananoja, M.: Collection of change management tools – an opportunity to make the best choice from the various organizational transformational techniques. GSTF Int. J. Bus. Rev. **3**(3) (2014)
25. TOC
26. PROSCI: Best Practices in Business Process Reengineering Report (2002). http://www.prosci.com/bprbestpractices.htm
27. Kotter, J.P.: Leading change: why transformation efforts fail. Harvard Bus. Rev. **73**(2), 59–67 (1995)
28. Kübler-Ross, E., Kessler, D.: On Grief & Greving: Finding the Meaning of Grieving Through the Five Stages of Loss. Scribner, New York (2014). ISBN 9781476775555
29. Gábor, A., Szabó, Z.: Semantic technologies in business process management. In: Fathi, M. (ed.) Integration of Practice-Oriented Knowledge Technology: Trends and Prospectives, pp. 17–28. Springer, Heidelberg (2013). https://doi.org/10.1007/978-3-642-34471-8_2
30. Vas, R.: STUDIO: ontology-centric knowledge-based system. In: Gábor, A., Kő, A. (eds.) Corporate Knowledge Discovery and Organizational Learning. KMOL, vol. 2, pp. 83–103. Springer, Cham (2016). https://doi.org/10.1007/978-3-319-28917-5_4
31. Kalpic, B., Bernus, P.: Business process modeling through the knowledge management perspective. J. Knowl. Manag. **10**(3), 40–56 (2006)
32. Weske, M., van der Aalst, W.M.P., Verbeek, H.M.W.: Advances in business process management. Data Knowl. Eng. **50**(1), 1–8 (2004)
33. Szabó, I.: Future development: towards semantic compliance checking. In: Gábor, A., Kő, A. (eds.) Corporate Knowledge Discovery and Organizational Learning. KMOL, vol. 2, pp. 155–173. Springer, Cham (2016). https://doi.org/10.1007/978-3-319-28917-5_7
34. Gábor, A., Kő, A., Szabó, Z., Fehér, P.: Corporate knowledge discovery and organizational learning: the role, importance, and application of semantic business process management—the ProKEX case. In: Gábor, A., Kő, A. (eds.) Corporate Knowledge Discovery and Organizational Learning. KMOL, vol. 2, pp. 1–31. Springer, Cham (2016). https://doi.org/10.1007/978-3-319-28917-5_1
35. Drakos, N., et al.: Predicts 2018: Digital Workplace Programs to Boost Digital Dexterity. Gartner Research, 23 November 2017. ID: G00325367
36. Schelder, K., Summermatter, L.: Customer orientation in electronic government: motives and effects. Gov. Inf. Q. **24**(2), 291–311 (2007)
37. Osborne, D., Gaebler, T.: How the Entrepreneurial Spirit is Transforming the Private Sector. Addison-Wesley Publishing Company, Boston (1992)
38. Riegraf, B.: Der Staat auf dem Weg zum kundenorientierten Dienstleistungsunternehmen? In: Aulenbacher, B., Funder, M., Jacobsen, H., Völker, S. (eds.) Arbeit und Geschlecht im Umbruch der modernen Gesellschaft. VS Verlag für Sozialwissenschaften (2007)
39. Tabrizi, B., et al.: Digital transformation is not about technology. Harvard Business Review (2019). https://hbr.org/2019/03/digital-transformation-is-not-about-technology. Accessed 15 Mar 2019
40. Robertson, B., Thomison, T.: Holacracy – discover a better way of working, pp. 1–10. White Paper, HolacracyOne, LLC, Spring City (2015)

Author Index

Printed in the United States
By Bookmasters